# KANT'S THEORY OF KNOWLEDGE

# KANT'S THEORY OF KNOWLEDGE

An Outline of One Central Argument in the
*Critique of Pure Reason*

by

## Graham Bird

*Lecturer in Logic*
*University of Aberdeen*

NEW YORK
HUMANITIES PRESS
1973

*First published* 1962

*Reprinted 1973 by Humanities Press*
*by Arrangement with the*
*Original Publisher*

Library of Congress Cataloging in Publication Data

Bird, Graham.
  Kant's theory of knowledge.

  Original ed. issued in series:  International
library of philosophy and scientific method.
  Bibliography:  p.
  1.  Kant, Immanuel, 1724-1804.  Kritik der reinen
Vernunft.  I.  Title.  II.  Series: International
library of philosophy and scientific method.
[B2779.B55  1973]          121        73-84345
ISBN 0-391-00316-X

*Printed in the United States of America*

To Jean

# CONTENTS

vii

# CONTENTS

# PREFACE

THIS book is intended as a limited account of one central argument in the *Critique of Pure Reason*. It is not an elementary or introductory account of the *Critique*, and presupposes some acquaintance with the main features of Kant's theory of knowledge. It is not simply a commentary on Kant's text, but an attempt to pursue one continuous argument through the *Critique*. That this argument extends from the Prefaces and Introduction, through the Aesthetic and Analytic, to the Paralogisms and the Third Antinomy suggests that it forms a central part of Kant's doctrines. But there is much else in the *Critique* which has been left out here. In particular nothing has been said specifically of what we should call Kant's philosophy of science.

The *Critique of Pure Reason* has had some influence on recent British philosophy. Significant references to Kant have been made in several recent books (for example, Hampshire: *Thought and Action*, Strawson: *Individuals*, Stenius: *Wittgenstein's Tractatus*), in which Kant's views are either re-stated in modern terms, or compared with the views of modern philosophers, like Wittgenstein (Cf. Strawson: op. cit., Ch. 3, Stenius: op. cit., Ch. XI). It is true that Kant, perhaps more than other traditional philosophers, invites such interpretation and comparison, and there are good historical reasons for this. In this book an attempt is made to provide a basis for such interpretations by discussing Kant's arguments in terms of a modern philosophical idiom. But since much of it is concerned to explain what Kant said, the philosophic issues cannot be exhaustively discussed, and are only introduced through Kant's attitudes towards them. No reasonably comprehensive account of a traditional philosopher could do more without assuming from the start what his views actually are; and in Kant's case no such assumption can sensibly be made.

This book will, therefore, appear defective for two opposed reasons. On the one hand it will not satisfy those who look for the thoroughness of a commentary. On the other it will disappoint those who hope for exhaustive discussion of purely philosophical issues. It is very likely that any short account of the *Critique*, which does more than merely paraphrase the text, will fall somewhere between the two stools of history and philosophy. I have tried to fall nearer to that of philosophical interest. This recipe seems to me to be recommended by another book on Kant with a similar aim, namely Prichard's *Kant's Theory of Knowledge*. Prichard provided in his book more genuine philosophical interest and argument than most commentaries on Kant; but he almost always misunderstood Kant's views. I have tried to give an account of the *Critique* which is as sympathetic to Kant as Prichard's was unsympathetic to him.

I would like to thank the non-philosophers who have helped and encouraged me. I owe also very much to the late T. D. Weldon, and to the kindness and help of Professor R. C. Cross and Dr. W. Bednarowski.

# I

# PHENOMENA
# AND PHENOMENALISM

'. . . which constrains us to regard all appearances (Erscheinungen) as data of the senses . . .' (A 122).

THERE is no one passage in the *Critique of Pure Reason* where Kant develops his account of perception. Such an account is none-theless implicit in Kant's use of perceptual terms, and especially of his key term 'Erscheinung', which it is natural to translate either as 'appearance' or as 'phenomenon'. This lack of systematic development reflects important differences of aim and emphasis between Kant and modern philosophers of perception, which make it hard to attach any modern label to his account without adding some qualification. Yet both natural translations of the term 'Erscheinung' in English, as well as some of the ways in which Kant uses the term, strongly encourage the assumption that Kant must be a phenomenalist of some kind. Many philosophers, including Kemp Smith, Paton, Vleeschauwer, and Ayer, have indeed ascribed such a theory to Kant, although there is no guarantee that they have all understood this attribution in precisely the same way. For these reasons it is as well to be careful before classing Kant as an adherent of this, or any other, theory, however firmly such labels have stuck to him. In this chapter I want to indicate some difficulties in the way of at least some attributions of such a theory to Kant. It would not be sensible, in the space of one short chapter, to try to show that all such attributions are wholly wrong. It may nevertheless be useful to indicate defects in one such attribution, so that permission may be provisionally granted to produce some alternative interpretation. Prichard's account of Kant has been chosen as the most vigorous and clearest exposition of the view to be disputed.

## (i) PRICHARD'S THEORY

Prichard's account of Kant's perceptual terms can be found throughout his book *Kant's Theory of Knowledge*, and is neatly summarised in a passage from pp. 231–235. In this passage Prichard argues (p. 231) that the central question of the Transcendental Deduction, which he identifies as 'How does an apprehension become related to an object?', contains an absurdity. He claims that Kant manages to conceal this absurdity from himself by supposing that representations, or appearances, or sensations, both 'have a being of their own' and also represent something, namely the thing in itself. This latter point is reinforced by Prichard elsewhere (p. 137) through the claim, specifically about appearances, that 'though from the point of view of the thing in itself an appearance is an appearance or perception of it, yet regarded from the standpoint of what it is in itself, an appearance is a reality perceived of the kind called mental'.

Prichard's picture of Kant is thus one in which appearances, or phenomena, connect the real world of things in themselves with perceiving subjects, by representing the former and also belonging to the latter. Clearly on such a view something needs to be said about the relations of 'representing' and 'belonging to', and Prichard now reintroduces Kant's problem in this way. 'If a representation is taken to be an appearance, or sensation, the main problem becomes that of explaining how it is that, beginning with the apprehension of mere appearances or sensations, we come to apprehend an object, in the sense of an object in nature, which, as such, is not an appearance or sensation, but a part of the physical world' (p. 232). According to Prichard Kant's solution to this problem is simply to say that '. . . appearances, or sensations, become related to an object, in the sense of an object in nature, by being combined on certain principles' (p. 232); or, as he later puts it, by the construction or making of 'parts of the physical world, and in fact the physical world itself, out of elements given in perception' (pp. 233–234). Prichard explains, in a footnote, that the mathematical illustrations of this supposed 'construction' are the most plausible, for 'while we can be said to construct geometrical figures, and while the construction of geometrical figures can easily be mistaken for the apprehension of them, we cannot with any plausibility be said to construct the physical world' (p. 234). This constitutes Prichard's basic objection to Kant's principal claim, that on such an account the construction envisaged has to be of the physical world itself (*literally* (p. 233)), and, impossibly, out of materials of a mental kind, namely appearances, or sensations.

It would be easy to say that Prichard's is a very unsubtle account of Kant, and to leave the way open for a more sympathetic interpretation of 'construction' along more sophisticated phenomenalist lines. Prichard does not say that Kant is a phenomenalist, but it is not hard to see in Prichard's exposition the outline of a crude phenomenalist theory. Prichard's main point is that Kant's term 'synthesis' refers to a construction of physical objects out of appearances, or sensations. A more up-to-date phenomenalist view might be expressed by saying that physical objects can be 'reduced' to sense-data. Where Kant, on Prichard's view, speaks of the construction of the external world out of our sensations, phenomenalists speak of the 'reduction' of things in the external world to sense-data. One obvious difference is that, on Prichard's view, Kant's construction is literally of objects from sensations, while contemporary phenomenalists prefer to speak instead of the reduction of physical object statements to sense-datum statements. These similarities and differences would allow one to say either that Kant was a phenomenalist of a primitive type, as Prichard implies, or else that he was simply a phenomenalist, on the ground that Prichard exaggerates the extent to which Kant was misled by talking of the construction of objects instead of the analysis of statements. Certainly it is true that Prichard exaggerates the psychological flavour of Kant's claims, though it is also true that some things which Kant says appear quite strongly to support Prichard's interpretation. Indeed if this were not so it would be hard to understand the tenacity with which such an interpretation survives. Nevertheless, examination of Prichard's central theme shows that his account is defective at almost every point.

Prichard evidently believed that for Kant the physical world is one of things in themselves, as well as that this world is represented to us by appearances, or sensations, of these things. It is not worth spending much time on the first of these interpretations,

3

since it is indisputable that Kant persistently denies it throughout the *Critique*. One of his most important aims is to show that our knowledge of the physical world is not of things in themselves, but is restricted to what he variously calls objects of experience, sensible objects, or appearances. Even the knowledge which we have from Newtonian mechanics, to which Kant ascribes a status superior to that of our ordinary experience, is said to be restricted in this way (B 313). A characteristic passage where Kant makes it clear that on his view all our theoretical knowledge is so restricted occurs in sections 22 and 23 of the second edition Deduction (B 146–150), but the same point is made frequently elsewhere. Even in the first edition Deduction, where, as we shall see, support for Prichard's interpretation is at its strongest, Kant shows that his argument would be pointless if our knowledge was of things in themselves. At A 128 he says: 'If the objects with which our knowledge has to deal were things in themselves, we could have no a priori concepts of them.' The point of this assertion is to summarise Kant's argument that we can employ a priori concepts only because our knowledge is limited to phenomena, or appearances.

The second claim, that appearances represent things in themselves, loses some of its plausibility as an interpretation of Kant once Prichard's first claim has been rejected in this way. It is, nevertheless, a more disputable claim than the first, for Kant certainly seems on occasion to say things which support it. Yet it is also true that some such passages which naturally seem to support this view do not in the end do so. Two such typical passages occur at B 164 and A 109. In the former Kant says: 'But appearances are only representations of things which are unknown as regards what they may be in themselves.' And in the latter: 'But these appearances are not things in themselves; they are only representations which in turn have their object—an object which (therefore) cannot be itself intuited by us, and which may hence be called the non-empirical, i.e transcendental object = X.'

In the first type of case it must be noted that Kant does not say that appearances are representations of things in themselves, which are nevertheless unknown to us. He says rather that appearances represent things, which are unknown to us as regards what they may be in themselves. These are clearly quite different claims, for the second is compatible with the statement that appearances do

4

not represent things in themselves, while the first is not. There are other passages where the same distinction is easy to overlook (e.g. *Prol.*, Sect. 13, note II; *Prol.*, Sect. 36. Ak., Vol. 4, p. 289 and p. 318). The first construction of this passage, which is that required for Prichard's interpretation, is paradoxical if not inconsistent. For it is hard to understand how we could be entitled to say that appearances represent something, and also that that thing is un-known to us. It would not be surprising that Kant could be so easily dismissed by Prichard if this were what he meant. It is cer-tainly not what he here says. For what he says implies that while it is proper to speak of appearances' representing things in some way, it is not proper to speak of knowing things as they are in themselves. And this suggests that the things which it is proper to say that appearances represent are not things in themselves.

Such a view is confirmed by the second passage. For there Kant claims that appearances might be said to represent not things in themselves, but the transcendental object. Nothing would have been easier for Kant than to have said at this point that appearances *are* not things in themselves, but only represent them. Yet he chooses instead to say that appearances are not things in them-selves and may be said to refer to the transcendental object. Again, Kant's use of the term 'transcendental object' in the singular, and his use of it in other contexts (see below Ch. 5) show that he does not regard the known physical world as composed of such objects, as Prichard would have to claim that he did. It is worth noticing, too, that later in the same context Kant makes it clear that it is not so much the thing, to which the phrase 'transcendental object' purports to refer, which is so important, as the concept of such a thing.[1] These deviations from Prichard's interpretation are not conclusive, and yet they raise doubts about it, which Prichard never considered. This whole passage, from A 104 to A 109, is of great importance and difficulty, and will be considered carefully later (in Ch. 5, pp. 76 ff.). There it will be argued that the passage is in intention entirely opposed to such a view as Prichard's. For the present it is enough to notice how much it obstructs rather than supports this view.

What these examined passages admittedly show is that for Kant it was correct to speak of appearances as representations, and even,

[1] A 109: 'The pure *concept* . . . objective unity. This *concept* . . . relation to an object.'

in some way, to speak of them as representations of something. What they certainly do not show, however much they might seem to, is that for Kant it was just as correct to speak of appearances as representations of things in themselves. In fact Kant explicitly denies this on at least one occasion. At B 332 he says: 'But even if we could by pure understanding say anything synthetically in regard to things in themselves (which however is impossible), it still could not be applied to appearances, which do not represent things in themselves.' The same message appears, though much less clearly stated, in a passage at B 63 ('The rainbow . . . remains unknown to us'). This latter passage will be considered later (Ch. 3, p. 40).

Prichard also believed that Kant wished to talk of appearances, or representations, or sensations indifferently, though it is clear that Kant himself distinguishes between all three terms. Although it is true in some way, for Kant, that appearances are representations, it is hard to see what justification there is for the claim that he believed them to be sensations as well. If it is accepted that Kant's term for 'sensation' is 'Empfindung', then it is obvious that he distinguishes between appearance and sensation as early as B 34, where he says: 'The effect of an object upon the faculty of representation, so far as we are affected by it, is sensation. That intuition, which is in relation to an object through sensation, is entitled empirical. The undetermined object of an empirical intuition is entitled appearance.' This makes it clear that Kant did not mean simply to identify appearances and sensations, as Prichard suggests that he did. Yet Prichard's basic objection to Kant turns essentially upon the claim that Kant speaks of appearances as sensations, so that there is an absurdity in talking consequently of constructing the physical world literally out of sensations. It is quite true that to reveal these defects in Prichard's interpretation is only to raise problems about the way in which Kant did understand these terms. But Prichard claimed to disclose mistakes in Kant's view and not merely difficulties; and this claim is open to all the objections stated so far to Prichard's understanding of Kant.

## (ii) LITERAL CONSTRUCTION

So far the criticism of Prichard has dealt only with mistakes or inadequacies in his account of the terms of the allegedly Kantian

6

construction of the physical world. But his account of the notion of construction itself is also defective. Prichard's view was that Kant envisaged a literal construction of the world of the same kind as the literal construction of a geometrical figure on a piece of paper. Nobody would deny that Kant intended some connections between synthesis and construction in geometry, but the fact that Kant uses two terms ('Synthesis' and 'Construction') suggests that he also wished to distinguish between them. The term 'Construction' is explicitly restricted by Kant to use in the context of mathematics (B 867), and elsewhere (e.g. B 741 ff.) is treated as a concept referring quite specifically to mathematics.

More important even than this is the proviso Kant attaches to the term 'Construction' in his polemic against Eberhard (Ak., Vol. 8, pp. 190–193). For there Kant insists that the term, even in the restricted context of geometry, is not to be taken literally. This intention is reinforced by Kant's wish to extend the term's use to cover procedures in algebra as well as those already accommodated in geometry. From these passages it seems clear that although Kant derived his term from the field of literally constructed figures in geometry, he nevertheless used the term in contexts where it could not be taken quite literally, and that even in the central context of geometry itself it was not meant to be so taken. Generally, indeed, when Kant speaks of construction he speaks of it in connection with concepts or principles, or geometrical figures in imagination (cf. B xi–xiii; A 24; B 271; B 741–742). These ways of talking about construction involve a concern with modes of describing objects or appearances, rather than with ways of constructing such objects literally.

The places where Kant typically connects the notions of construction and synthesis are those in which he tries to justify the ascription to phenomena of quantitative predicates. These occur mainly in the Analytic of Principles. But in these passages Kant deals with the description of phenomena in quantitative terms, rather than with the construction of the phenomena to which such descriptions are applied. In the argument at B 221, for example, Kant says: 'For instance I can determine a priori, that is, construct the degree of sensation of sunlight by combining some 200,000 illuminations of the moon.' In such a claim Kant evidently does not envisage anything so drastic as the construction of the sun or the moon themselves, but only of a comparison or measure of their illuminative power. If it is sensible to speak of the construction of phenomena in such a context, then these phenomena are not the things to which such magnitudes are ascribed, so much as the magnitudes themselves, or the models in accordance with which such comparisons of magnitude may be made, for example in photometry (cf. Vuillemin: *Physique et Metaphysique Kaintiennes*, pp. 129 ff.).

These points argue that Kant's account of construction, even in the context of the application of mathematical concepts or models, is not a straightforwardly literal construction of objects in the physical world. They argue also that Kant was well aware of differences between the mathematical context of construction, and the general context of synthesis, however similar or closely connected these may have been for him. The mathematical sense of 'construction' reflects an interest in our ability to employ quantitative descriptions, and to construct models of numerical comparison; the more general sense of 'synthesis' reflects a similar interest in equally basic non-quantitative types of description as well. Arguments such as these certainly throw some doubt on Prichard's simple account of Kant's idea of construction. They might also be used to dispute Prichard's claim that Kant speaks materially of the construction of the physical world itself, rather than formally of the construction of concepts applying to, or principles governing, such a world. They would then provide some general grounds for the view that even if Kant was a phenomenalist of some sort, he was not so naive an adherent as Prichard believed.

Prichard's ascription of a naive literal construction to Kant is in part a result of an over-simple interpretation of Kant's psychological terminology. Some commentators (particularly Vleeschauwer) have insisted that Kant's central claims have a logical importance, even though they may be expressed in psychological terms. It is not always made clear what is especially logical about these claims, or what exactly the contrast between psychology and logic in this context amounts to; but there is support in Kant's writings for the view that even where his argument deals with, or is expressed in, psychological terms, it should often be understood as an argument about the status, force, or sense of concepts. To say simply that Kant was not concerned with psychology is wrong, for there is no doubt that Kant was deeply interested in psychological concepts.

What Kant himself seems to have been clear about was that he was not investigating psychological phenomena empirically, but in some other way which we might call logical or conceptual. Prichard, by adopting the view that Kant's construction has to be taken literally, makes no concession to these points, so that it may be worth while briefly to review them.

Kant helps to give the impression of investigating construction or synthesis empirically by his persistent use of a chronological metaphor. For example, at B 101, he describes what is a logical classification of modal terms in a chronological way by saying: '. . . we first judge something problematically, then maintain its truth assertorically, and finally affirm it as inseparably united with the understanding.' At B 730 he similarly distinguishes between certain types of knowledge or statement by saying: 'Thus all human knowledge begins with intuition, proceeds from thence to concepts, and ends with Ideas (Idee).' The same modes of expression are used in the famous slogan which opens the Introduction at B 1, and more misleadingly in Kant's account of the three-fold synthesis. This makes it very easy to associate the particular aspects of synthesis with successive stages in some learning process, although it is clear that the three aspects can be so separated only artificially. Paton (*Kant's Metaphysic of Experience*, Vol. I, p. 548) expresses this concisely by saying that the three syntheses are not 'stages on the way to experience, but elements in experience'. Kant himself makes a similar point in the *Prolegomena* (Ak., Vol. 4, p. 304). Nevertheless Kant's use of such metaphors invites an unfortunate comparison with Locke's badly named enquiry into the 'origin' of our ideas.

Kant's equally artificial separation of categories and intuitions provides the opportunity for a completion of this metaphorical account of our experience. For Kant sometimes speaks (particularly in the Schematism) as though some mechanism were needed to connect the pure categories with ordinary empirical experience, since the categories are supposed somehow to be independent of such experience. It is tempting to fit this aim onto the chronological metaphor and explain Kant's task as that of sketching a mechanism through which certain concepts enable us to organise our initial experiences, so that we come to acquire or construct the knowledge that we ordinarily claim to have. On this story the schematism is a kind of clutch ready to engage the categorial

9

engine so that it may drive the wheels of our experience. Such a mechanistic account may be intelligible in physiological terms, which Kant was not concerned with, but to extend it beyond them would be to commit the same speculative incoherence that Descartes committed (in the *Regulae*, Rule XII) when he tried to account for non-physical phenomena on the model of physical explanations. However tempting such a view of Kant may be, it certainly pushes the metaphors very much farther than Kant wished them to go. For example, although Kant talks of the pure categories as independent of experience, he is careful to insist that properly they have no sense except in conjunction with experience (cf. B 148–149), and can be identified or defined only in such a context (B 300). Once again the separation which causes the simple metaphorical interpretation is recognised by Kant to be artificial in a way in which the engine's separation from the wheels is not.

Kant tried hard to avoid the misleading features of his terminology by explicitly distinguishing his task from that which he believed Locke to have undertaken. In the passage at B 118–120 Kant distinguishes between an empirical enquiry into the origin of ideas, such as Locke's, and a transcendental enquiry into the status of concepts, such as his own. From what Kant says in this passage it is natural to read this distinction as a denial that the *Critique* is concerned with the aims or methods of empirical psychology. A similar distinction, between an empirical and a transcendental enquiry into the subjective sources of our knowledge, is made at A 97 in the first edition Deduction, where Kant introduces the three-fold synthesis. Once again Kant rejects the empirical and chooses the transcendental enquiry. Whatever this distinction amounts to it is plain that Kant spent much time considering what kind of enquiry he was engaged on, and firmly rejected the claim that it was an empirical investigation into the origin of our ideas. Vleeschauwer cites two important items which bear on this issue, and testify to Kant's interest in the status rather than the origin of concepts. In the first of these Kant says: 'I concerned myself not with the evolution of concepts, like Tetens (actions through which concepts are generated), nor with the analysis of them, like Lambert, but merely with their objective validity. I am no rival to these men.' (Reflexion 4900). And in the second: 'Tetens investigated the concepts of human reason merely subjectively (human nature), but I investigated them objectively. The former analysis is empirical, the latter transcendental' (Reflexion 4901). Kant exploits the same distinctions for the same purpose in a passage in the *Prolegomena* (Sect. 21a, Ak., Vol. 4, p. 304) where he says: 'To put all this in a nutshell, it is first necessary to remind the reader that we are not here talking of the origin (Entstehen) of experience, but of what is in it. The former task belongs to empirical psychology, and would never be able to be developed but for the latter, which belongs to a critique of knowledge,[1] and especially of understanding.' This passage is parallel in the *Prolegomena* to the Transcendental Deduction in the *Critique of Pure Reason*, and it is important not only because it so clearly separates the empirical enquiry from Kant's, but also because it reveals a connection between them. This connection is also emphasised elsewhere in the *Critique* (e.g. A 113–114), and is, as we shall see later, of importance in understanding some of the argument of the first edition Deduction.

These points raise a serious problem, which did not arise for Prichard, since he believed that Kant's construction was literally of the external world and in terms of entities naturally dealt with in empirical psychology. For they point to the important Kantian distinction between empirical and transcendental, though they make it clear only in a negative way, that is, as the instrument by means of which Kant rejects the aims and methods of empirical psychology for his own enquiry. It is essential, however, to recognise the limits which Kant's rejection of such a programme places on the interpretation of the *Critique*. It argues that any exclusively psychological account of the *Critique* will be not only incomplete, but even residual and incidental to Kant's main theme. Kant often suggests that claims which he naturally expressed in an inherited psychological terminology are based on logical or conceptual distinctions (cf. B 81 and B 316 f.). The distinction between a transcendental and an empirical enquiry strongly reinforces the view that his main theme was of this conceptual kind. Certainly these passages only encourage, and do not compel, the translation of Kant's terminology into a more modern language of conceptual analysis. They constitute, nevertheless, an obvious invitation to try this which Prichard never acknowledged, and perhaps never noticed.

---

[1] The phrase 'critique of knowledge' is also used at B 81, where it is associated with the contrast between empirical and transcendental.

## (iii) THE FIRST EDITION DEDUCTION AND PHENOMENALISM

Although some criticisms of Prichard's theory have arisen from his account of the first edition Deduction (referred to as (A) in future), most of them have appealed to other sections of the *Critique*. But Prichard's view is stated chiefly as the result of his reading of the Deduction (A), and particularly of the passage at A 119–121. This passage is closely connected with another at A 97, and this with one at A 99, which Vleeschauwer (*La Déduction Transcendentale*, Vol. II, p. 240) found committal to what he called 'phenomenalist idealism'. The extent of Kant's commitment in these passages to phenomenalism may be measured by Ayer's claim (*Foundations of Empirical Knowledge*, p. 117) that phenomenalists aim to 'make the distinction between sense-data and material things as sharp as possible'. What is, in this way, distinctive about a phenomenalist construction is its attempt to restrict description of the proper objects of perception to a level below that of our ordinary descriptions of material objects. This is one reason why Prichard's view that Kant attempts to construct physical objects out of sensations is a recognisably phenomenalist attribution.

In the first of these passages (A 97: 'If each representation . . . a three-fold synthesis') Kant introduces the three-fold synthesis on the basis of two claims. The first of these is that no knowledge could ever arise under the hypothesis that all our representations were completely independent of each other; and the second is that if we deny this hypothesis, by ascribing what Kant calls a 'synopsis' to the senses, then we have to accept that a synthesis corresponds to it. It is easy to think that Kant is here committing himself to a Prichardian construction, on the obvious ground that the three-fold synthesis is supposed necessary for the building of knowledge from isolated and disconnected representations. What tempts the attribution of phenomenalism in this passage is the envisaged construction of objects, or our knowledge of them, from the low-level resources of isolated representations. However tempting this reading is, it is not what Kant strictly says. Kant is not here asserting that the described situation in which representations are quite independent of each other is our own originally, from which our knowledge is constructed by synthesis. He is, on the contrary, denying that such a situation is our own by supposing both that we have knowledge and that *if* this situation had been ours, such

12

knowledge would be impossible. Kant argues that since such knowledge is not impossible, it follows that our senses are not presented with independent representations, but with a manifold or multiplicity of them. Kant does not dispute that some arrangement of this presented manifold is required for our knowledge, and this is why a synthesis is said to be necessary, but this claim by itself does not commit him to phenomenalism. Kant's argument favours rather the language of discrimination between the multiplicity of things perceived than that of construction out of individual sensations.

The second passage continues the argument by claiming that the very supposition of such a multiplicity in intuition presupposes an ability to discriminate between the items in it (A 99: 'In order that unity . . . such a synthesis'). Successful discrimination, which Kant refers to as 'unity of intuition' presupposes, on his view, a synthesis of apprehension. This synthesis is explained here only through the 'metaphors of 'running through' and 'holding together', and this may again suggest a phenomenalist construction. But when Kant later (A 100–101) gives examples of a synthesis 'inescapably bound up with' the synthesis of apprehension, they do not seem to support such a view. For in these cases Kant envisages the construction not so much of an object as of a statement or belief about an object, for example, to the effect that cinnabar is red. What these are 'constructed' out of, or as we should naturally say 'based on', seem not to be simply sensations nor items which are not describable in material object terms, but rather particular experiences in which some identified material thing (the cinnabar) was perceived to have a certain property. Kant indeed seems to be talking on a level at which statements about the properties of objects are asserted on the basis of features they are perceived to have, and not on a level at which physical objects themselves are constructed out of lower-level elements sharply distinguished from physical objects.

These passages do not show that Kant certainly was not a phenomenalist; but they do not show either that he unequivocally was. The final passage (A 119–120: 'We will now, starting from below . . . that is, have apprehended them') is much more seriously committal. In this passage Kant expresses his argument in the form of a step by step account of what is involved in our experience. The conditions which he mentions are of two kinds, those that are empirical and subjective, and those that are objective and transcendental. Kant begins with what he regards as empirical conditions and since the division between the empirical and transcendental occurs at A 121 ('Now if this unity . . .') in the passage we are concerned with Kant is still evidently occupied with the former. What he says about these differs in one way from the account so far given of A 97 and A 99. Kant reproduces the same argument at A 120, claiming that the multiplicity of intuited features requires that there should be some faculty responsible for discriminating between them. At this point he connects the original first two syntheses by making 'imagination' responsible for such operations and calling the result of them 'apprehension'. This procedure is innocent enough so long as it is understood that the three aspects of synthesis are properly inseparable. But now Kant in the final sentence and a footnote complicates his argument by speaking not of appearances or perceptions, as he had done up to this point, but of impressions ('Eindrücke') and the imagination's effect upon them. It is not difficult to see in these final remarks an attempt to get below the level of material object discourse, which would satisfy one criterion for a phenomenalist view.

Although this passage seems to contain a commitment of this kind, it does not support Prichard's view. For Prichard argued that what was constructed on Kant's view was a physical object, whereas Kant, even in this passage, speaks of the production of an image of an object, which would enable us to recognise or discriminate between items in our perception. Even so, to elaborate the supposed procedure in which impressions are combined to produce such images would be to produce a crude phenomenalist theory. Kant, however, does not elaborate this procedure. He merely mentions it and goes on instead to consider what for him are the important transcendental conditions of experience. It has been suggested already that Kant's central theme was neither empirical nor psychological, yet in this passage where he seems most clearly committed to a phenomenalist view, he is on his own admission dealing with empirical and psychological features of experience. Such a commitment to what nowadays would be recognised as a basic phenomenalist position was evidently for Kant something which he held as a background psychological view about the empirical conditions of our learning ability. But if what has been said earlier about Kant's aims is at all correct, then this background view was subsidiary to the transcendental aim which he set himself, and which was distinct from any empirical enquiry. Although it is natural to say that Kant is a phenomenalist on the basis of such evidence, it should be added that the evidence also shows one respect in which Kant's account of perception differs in aim and emphasis from that of his phenomenalist successors. For Kant is not interested in the elaboration of the empirical conditions which commit him to such a doctrine. That he points them out at all seems to be the result of the connection between the two kinds of enquiry. It was noticed earlier that Kant thought empirical enquiry in psychology to be dependent in some way upon his transcendental enquiry, so that it is not surprising to find him pointing an incidental empirical moral on the way to his central transcendental aim. It is worth noticing a passage at A 118–119 ('We can however . . . modes of knowledge'), and another at B 117 ('The explanation of the manner . . . de facto mode of origination') and considering whether what is there rejected as the main task of the transcendental deduction is not that which Kant incidentally performs at A 120.

In what has been said of the passages from the Deduction (A) it has been supposed that Kant's term 'Erscheinung' was not equivalent to phenomenalists' 'sense-datum'. Certainly the examples given of appearances at A 100–101 supported this, and yet when Kant speaks of appearances as 'data of the senses' (A 122) or as 'the first things given to us' (A 120) or as 'representations', it is natural to wonder whether this equivalence does not hold. On the criterion that has so far been used, however, there is no such equivalence. For what Kant means by 'appearance' certainly does not exclude physical objects. Appearances are frequently called 'objects' by him (B 34, A 109), they are indeed throughout the *Critique* the only objects to which our knowledge, even of the physical world, is directed; they are quite certainly spatial, and even said to be 'distinct from all my ideas' (B xxxix, note). When Kant describes appearances as data of the senses, he therefore uses this description in a quite untechnical and neutral sense, to cover whatever is given to the senses unrestricted in any phenomenalist way. It is worth noting, too, that the term 'appearance' is not intended by Kant to cater for illusory situations, as the term 'sense-datum' is (see Ayer: *Foundations of Empirical Knowledge*, pp. 68–69). Kant explains frequently that illusions can be dealt with only empirically, and should not be allowed to influence, still less initiate, a philosophical account of perception.[1]

Enough has been said to cast serious doubt on the accuracy and fruitfulness of Prichard's interpretation. Enough has been said, too, to explain why such a theory is so tempting, even though it is defective. Although there is some evidence on which to hang an attribution of phenomenalism to Kant, it has been argued that he should be regarded as an incidental and unorthodox adherent. This is borne out also by the numerous passages where Kant rejects what he calls 'idealism', and with it any theory of the kind he believed Berkeley to have produced.[2] But although Prichard's theory is defective, nothing has yet been suggested to replace it. What has been done is rather to disclose some of the conflicts and confusions which surround Kant's terms, and particularly 'Erscheinung'. Prichard's account was defective because he grasped only one half of Kant's stated doctrine, and to show this at least reveals the problem of disentangling Kant's terminology. It does not much matter whether Kant is a phenomenalist or not, but it is important to see how his conflicting claims about appearances can be reconciled. For appearances are objects, spatial, and distinct from our ideas, and yet they are also representations, mere modifications of the mind, and in us. Prichard's view simply concentrated on the latter claims to the exclusion of the former. Other commentators have viewed the problem as though it could be settled only by regarding Kant as inconsistent (Vaihinger, *Kommentar*, Vol. II, pp. 42 ff.) or as the helpless victim of conflicting tendencies (Kemp Smith, *Commentary*, p. 83 f.). There is a long history of bewilderment both on Kant's and his critics' sides about this issue, and one task to be performed in the following chapters is to see how this apparent conflict should be understood.

Two guides to the solution of this problem have been already found. One is the distinction between transcendental and empirical, and the other is the puzzling passage about the 'object of repre-

[1] There are many important passages of this kind. See particularly A 376–377, B 277, note, B 278–279, B 69–70, and B xxxix, note. It is interesting to compare what Kant says in these passages (especially the first three cited) with the current, and mistaken, doctrine that the existence of illusions shows that some experiences must be veridical. (Cf. Ryle, *Dilemmas*, pp. 93–95.)

[2] For example the passage in the *Prolegomena*, Sect. 13, where Kant says of his theory: 'Can one call this idealism? It is in fact precisely the opposite' (Ak., Vol. 4, p. 289).

sentations' at A 104–109. Of the latter it can be suggested that perhaps, since Kant regards appearances both as objects and as representations, the attempt to explain the phrases 'object of representations' and 'transcendental object' will throw some light on this apparent conflict. The former distinction has already often been recognised as of importance in understanding Kant, but no very convincing account of its force has yet been given. Both these guides will be employed and examined later (the distinction in Ch. 3, and the passage in Ch. 5 and 9). This whole problem also points, of course, to the pervasive difficulty of understanding what is meant by Kant's often metaphorical language about constructions, and synthesis, or the making possible of objects of experience. But this task is too complex to be accommodated in any single chapter. All the chapters which follow may be seen as an effort to grapple with it.

# 2

# NOUMENA
# AND NOUMENALISM

'This latter must therefore be an external thing distinct from all my representations . . .' (B xli).

'. . . we shall never dream of seeking to inform ourselves about the objects of our senses as they are in themselves, that is, out of all relation to the senses' (A 380).

IT has often been supposed that Kant distinguished his theory from that of Berkeley only by admitting the existence of things in themselves or noumena, which served to explain and guarantee regularities to be found in the appearances immediately presented to our senses. Adickes, for example, held a view of this kind (*Kant und das Ding an sich*, Ch. 3, p. 35), and Prichard's theory, outlined above, also ascribes it to Kant. Passages like that at A 109 (Ch. 1, pp. 4 ff.), in which Kant appeals to the notion of a transcendental object, might, mistakenly, be understood in Prichard's way. But there are many other passages in which Kant appears to speak, even more committally, of a causal relation between things in themselves and appearances, or of appearances as appearances of such noumenal objects. At the very start of the Aesthetic (B 34) Kant talks of objects affecting our senses, and although he does not there identify these objects as noumena, it has very often been supposed that they are identifiable in this way. In this chapter a number of passages will be examined which argue against the ascription of such views to Kant.

Before these passages are considered it is as well to project something of the background in which Kant uses the terms 'noumenon', 'thing in itself', or 'intelligible object'. There are, in the *Critique*, two apparently conflicting views with regard to these notions. First there is Kant's evident desire to fasten on such concepts a good part of the blame for mistakes in previous (particularly dogmatic) philosophy. This is obvious from the Dialectic alone, but is also made clear in the Amphiboly of Concepts of Reflection (B 316 ff.). Kant held, briefly, that mistakes arise through the belief that such concepts refer to known and existing objects, and also that once this temptation is eliminated many issues in traditional metaphysics can be seen to be futile. Second, however, Kant appears willing to make two concessions to such metaphysical issues. The first arises partly from the view that these mistakes are inevitable and perhaps can never be wholly eradicated (*Prol.*, Sect. 40, Ak., Vol. 4, 328. B 397: '. . . Even the wisest of men cannot free himself from them'), and partly from his admission that some concepts, which stimulate these mistakes, have a genuine and indispensable use. The second concession arises from the argument in the transition to moral philosophy in the Antinomies (B 560–586), for this argument requires, in some way, the admission of things in themselves. In this context it is not the dogmatic rationalists who are at fault, but the cautious empiricists, for whom the idea of 'freedom' is a 'stumbling-block' (Ak., Vol. 5, pp. 7–8). Each of these concessions needs to be examined later (the first in Ch. 5, and the second in Ch. 12). They are mentioned here only as a background to the present problem of things in themselves, or noumena, in the context of Kant's account of perception.

The part for which things in themselves are often cast, in this context, can be simply explained. Kant is indisputably committed to a causal relation of some kind between external objects and our senses. It is easy to reject the view that these external objects are mere appearances, for appearances are said to be ideas or, as Prichard supposed, sensations; and this seems to leave only the alternative that such external objects are noumena, whose sensible effects in us are appearances. Such an account as this raises the problem of explaining how we ever come to know about noumena, when the only things we perceive immediately are their appearances. It is, then, natural to try to solve this problem by supposing some relation (for example, resemblance or causality) in accordance with which to reconstruct the link between what is presented to our senses (appearance) and the external objects (noumena) which present them to us. Kant is, on this view, committed to the following claims:

(i) That things in themselves are the causes of appearances in our sensibility.

(ii) That what is strictly, or immediately, presented to our senses are appearances, i.e. the effects of noumena on us.

(iii) That knowledge of such noumenal objects can be achieved or explained by exploiting the inference from given sensible effect (appearance) to presumed objective cause (noumena). The exploitation of such an inference might naturally be thought to be implicit in the construction of objects from sensations, which Prichard criticised. A view of this kind can be conveniently called 'noumenalism'.

Kant's position is made worse, once this view has been attributed to him, by his frequent claims that noumena are quite unknown to us, and that our knowledge (not merely perception) is limited (permanently and not initially) to appearances. For this directly conflicts with the premiss of the whole theory that noumena are known or supposed to affect our senses. Thus when Kant speaks of the causal series as restricted to appearances, for example, he reinforces the difficulty he already has over this premiss, which presupposes that a causal series may have a non-phenomenal member. It would be possible, superficially, to drop the claim to reconstruct knowledge of noumena, and so to produce a phenomenalism of the kind Prichard ascribed to Kant. But even if this ascription had not been shown to be inadequate in the previous chapter, Kant's position would still be open to the fatal criticisms which Prichard himself raised against it. These conflicting features indicate an apparent muddle in Kant's thought, which could be put generally by saying that on his view the objects which affect us must be noumenal, since they cannot be appearances, and yet that such objects could not be known to affect us. This is the traditional puzzle in Kant's account of perception and knowledge (see Vaihinger, *Kommentar*, Vol. 2, pp. 35–55). It may incline one to say that Kant was trying to extricate himself from the theory outlined above, and failing to do so; but in any case such conflicts should induce caution in the ascription of such a theory to him. The following passages suggest the total failure of such an ascription.

## (i) (a) A 366–373

This first passage occurs in the opening of the Fourth Paralogism in the first edition. The Paralogism itself, to be discussed in the whole of this section of the *Critique*, argues to the conclusion that the existence of outer objects is doubtful from the premiss that such objects are not immediately perceived but are inferred as the cause of given perceptions. Since Kant intends to reject this argument, it might seem as though he wished to assert in contrast that there is nothing doubtful about the supposed inference from given perception to its presumed cause. And if he had meant to reject the paralogism in this way, then this would amount to evidence that he was himself adopting a form of noumenalist theory. But his disagreement with the argument is not of this kind, and turns instead on his claim that outer objects are not *inferred* from given perceptions at all, but are immediately given in such perceptions (A 371: 'In order to arrive . . . but is immediately perceived', A 375). This by itself argues strongly against the ascription of noumenalism to Kant, but the importance of the passage lies more in the detail of Kant's discussion than in this summary conclusion to it.

Kant's discussion of the paralogism is, formally, very badly presented. Since he has chosen to express the rejected argument in an artificially formal way, and since it is his view that the argument so expressed commits a formal fallacy, it would be natural to expect a detailed analysis of the argument's logical structure. What is provided, however, amounts rather to an extended digression on his own account of perception in contrast to a doctrine (transcendental realism) which is not strictly concerned in the paralogism at all. This general air of confusion is present also in the misleading way in which Kant begins by appearing to agree with the premisses of the argument. Kemp Smith overcomes this difficulty by adding a parenthetical 'it is argued' in the translation, to suggest that Kant is merely rehearsing a view with which he wholly disagrees. It seems possible, however, that this unclarity arises because Kant regards the premisses, and their elaboration, as ambiguous, so that he might accept them in some constructions, but not in others, while the central point of the following discussion is to list these important ambiguities. Certainly his procedure in other paralogisms consists in detecting ambiguities in the premises (cf. B 410–411), and just such an ambiguity in the terms 'inner' and 'outer' is revealed in the centre of the present argument (A 373). These formal defects of presentation are not of great importance, and should not be allowed to obscure the doctrine which does emerge from the discussion. It is more useful to have Kant's unhampered account of perception than to disentangle the exact pattern of his formal thesis.

The discussion opens properly at A 369 ('Before exhibiting . . .') with Kant's distinction between transcendental idealism and transcendental realism. The transcendental realist is said to represent outer appearances as things in themselves, which are described as 'existing independently of us and of our sensibility' and 'outside (or separate from) us' in some special sense. Kant goes on (A 369): "It is, in fact this transcendental realist who afterwards plays the part of empirical idealist. After wrongly supposing that objects of the senses, if they are to be external, must have an existence by themselves, and independently of the senses, he finds that, judged from this point of view, all our sensuous representations are inadequate to establish their reality.' Transcendental realism is thus associated with an empirical idealism in which the limits of our perception of ideas fall far short of establishing the reality of any external object. Kant declares himself to be a transcendental idealist (A 370: 'From the start . . .'), and is therefore radically opposed to the stated realist view. But what Kant calls transcendental realism, in association with empirical idealism, is simply what we have called noumenalism. For adherents of the former doctrine, as Kant describes it, hold that external objects are things in themselves, that what is immediately presented to us are empirical ideas, and that an inference from the latter to the former is required. In rejecting this theory Kant is rejecting the theory of noumenalism.

It may seem that too much has been read into Kant's description of the transcendental realist. But Kant later elaborates the same argument (A 372) and puts this reading beyond doubt. He there says:

Since so far as I know all psychologists who adopt empirical idealism are transcendental realists, they have certainly proceeded quite consistently in ascribing great importance to empirical idealism, as one of the problems in regard to which the human mind is quite at a loss how to proceed. For if we regard outer appearances as representations produced in us by their objects, and if these objects be things existing in themselves outside us, it is indeed impossible to see how we can come to know the existence of the objects otherwise than by inference from the effect to the cause; and this being so it must always remain doubtful whether the cause in question be in us or outside us.

It is after this that Kant produces his distinction between two senses of the terms 'outside us' or 'external object'. In the first sense these phrases mean only 'what is spatial' or 'what is in space', and refer to appearances; in the second sense they mean 'what is totally independent of, or out of all relation to, the senses', and refer to noumena. Kant's own view about the objects described in these ways is, in contrast to that of transcendental realism, that we perceive appearances (spatial objects) immediately, and that no inference to noumena from what we perceive can be legitimate.

There can be no doubt that in this passage Kant consistently rejects what is a noumenalist theory. The efforts of the transcendental realist to establish truths about noumenal objects on the basis of our perceptions, sensations, or empirical ideas, parallel exactly those which Prichard supposed Kant himself to be making. Kant clearly identifies and rejects the claim that the objects said to affect us are noumena, and implies instead that if these objects are external in the spatial sense, as we ordinarily require and believe them to be, then they must be phenomenal objects or appearances. The puzzle which Kant leaves behind in all this is not whether he is secretly adopting a theory which he here explicitly rejects, but rather how to understand the theory he advocates in place of transcendental realism and empirical idealism. It is not yet clear what can be meant by his claims that he is a transcendental, and not empirical, idealist; that appearances are ideas, or representations, not in an empirical, but in a transcendental way; and that his theory eliminates the need for such a hopeless inference as that involved in noumenalism.

(*b*) B 333-334 ('The remaining concepts . . . their non-sensible cause')

Kant's central points in this passage are first that we have no knowledge of a transcendental ground or cause of appearances, and second that it is quite pointless to complain of this that we can therefore never know the inner nature of things in themselves. Once again Kant insists on the impossibility of inferring from appearances to noumenal objects, identified as the non-sensible or transcendental cause of appearances. These points are directed against Locke and Leibniz, who had been criticised in an earlier passage at B 326–327 for their attempts to establish knowledge of such noumenal objects. It has been noticed already (Ch. 1, p. 6) that Kant denies that appearances represent things in themselves, and these passages show that this denial is directed primarily against Leibniz' alleged view that appearances represent such things confusedly (cf. B 326 and B 332). A similar point against Leibniz' noumenalism is made at B 62, where Kant says: 'It is not that we cannot know the natures of things in themselves by our sensibility in any but a confused way; we do not apprehend them in any way whatsoever.' Again in the polemic against Eberhard (Ak., Vol. 8, pp. 207–209) Kant dismisses the temptation to believe that advances in scientific knowledge bring us nearer to knowledge of things as they really are, and so to knowledge of noumenal objects. He denies that a progress in enquiry from appearances to their noumenal ground is just like that from a distant view of a crowd to a close view of the individuals composing it. Kant held that scientific advances could not lead to knowledge of a different kind of object from those presented to the senses; they could lead only to a more extensive knowledge of sensible objects. The temptation to adopt a form of noumenalism on the basis of the view that science teaches us to see behind appearances to the way things really are is very powerful. Radical advances in science, such as those embodied in atomic theory or Newtonian mechanics, encourage metaphors like that of the crowd scene, and the adoption of noumenalism. That Kant did not succumb to this temptation and criticised Eberhard (and Leibniz) for adopting such a view shows once more that he himself rejected it.

Perhaps of even more importance in revealing Kant's attitude to noumenalist theories of perception is the reference to, and criticism of, Locke. For Locke, in his doctrine of primary and secondary qualities, undoubtedly held a noumenalist theory based partly on his belief in the special insight and status of scientific explanations. Locke's belief that our ideas of primary qualities can be held to resemble the qualities themselves is a noumenalist attempt to reconstruct the link between what we immediately perceive and the real objects themselves. This passage makes it clear that Kant ascribed such a theory to Locke and himself rejected it. He also makes clear that the restriction imposed on the scope of our knowledge by the failure of such an inference as Locke's, is not one about which it makes sense to complain. It imposes no practical limit on scientific investigation, but leaves open an indefinitely large area for further scientific advance (cf. *Prol.*, Sect. 57; Ak., Vol. 4, pp. 350–357). Kant seems to have noticed that such a *philosophic* failure to establish contact with an external world, and the consequent *philosophic* limitation on our knowledge, was not to the detriment of our ordinary and scientific beliefs about external objects. The same point is made in a passage in the *Prolegomena* to be discussed later (Sect. (*d*) below).

These implied criticisms of Locke and Leibniz amount to the claims that appearances are not representations of things in themselves; that we have no knowledge of the noumenal causes of appearances, even in the most spectacular scientific theories; that we are limited to knowledge of appearances, but that this limitation in no way prejudices our ordinary beliefs in the existence and properties of external objects. These claims together are quite incompatible with noumenalism. They would still leave it open to Kant to say either that it is proper to speak of a causal relation between phenomenal objects and our senses in empirical science, or that we may speak of the transcendental causes of our perceptions, in a non-literal way, to express a general intention to continue causal enquiries. They would not leave it open to him to say that things in themselves are literally or known to be the causes of appearances. Nor, consistently with this passage, could Kant have thought it worth while to attempt a reconstruction of the noumenal world through an inference from its sensible effects on us.

(*c*) B 342–346 ('If by merely intelligible objects . . . limited to our senses')

In this passage Kant repeats the claim that to speak of a noumenal cause of appearances is to talk emptily. He also indicates the mistake, which 'may excuse but cannot justify' the misuse of such a notion. The concept of a thing in itself is shown to have a peculiar force and to require careful handling. Although it may masquerade as the concept of a genuine object, its only proper use is to restrict our knowledge to appearances. This function it performs by purporting to name things of which we can have no knowledge, and it is therefore said to be not a concept of a genuine object, but a problem. This problem is simply that of saying whether there are such objects for intelligences other than ours; but this problem, as Kant is careful to explain, is not a genuine problem, since we have no means of settling it. Although we have no right to say that there are objects other than those which we experience sensibly, we have no right to deny this either. On this score the theory of noumenalism, if it were accepted by Kant at all, must be admitted only as a theory of this curiously problematic kind. Such a theory certainly could not be held to make any contribution towards explaining or guaranteeing our ordinary knowledge of appearances.

The temptation to conceive the idea of a noumenal cause arises because if we restrict our knowledge to appearances, then there is a compulsion to label, and therefore to seem to identify, what stands outside this limitation. It is not difficult to see how this temptation applies particularly to any causal account of perception. Kant concedes that once we acquire this conception we may use the term 'noumenon' to stand for it: 'If we are pleased to name this object "noumenon" for the reason that its representation is not sensible, we are free to do so. But since we can apply to it none of the concepts of our understanding, the representation remains for us empty, and is of no service except to mark the limits of our sensible knowledge.' Kant also, however, adds a warning against the pointless attempt to operate with such concepts of intelligible objects, as though they were genuine concepts of objects.[1] The mistake which we may make in speaking of or producing such notions is that of becoming too abstract in thought until we abandon the world of sensible objects altogether. It is as though in understanding the phrase 'the cause of our perceptions' we should think that this refers to some unique super-sensible object, instead of recognising that it is a compendious way of referring to

---

[1] Kant says (B 345): 'Die Kritik . . . erlaubt es . . . sogar nicht einmal in ihren Begriff auszuschweifen.' Kemp Smith translates this as 'it does not allow of our entertaining even the concept of them', although Kant clearly admits that we can conceive such things. What Kant means would therefore be better expressed by saying that we ought not to *operate* with these concepts, even though, in some way, we clearly have them.

a range of possible objects that can themselves be perceived. This account again makes it evident that Kant would admit the premisses of noumenalism only in a way which recognised the dangers of misconstruction in them. In particular to admit that we may, if we wish, speak of a transcendental cause of appearances, is not to suppose that we have or could have any knowledge of such a relation, in the way that a transcendental realist might claim.

## (d) *Prolegomena*, Sect. 13, Note II (Ak., Vol. 4, pp. 288–290)

In this passage Kant again refers to Locke's doctrine of primary and secondary qualities, with the intention of rejecting both this theory and the idealism, which Berkeley produced as a result of his criticism of Locke's doctrine. Much of what Kant says in this passage, however, appears ambiguous, and some of it can be, and almost certainly has been, taken as a statement rather than as a denial of this latter Berkeleyan theory. The temptation in the passage is not only that it may be understood to commit Kant to idealism, but also that he may be thought to have avoided this theory only by committing himself to the existence of things in themselves. Kant says:

> That we can say, without prejudice to the real existence of outer things, of a number of their predicates that they belong not to these things in themselves, but only to their appearances, and would have no existence apart from our ideas,—this is something recognised and admitted long before Locke's time, though mostly only after it. In this class belong warmth, colours, taste, etc. That I ascribe to mere appearances over and above these the other qualities of bodies which are called 'primary', extension, location, space and all that goes with these (impenetrability, materiality, figure, etc.) against this nobody can cite the least objection. (Kant goes on to say that this does not make him an idealist.)

On a cursory reading of this it would be natural to conclude not only that Kant believed all properties of objects to be ideas or sensations, but also that he accepted the existence of things in themselves, which produce these ideas in us. If it is objected that Kant certainly means to deny that he is an idealist, then the answer simply is that his assumption of the existence of things in themselves constitutes his denial of this idealist theory. In this way such a passage seems to reinforce the ascription of noumenalism to

Kant, even though it is incompatible with the views outlined in the Fourth Paralogism.

The claims about the existence of things in themselves arise from the opening sentence. Kant does not say, however, that what is not to be prejudiced is the existence of things in themselves, but only and non-committally that it is the existence of 'outer things' that enjoys this privilege. If this phrase is understood to refer to things in space, as it was construed at A 372–373 (Sect. (*a*) above), then Kant would be committing himself afresh only to the existence of spatial objects, that is, appearances. What can be said without prejudice to the existence of outer things is that a number of *their* predicates do not belong to things in themselves. This seems to imply that Kant is consistently denying that we know properties of noumenal objects. But Kant says that such predicates do not belong to *these* things in themselves, as though the outer things previously mentioned must after all be noumena. Yet if the sentence is read in this way it becomes absurd, for it then states that some predicates which belong to things in themselves (*their* predicates) belong not to things in themselves, but to appearances. It would be easy to say that in this sentence Kant is outlining a view (Locke's) with which he really disagrees, and therefore that these apparent commitments to noumena apply to Locke, but not to Kant. Nevertheless there is, in the passage, a presumption that Kant's own view could be stated by altering the opening sentence, so that it applies not just to some predicates, but to all of them. In this case, once more, what Kant may seem to be saying is that we know properties of appearances only, and yet that this can be admitted without prejudicing the existence of outer things in themselves.

It is possible to clarify this difficulty by appealing to a different, and more revealing, way of distinguishing between things in themselves and appearances. Often (e.g. B 43, B 56, B 157–158, B 186, B 329–330, etc.) Kant speaks of things *as* they are in themselves, and by contrast of things *as* appearances. This mode of expression implies that, for Kant, there is only one set of objects, although philosophers for various reasons have sometimes ascribed to them a different status, now thinking of them *as* noumena, now *as* appearances. If this terminology is applied to the difficult passage above, it becomes more easily comprehensible. For Kant is then saying that some predicates, ordinarily ascribed to outer spatial objects, do not belong to these things as they are in themselves, that is, construed as noumena, but belong instead to these things as appearances. Locke's view that this is not true of all predicates is now accommodated by the implication that, for him, some other predicates do belong to these things construed as noumena. Kant's view on the other hand, is that no predicates belong to these things as they are in themselves, and that this can be held without detriment to the existence of outer things as appearances. On this account Kant is again consistently rejecting Locke's doctrine of the distinction between primary and secondary qualities, and with it a theory of noumenalism.

This account of the distinction between things in themselves and appearances is of some importance. Kant puzzlingly speaks sometimes (e.g. B xxvi–xxvii) as though these were intimately related, though he spends a good deal of time distinguishing them. Some commentators, for example Paton (*Kant's Metaphysic of Experience*, Vol. I, p. 422), have rightly insisted that these are not two different things, but only two different ways of looking at the same thing. While this usefully avoids the mistake of supposing that the two concepts name different objects, it may mislead by suggesting that appearances and noumena are simply two sides of the same coin, or equal partners in the same joint enterprise. The truth seems to be, however, that these are two ways of looking at the same thing only because, on Kant's view, there is only one thing at which to look, namely appearance. These metaphors, and with them the attempt to subsume both appearances and noumena under a common category, do not properly reflect Kant's position, and Kant himself discourages such illustrations of his distinction (Ch. 3, pp. 47 ff.). Nevertheless the belief that there is but one set of objects, although there are two ways of accounting for them, helps to explain why Kant sometimes speaks of the close link between appearances and noumena. It also helps to make clear some of the difficulties of expression which Kant inevitably had in discussing or using the distinction.

## (ii) A 381–393

The important part in this last passage to be considered occurs from A 389–392 ('So long as we hold . . . void and illicit'). This part cannot, however, be understood without reference to what precedes it both in the Fourth Paralogism and in the general summary to the Paralogisms (A 381). It has been already suggested that Kant's account of the objects said to affect our senses presents the general difficulty that these objects can apparently be neither appearances (for these are 'mere representations') nor things in themselves (for these are unknown to us). Yet it also seems that these objects must be either appearances or things in themselves. This traditional criticism of Kant is associated particularly with Jacobi's review of the *Critique*, in which he said: 'Without the thing in itself I cannot enter the Critical philosophy, and with it I cannot stay there' (F. H. Jacobi: *Werke*, Leipzig, Vol. II, p. 304. Vaihinger: *Kommentar*, Vol. 2, p. 36). This objection presumes that Kant relied on noumenal objects to produce modifications of our senses, and yet that on his account there is no ground to rely on such a relation, since noumena are unknown to us. Since Jacobi's time this same criticism has been persistently raised against Kant. In the present passage Kant seems to recognise and accommodate this difficulty.

Kant begins the section after the Fourth Paralogism (A 381) by discussing the differences between psychology and physics. The central point is to explain why rational psychology is a pseudoscience, and to recommend that this name should be used to stand, not for a supposed science, but for a critical discipline designed to restrain philosophic theories. Kant then (A 384) mentions three problems, resulting in philosophic theories of a type needing the attentions of the new discipline. These problems centre on the interaction or 'communion' of mind and matter, difficulties in accounting for which are, according to Kant, the result of a 'mere delusion' (A 384). It is plain from the elaboration of this delusion that it consists in mistaking what are appearances for things in themselves, totally independent of the senses. It is, therefore, the same mistake as that committed by what Kant had called the transcendental realist in the Fourth Paralogism. If material things are taken in this way, then they are quite heterogeneous to the mental ideas of our senses, and it then appears inexplicable that such material things should or could affect our senses. Kant argues, on the contrary, that mind and matter are not heterogeneous in this way: '(A 385): Matter therefore does not mean a kind of substance quite distinct and heterogeneous from the object of inner sense (the soul), but only the distinctive nature of those

appearances of objects—in themselves unknown to us—the representations of which we call outer, as compared with those which
we count as belonging to inner sense . . .' Hence for Kant the
problem breaks down either into a matter of empirical psychology,
or into transcendental philosophy (A 386, A 387), or else into a
question we have no means of answering at all (A 392–393).

Kant's account of this problem of interaction, and its illusori-
ness, leans heavily on what he has already established in the Fourth
Paralogism. The delusive hypostatisation, which Kant regards as
the mistake on which the alleged difficulties turn, is that associated
with the doctrines of transcendental realism coupled with empirical idealism (conveniently abbreviated to 'transcendental dualism'
at A 379 and A 389). On the assumptions of this doctrine, that
material things are noumena, while their effects in us are empirical
ideas belonging to the mind, the relation of mind and matter is
incomprehensible. Kant insists that the correct way to deal with
this difficulty is not to accept these assumptions and try to solve
the problem of interaction, but instead to replace the assumptions
so that the problem no longer arises. In this way Kant accuses
transcendental dualists of what can be called a category mistake.
For their pseudo-problem arises only because they wrongly assign
mind and matter to categories so different that it is impossible to
account for their interaction.

At this point (A 389) Kant returns to the specific theories designed to account for the interaction of mind and matter, which it
is the task of his rational psychology to discipline. It is explained,
in conformity with what has gone before, that these philosophic
theories are all held on the assumptions of transcendental dualism,
that is, that we are immediately presented with empirical ideas,
from which we are supposed to infer their noumenal causes. The
three theories now mentioned are that of 'physical influence', and
two others which arise as objections to this, namely those of
'predetermined harmony' and 'supernatural intervention'. In objection to the first of these it is argued by the others that:

> what appears as matter cannot by its immediate influence be the cause
> of representations, these being effects which are quite different in
> kind from matter. Now those who take this line cannot attach to
> what they understand by 'object of outer senses' the concept of a
> matter which is nothing but appearance, and so itself a mere repre-
> sentation produced by some sort of outer objects. For in that case

they would be saying that the representations of outer objects (appearances) cannot be outer causes of the representations in our mind; and this would be a quite meaningless objection, since no one could dream of holding that what he has once come to recognise as mere representation, is an outer cause. On our principles they can establish their theory only by showing that that which is the true (transcendental) object of our outer senses cannot be the cause of those representations (appearances) which we comprehend under the title 'matter'. No one, however, can have the right to claim that he knows anything in regard to the transcendental cause of our representations of the outer senses; and their assertion is therefore entirely groundless.

The most remarkable feature of this argument is the dilemma constructed by Kant against those who argue against the physical influence theory. The basic argument against them is that they (as transcendental dualists) have a choice between understanding by 'external object' either 'mere appearance (representation)' or else 'transcendental object (totally independent of the senses)'. If they mean the former, then their objection amounts to saying that representations of outer objects cannot be outer causes of representations in our minds. This objection is absurd, since no one who accepted the physical influence theory would ever have held that what is recognised as a representation could be an outer cause. Consequently such an objection must miss the point. If, however, they mean the latter, then their objection amounts to the claim that a (transcendental) thing in itself cannot be the cause of our representations. But in this case, since we have no ground for claiming to know anything about such objects, we have no ground either for accepting or rejecting such a claim. Hence such objections to the physical influence theory must be either irrelevant or untestable.

The use Kant makes of this dilemma is rather complex. What he intends to do is to show the futility of disputing among the three rival theories, so long as they are all constructed on the assumptions of the transcendental dualist. For the objections of one theory against another are defective precisely because they have to be made within the framework of these assumptions. Each of these theories was thus compelled to regard external objects either as things in themselves (in which case they are unknown to us) or as empirical representations (in which case they are not external). Thus when Kant concludes his argument (A 391) by claiming that the difficulties in these theories of the interaction of mind and matter are all due to this 'illicitly assumed dualist view', he is disputing that these are the only constructions of the term 'external object' open to him. The illicit assumption is that in the construction of this term there are only two categories to choose from, either noumenon or empirical idea. This alternative was also the basis of the doctrine ascribed to the transcendental realist-empirical idealist in the Fourth Paralogism, and in disputing it once more Kant is again rejecting a noumenalist theory.

It is not difficult to see how this argument bears on the criticism made by Jacobi of Kant. Jacobi's argument presents Kant with a dilemma which parallels exactly that which Kant himself has constructed against the transcendental dualists. Both arguments insist on the defects of saying either that outer causes are empirical ideas (appearances) or things in themselves. Jacobi's criticism presupposed that Kant had no other alternative but to regard external objects in one or other of these two ways. For if Kant had some other way of accounting for them, then the objection would be inconclusive against him. Yet the passage just examined shows that Kant himself regarded the same dualism as an illicit assumption, to which he was not committed. This argues that Kant had some alternative way in which to account for his notion of an external object affecting our senses, and this is confirmed also by the other passages examined above. For in them Kant makes it clear that he is not an *empirical* but a *transcendental* idealist. Part of what this seems to mean is that he is not committed, as an empirical idealist would be, to the view that appearances are merely empirical ideas. If appearances are said by Kant to be ideas or representations, then they must be so not in an empirical but in some transcendental way. In denying that appearances can be regarded as empirical ideas Kant provides a possible way of avoiding both the illicit dualism, and Jacobi's objection.

It would be wrong to think that these passages establish that Kant never held a doctrine such as noumenalism. They show nonetheless that Kant often expressed views incompatible with, and in conscious rejection of, such a doctrine in the *Critique*. There are many other passages in which it is possible to read a commitment to this theory, where Kant speaks of things in themselves and their appearances, or of appearances as appearances of unknown things in themselves (e.g. B xxvi–xxvii, A 391). These passages have always encouraged the belief that Kant was a noumenalist, even though such claims, and their mode of expression, are often curiously incidental to the main argument. They leave a puzzle for interpreters of Kant, however his doctrines are understood.

The examined passages do not solve this puzzle, but they point clearly enough to one solution. Their predominant message is that no causal relation between things in themselves and our senses can ever be established, and hence that any established causal relation between external objects and our senses must refer to appearances and not to things in themselves. Kant implies that he holds the 'physical influence' theory of A 390 so long as it is correctly interpreted in the light of a 'well-founded critical objection' (A 392). He regards it as a mistaken theory, so long as it is held under the assumptions of transcendental dualism, but as unobjectionable once these assumptions are abandoned. In its purified form the theory seems to be an empirical theory of optics and psychology, of the kind outlined at A 386 and A 387. Such a theory is concerned with empirical objects, appearances, and not with things in themselves. As an empirical scientific theory it is beyond reproach, and becomes objectionable only when it acquires the philosophic accretions of transcendental dualism.

There is therefore one clear way in which it is proper for Kant to speak of a causal relation between external objects and our senses. Kant also, however, admits the propriety of speaking in another way, as if noumena could be regarded as causes of our perceptions (passage (c) above). The difference between these claims is that whereas the first can be empirically established, the second can neither be established nor rejected, for we have no knowledge of things in themselves, and therefore no knowledge of the features they may have. Kant concedes that we may talk in this way, if we wish, but insists that we do not understand such claims as a genuine theory of perception. Such claims are, on Kant's view, empty but inevitable, and permissible only so long as the dangers of hypostatisation, and limits on their use, are clearly recognised. It is possible, in the light of these claims, to accommodate consistently the very different ways in which Kant speaks of such causal relations. Kant's rejection of noumenalism is therefore not of a kind which regards the theory as false, but of the kind which regards it as not a genuine theory at all.

Two further problems stand out from this account. Kant's intention to replace noumenalism is fulfilled in his account of the term 'appearance'. It has been suggested already that Kant hopes to avoid the assumptions of transcendental dualism by claiming that although appearances are ideas, they are not empirical ideas. In order to clarify this contention Kant's distinction between transcendental and empirical will be discussed in the next chapter. More generally, Kant raises a problem about the notion of an object. If, as Kant claims, our knowledge is restricted to appearances, then it is necessary to explain how we can speak of appearances of objects, or of appearances as objects. To put this in another way Kant is committed to providing an account of the term 'of' in such a phrase as 'appearance (or representation) of an object'. Kant certainly recognises this need, and the whole of the Analytic is designed to satisfy it. The question at A 104, in the opening of the transcendental Deduction, where Kant asks 'What is meant by the phrase "object of representations"?', contains an explicit recognition of the difficulty. That Kant admits the need to answer such a question, without appealing to a noumenalist theory of perception, argues finally that Kant was not committed to such a theory in the *Critique*.

# 3

# TRANSCENDENTAL
# AND EMPIRICAL

---

'All this clearly points to the conclusion that transcendental questions allow only of transcendental answers . . .' (B 665).

IT has been already suggested (Ch. 1, p. 16) that the distinction between transcendental and empirical bears directly on Kant's aim in the Deduction; and many commentators have recognised the importance of this distinction in the *Critique*. One of the earliest, Mellin, understood Kant to mean that the objects said to affect our senses do so in a dual way. On his view Kant thought that although these objects were themselves empirical, yet they had an effect both upon our empirical and our transcendental sensibility. Much more recently a similar position was reached by Adickes, who suggested a complex 'double affection' between appearances and things in themselves on one side and empirical and noumenal selves on the other. Such views are more simply illustrated by diagrams such as those which appear in Kemp Smith's *Commentary* (p. 281) or Weldon's *Kant's Critique of Pure Reason* (2nd ed., p. 253). Yet such diagrams presuppose that the objects drawn in them can be easily distinguished, when in reality nobody has been able to give a clear and unobjectionable sense to the notions of a transcendental object or a transcendental self.

There is at least one passage in Kant's writings where he notices and firmly rejects duplications of entities in this way. At the time when he was writing the *Prolegomena* he criticised Berkeley for needlessly duplicating mental phenomena, by bringing them into relation both with appearances and things in themselves. He said

(Ak., Vol. 23, p. 58): 'Berkeley found nothing constant, and could find nothing so, which the understanding conceived in accordance with a priori principles, so he had to look for another intuition, namely the mystical one of God's ideas, which required a two-fold understanding, one which connected phenomena in experience, and another which knew things in themselves. I require only one sensibility and only one understanding.' Whether this is a fair account of Berkeley or not, it clearly testifies to Kant's lack of intention to develop seriously complex relations between two kinds of object and two kinds of person, empirical and transcendental, along the lines of Adickes or Mellin.

In the *Critique* Kant certainly distinguishes between transcendental and empirical objects, transcendental and empirical syntheses, transcendental and practical freedom, and transcendental and empirical selves. But the central use of this distinction, which was noted earlier (in Ch. 1), is to separate two kinds of enquiries or questions or claims. Such uses of the distinction as those cited above should be taken to mean that we can investigate objects or synthesis, the self or freedom, either empirically or transcendentally. And this implies that we may also distinguish empirical from transcendental questions about these things, and empirical from transcendental claims in answer to them. Such phrases should be understood to refer not to two different kinds of entity, but instead to two different ways of talking about one and the same thing. The terms 'transcendental' and 'empirical' behave properly, for this reason, more like adverbs than like adjectives. In order to obtain a closer look at Kant's use of the distinction we shall consider two kinds of passage. In the first of these Kant talks generally of the contrast, and in the second it is applied particularly to his account of perception.

## (i) THE DISTINCTION IN GENERAL

There are many passages where Kant speaks initially of the special status of transcendental knowledge or transcendental philosophy. At B 25 he says:

As such, it should be called a critique, not a doctrine, of pure reason. Its utility, in speculation, ought properly to be only negative, not to extend, but only to clarify our reason, and keep it free from errors—which is already a very great gain. I entitle 'transcendental' all knowledge which is occupied not so much with objects as with the mode of our knowledge of objects in so far as this mode of knowledge is to be possible a priori. A system of such concepts might be entitled transcendental philosophy.

Similarly at B 40 Kant explains that by a 'transcendental exposition' he means the explanation of a concept as a principle from which the possibility of other a priori synthetic knowledge can be understood. These quotations serve only to show that a transcendental philosophy, or exposition, or knowledge is of a quite special kind, not to be classed with even a priori knowledge of a mathematical kind, still less with everyday empirical knowledge. Such higher-order enquiries tell us nothing about objects in the accepted ordinary or scientific ways, but only about the kinds, status, or limits of such ordinary or scientific knowledge. The same points are made forcibly in a passage at B 296–298.

These first passages are further elaborated in others at B 80–81, *Prol.*, Sect. 21a, B 117–118, and A 97, some of which have been already noted (in Ch. 1). In the last two of these, as we saw, Kant distinguishes his transcendental task from that empirical investigation of the formation of concepts, which he believed Locke to have undertaken. The same point is made in the *Prolegomena* passage, where Kant speaks of his aim as that of providing a 'critique of knowledge' as he does in the passage at B 25. This phrase occurs also at B 80–81, where Kant says:

> Not every kind of knowledge a priori should be called transcendental, but only that by which we know that—and how—certain representations (concepts and intuitions) can be employed or are possible a priori. . . . The distinction between the transcendental and the empirical belongs therefore only to the critique of knowledge; it does not concern the relation of that knowledge to its objects.

This should be linked with another passage from the *Prolegomena*, Sect. 13 (Ak., Vol. 4, p. 293), where Kant says: 'The word "transcendental" never signifies with me the relation of knowledge to an object, but only that to our faculty of knowledge.' Part of what Kant seems to mean by these denials that the distinction bears on the relation of knowledge to its objects is that, if we speak of transcendental knowledge, this must not be taken to mean that it is knowledge of any transcendental objects. This is part of the negative, limiting, aim of Kant's 'critique' of knowledge (see also B xxv, B 296–298), that it informs us neither directly about objects in our experience, nor about any special objects beyond it. This critical aim is well exemplified in the identification of the mistakes arising from the concept of a noumenal cause of appearances (B 344–345) as those of 'employing understanding transcendentally, and so making objects conform to concepts'. For this is to say that such mistakes arise from hypostatising what exists merely in thought (A 384) and so misusing the concept of a noumenon, which properly (B 344) is not a concept of an *object* at all.

Kant also means to suggest that his transcendental enquiry, or the claims it makes, is not intended to cast doubt on any ordinary beliefs about physical objects. The passage from the *Prolegomena* quoted above comes from a context in which Kant denies that his form of idealism makes the existence of external objects in any way dubious, and other passages at B 45 and A 393 show how Kant thought such empirical beliefs were insulated from transcendental claims. At B 45 he says: 'The true correlate of sensibility, the thing in itself, is not known, and cannot be known through these representations; and in experience no question is ever asked in regard to it.' And at A 393: 'In all problems which may arise in the field of experience we treat these appearances as things in themselves, without troubling ourselves about the primary ground of their possibility (as appearances). But to advance beyond these limits the concept of a transcendental object would be required.' Kant's point is that ordinarily we investigate phenomena, for example in science, without considering questions about the status of the objects referred to in such investigations. Such a concern about the status of our knowledge of phenomena is not itself of an empirical but of a transcendental kind. The differences between these are exemplified in the argument already discussed over the relation of mind and matter (A 384–394) (in Ch. 2, pp. 29–33). For this provides a concrete account of the way in which an indisputable empirical theory of optics may become extended so that it gives rise to apparently insoluble problems of metaphysics. This progress from empirical theory to metaphysics is precisely that which Kant refers to in his prefatory remarks (A vii–viii). In this case Kant evidently believed that the path away from the empirical theory led only to pseudo-problems, but it would be wrong to think that all transcendental problems could be resolved in this way. Such transcendental problems as those which Kant regards as arising from the status of mathematical or scientific systems (B 80–81) present difficulties which cannot be resolved in this way. These difficulties, nevertheless, are of a transcendental kind and cast no doubt on the empirical validity of such systems (cf. *Prol.*, Sect. 13, Ak., Vol. 4, pp. 293–294; and B 56: 'This ideality . . . our intuition of them').

These passages help to show how Kant's distinction should be understood in general terms. Now two important passages must be carefully examined which apply this general account to problems about perception. These occur at B 62–63 and B 235–236, and may be regarded as introducing Kant's complete account of perception in the Paralogisms and the Aesthetic. The first of these runs:

> We commonly distinguish in appearances that which is essentially inherent in their intuition and holds for sense in all human beings, from that which belongs to their intuition accidentally only, and is valid not in relation to sensibility in general, but only in relation to a particular standpoint, or to a peculiarity of structure in this or that sense. But this distinction is merely empirical. If, as generally happens, we stop short at this point, and do not proceed, as we ought, to treat the empirical intuition itself as mere appearance, in which nothing that belongs to a thing in itself can be found, our transcendental distinction is lost . . . The rainbow in a sunny shower may be called a mere appearance, and the rain a thing in itself. This is correct if the latter concept be taken in a merely physical sense . . . But if we take this empirical object (*the empirical in general*) and ask, without considering whether or not it is the same for all human sense, whether it represents an object in itself (and by that we cannot mean the drops of rain, for they are already as appearances, empirical objects) the question as to the relation of the representation to the object becomes transcendental.[1] (And to this question Kant's answer is 'No' or 'We have no means of knowing'.)

There is no real need to examine carefully what Kant says of the distinction between rainbows and raindrops. It is true that we ordinarily regard the latter as more substantial than the former, and that there are simple differences in the ways in which we might test other people's claims to have seen these different types of thing. The important point in this passage is not, however, the exact distinction between these, but the distinction Kant draws

[1] It is well worth-while to compare this passage with another at B 401–402: 'For inner experience . . . which is certainly a transcendental enquiry.'

between empirical and transcendental questions about the objects of perception. For Kant both rainbows and raindrops are empirical objects of perception, and these terms are both contrasted with answers that might instead be given to a transcendental question about the things that we perceive. The fact that Kant also distinguishes two different kinds of empirical answer to such a question is irrelevant to his claim that both such answers are to be distinguished, as empirical, from another which is transcendental.

The question which invites such different answers can be represented simply as 'What do you perceive?' or more particularly 'What can you see?' Such questions as these might be asked in a context where the interest lay only in finding out whether some person had seen the rainbow as well as the rain. In such a case the appropriate answer would be one which served to distinguish between the things which as a matter of fact it would be true to say that the person could now see, or one which served to distinguish the whole scene now presented to him from others that he might perceive or see on other occasions. If the person's reply did distinguish in this way between such things, then he would have given an empirical answer to the original question. Since either answer 'I can see a rainbow' or 'I can see (or hear) the rain' would distinguish between such things in this way, both would count as empirical answers.

The same question understood in a transcendental way does not invite this kind of answer, but instead one about the general status of things perceived. In this way such a question would be designed to ask not what is perceived on some particular occasion, but rather what kind or type of thing is perceived when we perceive anything whatever. Kant does not put the difference between the two questions in quite this way, though this is one way of putting it. For him the contrast is between asking of an intuition whether it represents a rainbow, or rain, which are, for Kant, empirical descriptions, and asking whether it could be said, however it might be described empirically ('*the empirical in general*'), to represent a thing in itself totally independent of the senses. To this question Kant's answer is either that it cannot be said to represent things in themselves of this (transcendental) kind, or else that we have no means of knowing whether it does, since we know of objects only through our senses, and these objects all have the status of appearances. Hence Kant's answer to the transcendental question as we expressed it above would be to say that the type of thing that we perceive when we perceive anything is an appearance, and not a transcendental thing in itself. Kant allows that empirically we may treat appearances as things in themselves in a physical sense, and this is to insist once more that his transcendental enquiry is insulated from our empirical beliefs in the way indicated in the passages quoted above (B 45, A 393, B 56).

Kant's answer to the transcendental question is for the moment less important than the question itself. The contrast between the two kinds of answer to it can be shown by the absurdity that would result from giving the transcendental answer to the empirical question, and the inadequacy that would result from giving an empirical answer to the transcendental question. For in the former case, if someone were asked to say what he particularly perceived on this occasion, and gave the right transcendental answer ('appearance'), it would be totally uninformative since it would not distinguish between all the things which it would be possible for him to perceive on this or any other occasion. If he gave the wrong transcendental answer ('noumenon'), and as it is fair to suppose we never could perceive what he now claims to see, his answer would be no more informative. In the latter case to give an empirical answer to the transcendental question would always be inadequate, since it would be one which discriminated between the things that might be perceived on any occasion, and so would inevitably fail to cover all the things that we perceive when we perceive anything whatever. As soon as a description, in answer to such a question, becomes so general that it does not serve to discriminate between what is perceived on different occasions, then it ceases to be an empirical and becomes a transcendental answer.

Kant also distinguishes between this transcendental question and a further problem which arises out of his answer to it. This further problem is stated most clearly at B 234–236 ('The apprehension of the manifold . . . necessary rule of apprehension'). (See Chap. 10, pp. 154 ff.) In this passage Kant begins by saying that every intuition may count trivially as an object, but that it is a further matter to say what such intuitions represent. This question, which is again the transcendental question aired at B 62–63, is now summarily answered (B 236): 'Now immediately I unfold the transcendental meaning of my concepts of an object, I realise that the house is not a thing in itself, but only an appearance, that is, a representation, the transcendental object of which is unknown'. Now, however, it appears that this answer, although right, is itself inadequate in respect of the further question of what the word 'object' signifies in regard to appearances. For, as Kant goes on to say, in order to count an appearance as an object it must be distinguished in some way from other objects. That is, part of what it means to be an object in this case is to be an appearance of some discriminable and objective kind. Hence the right general answer to the transcendental question cannot help here, for it was a condition of its being the right answer that it should fail to discriminate one apprehended thing from any other. The same points about the need for discrimination between what is presented to the senses, expressed in the language of a 'manifold of intuition', are made in the early passages of the Deduction (A) (A 97, A 99; see Ch. 1, pp. 12–15). Kant's general intention in the Analytic of Principles is to solve this further problem by showing how the categories and their associated principles enable us to discriminate between phenomenal objects in certain allegedly basic ways. This aim cannot be discussed now (see Ch. 10), and for the present it is enough simply to notice the emergence of this further problem.

### (ii) THE FOURTH PARALOGISM (A)

In the Fourth Paralogism (A 366–380) as we have already seen (Ch. 2), Kant dismisses the view that the existence of external objects is doubtful, because based insecurely on a causal inference from the representations that are immediately perceived. Kant's view on the other hand explains that (A 371): 'The transcendental idealist (Kant) is therefore an empirical realist, and allows to matter, as appearance, a reality which does not permit of being inferred, but is immediately perceived.' For Kant the appearances of inner and outer sense are both immediately perceived, and the distinction between them is a merely empirical one, which is only mistakenly turned into a transcendental distinction by those who think of external objects as things in themselves. For Kant (A 372–373): 'The transcendental object is equally unknown in respect to inner and to outer intuition. But it is not of this that we are speaking, but of the empirical object, which is called an external object if it is represented in space, and an inner object if it is represented only in its time relations.' At this point Kant notices that the difference between transcendental realism, which he rejects, and transcendental idealism can be put in terms of the distinct senses which each theory gives to the phrase 'external object'. To be external in the empirical sense (in which Kant admits the existence of external objects) is to be in space, or have spatial properties; to be external in the transcendental sense (as in transcendental realism) is to be entirely separate from our sensibility in the way that the transcendental cause of appearances is supposed to be. Kant then attacks the argument from illusion (A 376–377), distinguishes his empirical dualism from transcendental dualism as before, and concludes by arguing (A 380): 'If then, as this critical argument obviously compels us to do, we hold fast to the rule above established, and do not push our questions beyond the limits within which possible experience can present us with its object, we shall never dream of seeking to inform ourselves about the objects of our senses as they are in themselves, that is, out of all relation to our senses.' This critical restriction on our powers of investigation is clearly the same as that made at B 62–63.

The central feature of this argument is Kant's denial of transcendental realism–empirical idealism (which I shall call transcendental dualism) and his adoption of transcendental idealism–empirical realism (empirical dualism). The force of the denial can be explained, as Kant explains it, through the detected ambiguities in the (transcendental or empirical) senses of the term 'external' as applied to objects. The disagreements between the rival theories can then be stated in terms of the different ways in which they subscribe to the following claims: (a) That there are external objects of which we have knowledge. (b) That we are immediately aware only of our ideas, or representations. For Kant the first claim is transcendentally false, but is empirically true; and the second is false empirically, but true in a transcendental sense. This is to say that for Kant external objects must be admitted to exist as a matter of empirical fact (empirical realism), but not as a transcendental claim (transcendental realism); and that although it is false as a matter of fact that we are aware only of our ideas (empirical idealism), this is transcendentally true (transcendental idealism).

In claiming that the first statement is empirically true Kant is asserting that we know about objects of a spatial kind, and that ordinarily we discuss and investigate their properties unconcerned about the philosophic (transcendental) problems which may arise out of such ordinary beliefs (cf. B 45 and A 393). To say that such a claim about external objects is false if it is taken in a transcendental sense is to deny that we have any knowledge of objects inaccessible to the senses, such as were supposed to exist in the theory of transcendental realism. This denial must be distinguished from the claim that we may on occasion acquire knowledge of things inaccessible to the senses so far in scientific empirical enquiries. For Kant admits that we may properly speak of things which are imperceptible to us in cases where these have been inferred from given perceptions in accordance with accepted physical laws. The example which he gives of this is at B 273, where he says: 'From the perception of the attracted iron filings we know of the existence of a magnetic matter pervading all bodies, although the constitution of our organs cuts us off from all immediate perception of this medium.' This special case is quite different from the radical supposition that all our appearances, and not just those of magnetic phenomena, stand to an imperceptible cause in this way. Morever this particular inference rests on the assumption that the things from which the magnetic matter is inferred are immediately perceived empirical objects, namely iron filings, and not the mere ideas of the transcendental dualist. Kant suggests that in this limited kind of case a hypothetical analysis would be appropriate; that is, that we should explain what was meant by such an inference by saying that we should, were our senses more refined, come also upon an immediate intuition of the inferred entity (B 273). A similar analysis is suggested by Kant for the claim that there are men on the moon (B 521), but he indicates such analyses only for particular cases of these kinds, and not, as a phenomenalist would, for all perception of objects.

Kant's approach to the second statement is dictated by his account of the first. For if empirically we are immediately aware of external spatial objects, then empirically we cannot be aware only of our ideas. The claim, therefore, that we are aware only of our ideas is, for Kant, empirically false. In the empirical sense of the word 'idea' or the term 'in us', an idea or inner intuition is specifically distinguished by Kant from any empirically external object. This is the basis of Kant's empirical dualism, which adheres to the ordinary conviction that discriminates between mental phenomena, images or sensations, and spatial objects. Empirical idealism claims that the only things we perceive (properly or immediately) are those belonging to inner sense, and for Kant this is simply false. It is, on his view, empirically false that I do not (and immediately) perceive chairs and tables, and false to allocate such things to inner sense. For to do this would be to say that they are not in space, but only in time, and this is simply not so.

Since Kant is here supporting the answer he gives to the preliminary question about the status of the objects we perceive, it is natural to understand his account in a negative way. It can be said, therefore, that Kant is an empirical realist because it is false to suppose that we perceive only ideas in the empirical sense, that is, sensations; and that he is a transcendental idealist because it is quite unwarranted to make claims about objects which are not open to any sort of perceptual inspection. Or we could say that Kant is an idealist because we can know nothing of (transcendental) things in themselves, and a transcendental idealist because our knowledge is not limited to ideas in the empirical sense.

Because of this important difference between what empirical and transcendental idealism deny, Kant's claims that space time and appearances are transcendentally ideal, or ideas in a transcendental sense, cannot be understood in terms of our ordinary use of 'idea' or 'appearance'. To call the objects of our perception 'appearances', or space and time 'ideal', is to treat them neither as mere sensations, nor as only illusory guides to reality. The force of the claims in which Kant speaks of appearances or space and time in this way is primarily to deny that such things either are, or belong to, things in themselves totally independent of the senses. To call the objects of our perception appearances or ideas, in this transcendental way, is to make no claim about their empirical status. Some appearances are empirical ideas, like sensations, belonging to inner sense; but others, those of outer sense, are not empirical ideas at all, but just what these are contrasted with ordinarily and in empirical dualism.

It would be natural to object to this by saying that although Kant talks of the ideality of space and time, he does not talk of the ideality of appearances; or that when he describes appearances as ideas, or representations, he does not say that this is to be understood in a transcendental and not empirical way. It is true that Kant talks of the ideality of space and time much more than of that of appearance, and true that he most often says only that appearances are ideas, and not ideas in the transcendental sense. But it would be wrong to think that he never talks of the transcendental ideality of appearances, or that there are no grounds for the view that to call appearances ideas is to speak transcendentally and not empirically. Two passages where Kant refers to the ideality of appearances occur at B 535 and B 66. In the former Kant says: 'From this it then follows that appearances in general are nothing outside (apart from)[1] our representations—which is just what is meant by their transcendental ideality.' At B 66 Kant refers to the 'theory of the (transcendental) ideality of both outer and inner sense, and therefore of all objects of the senses, as mere appearances'. Moreover, as this last passage suggests, it is a natural inference from the status ascribed to space and time, that this status should be ascribed also to the objects, appearances, which are in them. Again Kant almost always calls appearances ideas in contexts where the rejected alternative would be to call them things in themselves (e.g. A 129–130). But to call something a thing in itself, or to rely on the distinction between things in themselves and things as appearances, is to employ a transcendental, and not empirical, distinction. Since Kant clearly wishes to reject empirical idealism, it seems certain that to call appearances ideas in such contexts is to talk transcendentally and not empirically. The most that could be said for such an objection in general would be that, although it does not show Kant to be an empirical idealist, it helps to show why he has been thought so often to be one.

### (iii) THE AESTHETIC

There remain to be considered only the important and often misunderstood passages in the Aesthetic where Kant elaborates his view that space and time are transcendentally ideal. The first of these is at B 44–45. Here Kant begins by stating the negative force of his transcendental doctrine: 'We assert then the empirical reality of space, as regards all possible outer experience; and yet at the same time we assert its transcendental ideality—in other words that it is nothing at all immediately we withdraw the above condition, namely, its limitation to possible experience, and so look

[1] Since Kant clearly admits the existence of outer spatial objects it is better to translate the term 'ausser' more neutrally as 'apart from'.

upon it as something that underlies things in themselves.' After this comes a passage which differs in the two editions of the *Critique*. In the first edition Kant expresses a difference between space on one side and tastes and colours on the other by saying that while space is a necessary condition of all outer appearances this is not true of tastes or colours; or again that while we have a priori knowledge of spatial features, in geometry, there is no comparable a priori account of tastes or colours. It is explained that this account of the difference is designed to prevent a misunderstanding of the doctine of the transcendental ideality of space.

In the second edition this aim is made much more clear. For Kant indicates that the difference was designed to prevent any comparison between space and such things as colours. On Kant's view it would be quite wrong to use this comparison to illustrate the ideality of space, because in speaking of colours we tacitly assume an (empirical) object to which such colour properties are ascribed. The whole point of calling space transcendentally ideal just is to deny a comparable assumption about transcendental objects. And so Kant says:

> In such examples as these, that which originally is itself only appearance, for instance, a rose, is being treated by the empirical understanding as a thing in itself, which nevertheless in respect of its colour can appear differently to every observer. The transcendental concept of appearances in space, on the other hand, is a critical reminder that nothing intuited in space is a thing in itself . . . that space is not a form inhering in things in themselves as their intrinsic property. . . .

What, then, is wrong with such comparisons is not so much that in one case we have a priori knowledge, which in the other we lack, but rather that the empirical contrast between a rose and its apparent colour is inevitably misleading as an illustration of the transcendental contrast between appearances and things in themselves. To try to understand this transcendental contrast in such an empirical way is to falsify it, in the way in which earlier it was argued that any empirical answer to the transcendental question about the objects of perception will be inadequate. For whereas empirically we are entitled to distinguish the rose as an object, from one of its apparent properties, the transcendental distinction between appearance and things in themselves is meant to show that we are precisely not entitled in the same way to suppose a transcendental object distinct from spatial appearances. To say that a rose has an apparent colour is to assume the existence of a rose; to say that spatial objects are appearances is to deny the comparable assumption about a transcendental thing in itself.

At B 53 the same point is made for time:

> This ideality, like that of space, must not however be illustrated by false analogies with sensation, because it is then assumed that the appearance, in which the sensible predicates inhere, itself has objective reality. In the case of time, however, such objective reality falls entirely away, save in so far as it is merely empirical, that is, save in so far as we regard the object itself merely as appearance. On this subject the reader may refer to what has been said at the close of the preceding section (B 44—45).

Evidently it would be a mistake to understand the transcendental contrast between appearances and things in themselves as in any way parallel to the empirical contrast between sensible predicates and empirical objects. Kant again makes it clear in the passage at B 62–63, examined above, that the similar attempt to understand the transcendental distinction by means of the contrast between a rainbow and a raindrop is mistaken for just the same reason. Later, in the extended passage at B 69–70 he places the same veto on the comparison between illusory and veridical perceptions. To speak of appearances is not to suppose that such things are in any way illusory, and still less to suppose that any veridical experience relates to transcendental things in themselves. When Kant says that appearances are spatial he does not mean to say that bodies only seem or appear to be in space. The transcendental notion of an appearance is evidently unlike the empirical notion of appearing. And the central reason for rejecting any such comparison between the two notions is, once again, that the empirical concept presupposes the existence of an object, while the transcendental notion expressly rejects the existence in our experience of any such counterpart (transcendental) object.

This account of Kant's distinction between the empirical and transcendental enables us to estimate the peculiar character of Kant's account of perception, and also to resolve some of the paradoxes noticed earlier (Ch. 1 and 2) about the notion of an appearance. In his use of this distinction Kant seems to have recognised something of the special status which attaches to a philosophic account of perception. He recognised that his key term 'appearance' had a special sense different from its conventional empirical meaning, since it stipulated rather than described the objects given to us in perception. Unlike the phenomenalists' term 'sense-data' (see Ch. 1, p. 15), Kant's term 'appearance' for whatever is presented to the senses, places no limit on the empirical descriptions which we ordinarily give of perceived objects. On Kant's view it is not correct to say that only objects of inner sense, such as sensations, are given to us immediately. Even the physical objects of outer sense are immediately given, and count just as much as appearances. Such ordinary empirical descriptions are, on his view, insulated from the transcendental enquiry which required the term 'appearance' to be coined.

What Kant wished mainly to avoid was the suggestion that we might on occasion have knowledge of objects that were inaccessible to or beyond our senses. He believed that we certainly had non-empirical knowledge of various kinds, but rejected the inference from this belief to the claim that we have knowledge of non-empirical (intelligible or transcendental) objects. On his view it was mistaken to regard our experience as including any such reference to transcendental things in themselves, out of all relation to the senses. Kant's empirically neutral term 'appearance' was thus designed to limit the range of our possible experience to the objects that can be presented to our senses. This is one reason why the provisos about empirical illustration of the contrast between appearances and things in themselves are so important. There are in our empirical experience cases of rainbows as well as of raindrops, of illusory as well as of veridical experiences, of colours as well as of roses. But the analogous transcendental claim, that there are in our experience appearances as well as things in themselves, is just what the transcendental theory of ideality is intended to deny. There may be a sense in which we can admit that there are things in themselves (cf. B 308–309), but it is not one which supports their existence in experience, and consequently is quite unlike the way in which we cheerfully admit the existence of rain and roses. Kant's central aim, so far, in employing the term 'appearance' is thus largely negative, to deny knowledge of transcendental things. Few contemporary philosophers can ever have been seriously tempted to dispute such a denial, so that Kant's argument might nowadays seem trivial. Such a conclusion was not a triviality in Kant's time, and was for Kant in any case only a preliminary thesis required for the setting and solution of a further problem. It is nevertheless worth while to stress this evident divergence between the aims and assumptions of Kant and modern philosophers of perception. For it may help to explain some of the difficulty of attaching to him a modern label such as that of phenomenalism.

The distinction helps also to resolve some of the paradoxes encountered earlier over the term 'appearance'. For appearances were said to be objects, spatial, and even distinct from our representations, while at the same time they were mere representations, modifications of the mind, and 'in us'. It is now possible to see that these conflicts arise because such predicates are understood in their empirical sense, and yet supposed also to provide defining features of an appearance. But if they are to be understood as providing such a defining characteristic, then the defining predicate must be taken in its transcendental, and not empirical, sense. For the term 'appearance' is part of a transcendental and not empirical contrast. Thus, if we take these claims empirically, then all they say is that the term 'appearance' must be understood to cover things that are spatial, and distinct from us, as well as things that are 'in us' and mere modifications of the mind, belonging to inner sense, such as sensations. In this case none of the claims will provide any defining characteristics of the term, and there will then be no conflict. For there is no logical reason why there should not be such a term to cover all the things that might be given to our senses, whether inner or outer. If, however, we take the second claim to provide a defining characteristic of appearances that they are ideas or representations, then this must be taken in the transcendental sense, and means no more than that appearances are not things in themselves, in the transcendental sense, out of all relation to our perception. In this case, too, there will be no contradiction; for to say that appearances are transcendentally ideas in this way is quite compatible with their covering what empirically we call spatial objects distinct from our empirical ideas. The conflicts arise because we think of the claim that appearances are ideas as a definition equivalent to saying that appearances are sensations, which is not compatible with their being also spatial and distinct from our ideas. Once the distinction between transcendental and empirical is understood this account of such claims can be rejected.

# 4

# SENSIBILITY

# AND UNDERSTANDING

'It is therefore just as necessary to make our concepts sensible, that is, to add the object to them in intuition, as to make our intuitions intelligible, that is, to bring them under concepts' (B 75).

THE distinction between sensibility and understanding is of an importance out of all proportion to the minute amount of space Kant formally devotes to it in the *Critique* (cf. B 29). It is, of all Kant's basic contrasts, between empirical and transcendental, synthetic and analytic, or a posteriori and a priori, the least carefully explained. Yet if the distinction made no evident sense, the central positive problem of the Analytic would be unintelligible. For this problem can be represented as arising out of the view that sensibility and understanding, although distinct faculties, produce knowledge only in partnership. Since Kant's aim is to explain certain general features of our knowledge he is directly involved in an explanation of this partnership. It is in the passages where Kant expresses his aim in the quasi-mechanical terms of a connecting link between the two faculties that his procedure and task seem philosophically most unclear. It is, even within psychology, difficult to give a sense to the claim that the two faculties are connected by imagination, as though the latter faculty worked like a clutch mechanism (cf. Ch. 1, pp. 9–11). Some philosophers (e.g. Prichard, op. cit., Ch. X; Warnock: *Analysis*, Vol. 9, pp. 77–82) have argued that Kant's problem expressed in this way (in the Schematism, for example) is not a genuine problem. Yet there are other clearer ways of understanding the distinction and the problem based on it.

Kant sometimes seems to admit that the distinction between sense and understanding, and the 'allocation' of terms to one or other faculty, is, or is based on, a logical classification of concepts. The distinction between appearances and things in themselves, clearly connected with the contrast between sense and understanding, is also associated with a logical classification of concepts at B 311: 'The division of objects into phenomena and noumena, and the world into a world of the senses and a world of the understanding, is therefore quite inadmissible in the positive sense, although the distinction of concepts as sensible or intellectual is certainly legitimate.' Yet Kant had also a motive for saying, as he does at B 62, that the contrast between the two faculties is not a logical but a transcendental distinction. For to deny the contrast to be merely logical was, for Kant, to deny the dogmatic view that the understanding gave us knowledge of intelligible objects. Kant admitted the existence of an intelligible contribution to knowledge, but denied that this provided knowledge of any intelligible objects. His views about the objects of sense and of understanding are contained in the three-fold distinction between appearances (Erscheinung), phenomena (Phänomen) and noumena.

The distinction between things as they appear and things as they are in themselves, between appearances and noumena, has been already loosely tied to the contrast between perception (sense) and thought (understanding). Appearances are the objects of perception, and so belong to sensibility, while the understanding is responsible for the problematic and deceptive concept of a thing in itself, or noumenon. But not all the uses of the understanding produce similar deceptions, and if it may be misused it has also, on Kant's view, a correct and invaluable employment. It is due to our understanding, to our modes of thought, that we are able to categorise, or determine, or discriminate between what is presented to the senses. This function of the understanding requires a further distinction, between what is strictly given to the senses (appearance) and the things into which appearances may be discriminated by means of the understanding. In this way Kant distinguishes between appearance and phenomenon, for example at A 249:

> Appearances in so far as they are thought as objects according to the unity of the categories, are called phenomena (Phaenomenon). But if I postulate things which are mere objects of the understanding,

and which nevertheless can be given as such to an intuition, though not to one that is sensible—given therefore *coram intuiti intellectuali*—such things would be entitled *noumena* (*intelligibilia*).

By using this further distinction Kant points, artificially but importantly, to the various contributions which the two faculties of sense and understanding make to knowledge. Our ability to be presented with appearances is due to sensibility, and our ability to discriminate between, name or describe, phenomenal objects is due to the understanding. Kant certainly did not wish to duplicate the world or objects by supposing that appearances and phenomena are two kinds of object. They are the same things, only viewed in different ways.

### (i) DATA OF SENSE AND PHENOMENAL OBJECTS

The contrast between appearances, which are the data of the senses, and phenomena, among which can be counted such things as material objects, tempts further ascriptions of phenomenalism to Kant. That Kant distinguishes between what is strictly given to the senses and what the understanding can construct out of this material, suggests at once a phenomenalist inference from sense-data to material objects. For since we name and describe such things as material objects at least part of our knowledge of them is attributable to the understanding, so that material objects cannot be strictly given to the senses. But if what is strictly given to the senses cannot be said to be a material object, it is naturally thought of as a sensation or sense-datum; and this is apparently to involve Kant in phenomenalism once more (cf. Ch. 1).

Such an argument begins rightly by supposing that there is, on Kant's account, some oddity in describing what is strictly given to the senses in material object terms, but it argues wrongly to a phenomenalist conclusion. The argument turns on the claim that since our concepts of material objects belong strictly to the understanding, it would be wrong to describe appearances, which belong to sensibility, in these terms. But in this case what prevents us from employing such a description is not the kind of description it is, so much as the fact that it is a description at all. Any attempt to describe what is strictly given to the senses in any ordinary empirical terms will be open to the same objection. The conclusion to the argument was made plausible only because it contrived to place a restriction on some such descriptions, but not on others. But the argument places a similar restriction on all descriptions. To describe appearances in terms of sense-data, where these are distinguished from material objects, is also ruled out on the same grounds. So long, therefore, as a phenomenalist conclusion would distinguish sense-datum descriptions from those of material objects, the argument does not lead to such a conclusion.

Although the argument does not establish this conclusion, it points to the sense in which appearances are indescribable, on Kant's view. The suggestion was that appearances cannot be described simply because any description involves a concept, which will belong not to sensibility, but to understanding. Kant cannot mean, however, that it is never possible to describe appearances, for on his view it is of such things that we ordinarily speak and acquire knowledge. Phenomena, too, are called categorised appearances. Kant means only that although such descriptions are available empirically, there is some reason why they are not available transcendentally in talking about appearances. If someone genuinely wished to know what kind of things appearances empirically are, it would not be out of place to identify or exemplify them in terms of ordinary empirical descriptions, whether of sensations or material objects. Indeed it would be hard to understand what such a term was supposed to cover, if we were not allowed our habitual method of identifying the things we commonly say that we perceive. But such descriptive resources, however useful they may be in showing what kind of things are covered by the term 'appearance', will be inadequate to supply a general account of what an appearance strictly is. For such empirical descriptions always provide a contrast with some other kind of thing that can be presented in experience. The transcendental use of the term 'appearance' has to cover every possible empirical description, and can be contrasted only with something that is never found in experience, that is, a thing in itself.

Appearances are indescribable only because any empirical description will be inadequate to account transcendentally for them, and because it is part of the stipulation governing the term's use that we should not attempt to characterise them in any such specific ways. Such a stipulation is of philosophic importance in that it serves artificially to separate sense and understanding, but it places no empirical restriction on the ways in which we may describe or name what we perceive. It would be more accurate to say that appearances are nondescript, rather than that they are indescribable. To call them indescribable is to suggest that there is some substantial restriction to be placed on their empirical description, in the way that Russell or more recent phenomenalists have restricted the description of sense-data (cf. *Logical Atomism*, Ch. II; in *Logic and Knowledge* (ed. Marsh), pp. 200–203). To call appearances nondescript on the other hand emphasises that appearances cover indeterminately whatever can be presented to the senses, without implying any restriction on the ways in which we ordinarily identify or describe what we perceive. So long as the term 'sense-datum' has a substantial empirical sense, in which it is distinguished from other empirical descriptions, as, for example, sensations are distinguished from material objects, appearances cannot be said to be sense-data. It is only in the literal meaning of 'sense-datum', in which it refers indiscriminately to whatever is presented to the senses, that appearances can be identified with sense-data.

That Kant held such a view of appearances can be supported briefly by several short quotations. In the *Prolegomena* (Ak., Vol. 4, p. 290) Kant says: 'If appearances are given to us, then we are free to judge of them as we wish. For appearances rest on the senses, and judging on the understanding.' And again: 'In this way if we do not consider the origin of our ideas and link our intuitions of the senses, *whatever they contain*, in space or time, in accordance with the rules of the connection of all knowledge in experience, deceptive appearance or truth may arise, according to whether we are careful or careless.' At B 44 Kant says: 'Our exposition therefore establishes the reality, i.e. objective validity of space in respect of *whatever* can be presented to us outwardly as an object.' Finally and briefly, at B 34: 'The indeterminate (undetermined) object of an empirical intuition is entitled "appearance".' Similar points about the indeterminate character of appearances, and the way in which concepts bear on their 'determination', can be found at B 159 ('We have now to explain . . . making nature possible') and B 94 ('But concepts . . . not yet determined') and elsewhere (e.g. B 154, B 168–169, B 157–158, note).

In this account of the distinction between the objects of sense and of understanding, Kant makes much use of the contrast between what is indeterminate and what is determinate. He speaks generally of what is given to the senses as indeterminate until the understanding is able to determine, or discriminate between, what is perceived. Similarly, he speaks of 'determining' or 'determination' as the specific contribution which the understanding makes to knowledge (cf. B 157–158, B 168–169). The contrast between the objects of sense and of understanding is, therefore, best expressed in such terms as those of indeterminate and determinate, indiscriminate and discriminated, or nondescript and described, objects or appearances. The familiar distinction between what is *strictly* given and what is inferred or constructed from this basic material, is not exactly the contrast Kant has in mind. This is borne out, too, by his rejection in the Fourth Paralogism (A) (Ch. 2, pp. 21–23) of the supposed inference from immediately given ideas to external objects. On Kant's view, however we choose empirically to describe what we perceive, these things can be said to be given immediately to our senses. It is nevertheless important to distinguish perception from conception, natural consequently to draw a stipulated distinction between the nondescript or indiscriminate manifold of appearance and its description in terms of, or discrimination into, different kinds of perceived object. To stipulate the sense of 'appearance' in this way is to disallow any further question about the possibility of specifying its sense through ordinary empirical descriptions of what we perceive. Kant very rarely uses the special term 'phenomenon', but speaks instead of the things we know and investigate as appearances. This is entirely natural, so long as this latter term is understood to cover indiscriminately all the things we say we perceive, and not to refer to some favoured category of such things from which such others as material objects may be inferred or constructed. Kant's construction is not 'vertical', from low-level to higher level descriptions, but 'horizontal', from an indiscriminate manifold of sense to discriminated items within it.

When Kant comes to explain the problem arising from his distinction between the two faculties he seems to produce either contradiction or incoherence. In a passage at B 121–123 he contrasts the ease with which it can be shown that space and time relate necessarily to appearances, with the difficulty of showing how the understanding is necessarily related to objects given in intuition.

It is made clear in this passage, and later at B 125–126, that Kant wishes to say ultimately that categories (concepts belonging to the understanding) are related necessarily to objects. He indicates in the later passage that the reason for this is that without such concepts nothing is possible as an object of experience. Yet Kant also claims that there is no impossibility in supposing that appearances might be given in intuition independently of the understanding. He outlines a situation (B 122–123) where 'objects may appear to us, without their being under the necessity of being related to the functions of understanding'. It seems that Kant is saying inconsistently that appearances both are and are not necessarily related to categories.

The apparent contradiction in this passage can be nominally resolved by noticing that while Kant says that appearances may be presented uncategorised, it is objects of experience that are related necessarily to categories. It is natural to understand the term 'object of experience' to have the same sense as 'phenomenon', and so to signify something conceived in accordance with the categories. In this way the apparent contradiction reinforces the original distinction between appearances belonging strictly to sense, and phenomena discriminated in accordance with the categories. The argument would, on this account, be equivalent to stipulating once again that while appearances are not logically connected with categories, phenomena or objects of experience are. Since there is so far no ground to deny the possibility that we might be presented with appearances which never reached the status of, or were never discriminated into, objects of experience, the contradiction may seem to vanish.

There are, however, two grounds for thinking that this solution to the paradox is incomplete. The first of these results from the belief that the situation of appearances without categories, which Kant seems to envisage, is absurd if not contradictory. There is certainly something odd in envisaging a situation where appearances are presented but cannot be described, though it is not easy to pin down the kind of absurdity involved. It will not do to say *simply* that our habitual mode of identifying what we perceive involves the ordinary resources of description. For it is certainly possible to speak of creatures who are able to perceive, even when they have no such conventional resources. It is true that difficulties arise in such a case from the effort to explain what such a situation would be like, but there are many positions of this kind which do not involve absurdity. To promote such an argument against Kant more would have to be said of the kind of difficulty involved in such a situation. Even so, this does not produce a good enough reason for denying Kant's claim that it is logically possible to perceive without being able to describe what is perceived.

This side of the argument against Kant's distinction between the two faculties is, in any case, a blind alley. On the one hand it tempts fruitless efforts to exemplify a total separation of the faculties by appealing to the experiences of the animal world or to human mental defects. On the other it presupposes that Kant did not notice any difficulty in such a situation, when in fact he later makes much of this same difficulty (cf. Ch. 9, pp. 126–130). All that Kant wished to say was that there is no logical impossibility in speaking of a separation of the faculties. He did not wish to deny that there was any difficulty in explaining such situations; on the contrary he later argues that there is an important limit to be placed on our understanding of them. Nor did Kant wish to elaborate empirically cases which may seem to satisfy these strange conditions. That we speak of them at all is enough to establish prima facie that such a distinction between the two faculties is not logically impossible.

The second incompleteness in the resolution of the paradox is of more direct importance. The argument at B 121–126 may be represented as yielding the two stipulations that appearances are spatio-temporal[1] and that phenomena, or objects of experience, are categorised, or thought in accordance with categories. But these logical or stipulated connections do not exhaust Kant's argument; they are designed to introduce and not to settle his problem. The problem is that of explaining the relation of appearances to categories, once these stipulations are given. It is not a mere stipulation that appearances can be thought in accordance with categories, and Kant's aim in the Analytic is to explain how it is possible for them to be so conceived. Moreover, although Kant did not regard it as a logical truth that appearances can be so

---

[1] It is, of course, true that Kant argues in the Aesthetic that appearances are spatio-temporal, and does not simply stipulate that this is the sense to be given to the term 'appearance'. Nevertheless from the point of view of the argument in the Analytic this feature of appearances is presupposed, so that it is quite possible to represent the claim that appearances are spatio-temporal as a stipulation in this context.

conceived, he wishes in the end to say that it is in some way necessary that they should be. The original paradox may now seem to re-appear, since Kant says both that appearances are necessarily related to categories, and yet that it is not logically impossible for them to be uncategorised. The obvious way to resolve this paradox is to suppose that when Kant claims that appearances are necessarily related to categories, he is not denying that it is logically possible for them to be uncategorised. The kind of necessity involved in the former claim is not, then, a logical necessity.

To say this is to leave the sense of 'necessity' in Kant's claim unclear, and for the present this is inevitable. For the whole of the Analytic is needed to clarify the sense of such a claim. It would not be wrong to say that Kant is using the term 'necessary' in a conditional way, so that he is claiming that appearances must be related to categories, if knowledge is to be possible at all. This, however, merely indicates the possibility of an escape route, without showing where such a route might lead. A more reliable, though less simple, guide can be found in the claim, made above, that Kant insists on the oddity of the envisaged situation in which appearances may be presented uncategorised. It was suggested that Kant indicates a limit in our understanding of such a situation, and thereby shows the kind of oddity such a situation involves. The attempt to elucidate such a limit or such an oddity could help to explain why categories, or modes of thought or description, are of importance in our experience. It could consequently be used to support the claim that there is a necessity of some non-logical kind in relating appearances to such concepts. To show the kind of absurdity in, or the kind of limit set to our understanding of, such a situation, would be to show the kind of necessity attaching to such modes of thought or description in our experience. In the Transcendental Deduction (Chs. 8 and 9) Kant argues in this way that an examination of this envisaged situation leads to a recognition of the importance of categories in our experience, and so to the claim that categories are in some way necessary in or for that experience.

### (ii) THE 'REPRESENTATION' PROBLEM FOR CATEGORIES

Kant's distinction between sense and understanding, and the associated distinction between appearances and phenomena, are used to introduce a general problem about the relationship between our concepts, or language, and our perception. The origin of this problem, at least as it affects the *Critique of Pure Reason*, can be seen in a letter to Herz (Ak., Vol. 10, p. 125), where Kant explained his dissatisfaction with the argument in the *Dissertation* (Ak., Vol. 2, pp. 385 ff.). He wrote in the letter:

> I was content to express the nature of intellectual representations merely negatively in the Dissertation, by saying that they were anyway not modifications of the mind by an object. But I passed silently over the problem of how a representation, which refers to an object, is possible without being affected by the latter in any way. I had said: sensible representations present things as they appear, and intellectual representations present things as they are.

This early solution was incidentally dismissed in a passage in the *Critique* (B 313–314), where Kant exploits the distinction between the transcendental and the empirical senses of the term 'object'. He there said:

> When, therefore, we say that the senses represent objects *as they appear*, and the understanding objects *as they are*, the latter statement is to be taken, not in the transcendental, but in the merely empirical, meaning of the terms, namely as meaning that the objects must be represented as objects of experience, that is, as appearances in thoroughgoing inter-connection with one another, and not as they may be apart from their relation to possible experience (and consequently to any senses), as objects of the pure understanding.

The new way of expressing relations between 'intellectual representations' and objects in the *Critique* is that found at B 124–125 (and elsewhere) where Kant speaks of 'making possible the objects of experience'. The problem in this mode of expression is that of explaining how certain very general concepts, categories, come to bear on our experience, or to apply to the appearances presented to the senses. Kant seems to have thought that appearances themselves can be explained in terms of the capacity our senses have for being affected by objects, and he seems to have regarded the comparable question about ordinary empirical concepts as a merely 'physiological' problem to be settled by reference to an enquiry of an empirical kind, like Locke's (B 118–119). There remained, therefore, only the problem of explaining how the concepts called categories operate, and it is this problem which is tackled in the Transcendental Analytic.

There are many ways in which this problem may be crippled at the start, and two of these have been already noticed. It is, as we have seen, possible to argue that Kant either contradicts himself, or else is muddled, in his statement of the problem at B 121–126. This argument has not been conceded, but it has not been completely rejected either. All that has been done is to uncover a condition which must obtain if Kant is not to contradict himself, namely that the necessity in which appearances are said to relate to categories is not a logical necessity. Nothing, however, has yet been done either to establish that Kant's argument in the Analytic fulfills this condition, or to elaborate further the kind of necessity involved in Kant's claim. It has been suggested that Kant's argument later relies on an elaboration of this necessity, and this certainly points to a way out of the difficulty; but the path has not yet been followed. It could also be argued that to enquire into the connections between sensibility and understanding is properly a task of experimental psychology, and not philosophy. Something has been said already of this charge as it applies generally to the *Critique*. In this particular context there is no doubt that much of what Kant says of imagination and schematism could be interpreted in such a way. Yet it is also worth remembering the passages, quoted previously (Ch. 1, pp. 9–11), in which Kant firmly rejects this as his primary aim. Whether Kant's account of the connections between these faculties can be construed as an essay in experimental psychology or not, it certainly can be construed in other ways, for example, as an enquiry into the status and force of certain very general concepts. These arguments against the programme of the Analytic are not therefore wholly wrong, or have not yet been shown to be so, but neither are they wholly right. They may be allowed to point to features which hamper the development of Kant's argument, but they should not be allowed to cripple it permanently.

These are not the only objections that Kant's problem has to face. Even if he is taken to be concerned with the function or status of concepts, his task may still be regarded as a pseudo-problem, which arises only because of the artificial separation of sense from understanding, or concepts from objects. Kant sometimes (e.g. in the Schematism (B 177)) puts the problem by asking how it is possible for categories to apply to appearances, and this is a quite natural mode of expression. Yet it has been suggested (by Warnock: *Analysis*, Vol. 9, pp. 77–82) that this is a 'silly question' to which there properly is no answer. Warnock argues: 'To ask how I can apply a concept that I have is to ask how I can use a word that I know how to use. And this is a silly question, brought on by illegitimately separating the application of concepts from having them.' The failure of this argument, as an objection to Kant's programme, arises from the falsity of the claim that the question 'How can I use a word that I know how to use?' is silly. If this were a question about the conditions in which it is possible for me (or anyone) to use a word, then it is not obviously a silly question at all. The fact that I know how to use a word, or that a word's use is known, does not make an enquiry into the conditions of its use absurd; on the contrary, such an enquiry could be prosecuted only on the supposition that the word had a known use. It is not difficult to understand Kant's problem in somewhat this way, as an enquiry into the conditions in which certain concepts are, or can be, used.

Once these initial objections to the problem are avoided, all the different formulations of it can be seen to come to the same thing. To speak, as Kant does at A 97 and A 99 (Ch. 1, pp. 12–14), of the manifold presented to the senses is to draw attention to the need for discriminations among the items presented. To speak of appearances as nondescript or indeterminate is again to draw attention to the same need. To distinguish appearances as indeterminate from phenomena or objects of experience as determinate objects is to point to an examination of the ways in which such discriminations can be effected. The distinction between sensibility and understanding is thus implicit in all these contrasts between what is indeterminate in perception and what is discriminated within it. Yet the problem about these discriminations does not strictly require a rigid and artificial distinction between the faculties or their objects. It is an indisputable truth that we are able to discriminate items in our perception, and this is enough by itself to introduce a general problem about the ways in which we are enabled to do this. An enquiry into the means by which such discriminations are effected may naturally seem a part of empirical psychology. Yet Kant generally formulates his problem, as we have suggested, as an enquiry into the conditions in which such discriminations are possible, and this can naturally be regarded as an enquiry of a conceptual kind.

The other way of formulating Kant's problem emphasises this conceptual interest. His account of 'intellectual representations' and the claim that he wishes to examine the conditions in which certain concepts can be used supports this. Kant's problem about 'intellectual representations' reflects the fact that certain concepts in mathematics and some natural sciences play a complex and puzzling role. The superior status of claims in such sciences, and the peculiar authority they seem to possess, led Kant, as it led many other traditional philosophers, to consider how these concepts, centrally involved in such disciplines, operate. Kant's argument against Hume over the concept 'cause' reflects Kant's belief that there are many concepts of this kind, which similarly set a problem about their function or operation (Ak., Vol. 4, p. 260). Kant was therefore naturally led to enquire, as we have suggested, into the conditions in which such concepts can be used. Kant was not interested in all concepts, but rather in those which he took to be centrally embedded in mathematics and science and in our ordinary experience. These concepts he called categories, so that his task in the Analytic can be represented as an enquiry into the conditions in which categories can operate in our experience.

Once again this aim is not essentially different from that formulated in terms of the ways in which we effect discriminations in our perception or experience. Kant believed that to examine the conditions in which categories operate is to examine the ways in which we are enabled to discriminate items in experience. It is natural to say that what we discriminate in our experience is one category of object from another, and therefore just as natural to examine the ways in which we effect such discriminations by examining the concepts which mark or effect them. All concepts mark discriminations of some kind, and to examine categories is only to examine certain important or basic distinctions in our experience. Kant wishes to say, as we have seen, that there is a certain necessity in relating categories to appearances, that is in discriminating among items presented in our perception. But this is not a different enquiry from the one already mentioned. The data for a conclusion of this kind are contained already in the examinations of categories and discriminations projected above.

# 5
# INTELLIGIBLE OBJECTS

'Doubtless, indeed, there are intelligible entities, corresponding to the sensible entities . . .' (B 308–309).

'. . . But in that case a noumenon is not for our understanding a special (kind of) object, namely, an *intelligible object*' (B 311).

IN this chapter something is to be finally said about the notions of noumena, things in themselves, transcendental or intelligible objects, all of which have a common root in the *Critique*. What has been said so far concerned mostly the negative way in which Kant employed these terms; and some problems remain about other ways in which Kant uses them. Many philosophers have implied that Kant's views about such noumenal objects went far beyond the bounds of truth or sense. At least something has already been done to dispute the naive idea that Kant required the existence of things in themselves to counterbalance the paradoxical claim that all our immediate perception was of ideas or sensations, in the ordinary empirical sense. There have, nevertheless, been other criticisms of Kant's use of such terms, and some of these will be considered here. This discussion of Kant's account of noumena will not deal with their function in the context of moral philosophy, for Kant's views about such things in that context involve separate issues and deserve a chapter to themselves (see Ch. 12).

Kant indicates three general aspects of the use of such concepts, which are to be mentioned here. The first is his belief that such concepts arise predominantly from the need to adopt certain heuristic principles in any theoretical enquiry. The second is his belief that mistakes arise from this need through a failure to distinguish adequately between concepts and objects. The third is his belief that an important instance of this general temptation to misuse concepts can arise even in the field of transcendental philosophy. Kant certainly does not treat all such misuses of concepts as though they were exactly the same; the arguments in the various sections of the Dialectic clearly show sharp differences between such mistakes. But for the purposes of a general account of these notions it will be necessary to minimise the extent of the detailed differences between them.

### (i) THE OCCASIONS OF MISUSE

We have already seen (in Chs. 2 and 3) how mistakes may arise through a failure to recognise ambiguities in such a phrase as 'external object'. These mistakes could be occasioned by the misconstruction of a scientific theory about the working of our senses; and in this way they followed the pattern of illusory metaphysical speculation outlined by Kant at A vii–viii. In the Transcendental Dialectic Kant provides a range of somewhat similar instances of the same pattern, in which a concept is misunderstood or misused and gives rise to similar mistakes. These concepts Kant calls 'Ideas' ('Idee' not 'Vorstellung') and with their associated principles they cover many kinds of case from the ascription of immortality to persons to the Idea of an ultimate particle of matter or a necessary being.

Kant shows that such notions cannot be treated as ordinarily exemplified in our experience. Some of them produce conflicts or antinomies which evidently cannot be settled by inspection of experienced objects, and others produce claims which it is at best very difficult to understand in terms of that experience. It is natural, and tempting, to argue therefore that these concepts refer to a world, and to objects, beyond those which we normally experience. Such a world would be composed of what Kant calls intelligible objects, corresponding to these concepts. It has been suggested already that although Kant admitted the existence of a priori or intelligible knowledge, he rejected the view that this was knowledge of any special object of a non-empirical or intelligible kind. Kant shows in the Dialectic that the supposition of such a world beyond our experience could not solve the conflicts, and could not make more comprehensible the claims, which stimulated its invention. He did not, however, believe that nothing further could be said of these difficulties. On his view such Ideas and their associated principles were genuine aids to investigation, which were sometimes mistakenly thought to refer to objects of an inevitably non-empirical sort. Kant expresses this point often by using the contrast between regulative and constitutive notions (B 647–648, B 672) and less often by using that between heuristic and ostensive concepts (B 644, B 699). The Ideas which cause these difficulties are, for Kant, always regulative or heuristic, and never ostensive or constitutive. They serve to regulate or guide our enquiries, but do not refer to any objects dealt with in such enquiries. To treat them in the latter way is to invite all the mistakes of hypostatisation associated with the concept of a noumenon or thing in itself.

In the concluding note to the Antinomy of Pure Reason Kant sums up the general features of the process which engenders such contradictions (B 593–594):

> So long as reason, in its concepts, has in view simply the totality of conditions in the sensible world, and is considering what satisfaction in this regard it can obtain for them, our Ideas are at once transcendental and cosmological. Immediately, however, the unconditioned . . . is posited in that which lies entirely outside the sensible world, and therefore outside all possible experience, the Ideas become transcendent. . . . Such transcendent Ideas have a purely intelligible object; and this object may indeed be admitted as a transcendental object, but only if likewise we admit that for the rest we have no knowledge in regard to it.

Here Kant emphasises rather the limits placed on the use of these Ideas, or principles of the totality of conditions, though he also envisages a proper use for them in relation to the sensible world. Such a use, as he points out earlier (B 536), is only to encourage the continuation of a certain kind of enquiry, for example, into the series of empirical causes, or the basic particles of matter; any other employment is transcendent and a misuse. This heuristic function is very well expressed in a passage at B 672:

> I accordingly maintain that transcendental Ideas never allow of any constitutive employment. When regarded in that mistaken manner, and therefore as supplying concepts of certain objects, they are but pseudo-rational, merely dialectical concepts. On the other hand, they have an excellent and indeed indispensably necessary, regulative

67

employment, namely, that of directing the understanding towards a certain goal upon which the routes marked out by all its rules converge, as upon their point of intersection. This point is indeed a mere Idea, a *focus imaginarius*, from which, since it lies outside the bounds of a possible experience, the concepts of the understanding do not in reality proceed; none the less it serves to give these concepts the greatest (possible) unity combined with the greatest (possible) extension.

In other passages (B 710–717, B 699–700) Kant expresses this heuristic aim by saying that Ideas enable us to treat the genuine objects of our enquiries *as if* they had certain features, to which the Ideas point, although we have no knowledge of such features. For example, we may be helped in psychological investigations by treating the mind as if it were a simple substance, or in physical enquiries by treating causal connections as if the series of appearances were endless.

In the passage at B 593–594 Kant speaks puzzlingly of admitting an intelligible object as a transcendental object, so long as we also concede that we have no knowledge of such an object. What Kant means by this can be explained by reference to another passage at B 519–524 where Kant shows how transcendental Idealism can solve the problems of the Cosmological Dialectic. In this passage Kant reiterates the central doctrine of transcendental Idealism that objects of experience are never given as they are in themselves. He says (B 521): 'The objects of experience are never given in themselves, but only in experience, and have no existence outside it. That there may be inhabitants in the moon, although no-one has ever seen them, must certainly be admitted. This, however, only means that in the possible advance of experience we may encounter them.' Thus such cases in which we speak empirically of things to which we have no sensible access are not cases of reference to things in themselves, but only ways of talking about the kinds of appearances, or phenomena, we might meet in some future experience. He goes on (B 522–523):

> We may, however, entitle the purely intelligible cause of appearances in general the transcendental object, but merely in order to have something corresponding to sensibility viewed as receptivity. To this transcendental object we can ascribe the whole extent and connection of our possible perceptions . . . thus we can say that the real things of past time are given in the transcendental object of ex-

perience; but they are objects for me and real in past time only in so far as I represent to myself (either by the light of history, or the guiding clues of causes and effects) that a regressive series of possible perceptions in accordance with empirical laws conducts us to a past time series as a condition of the present time. . . .

In this passage Kant makes clear the force of the term 'transcendental object' in these contexts. It is evidently designed as a conceptual repository for our ways of referring to the remote past, distant regions of space, or the series of causal connections. To use the term in this way is to abbreviate what would be a longer claim about ordinary phenomenal objects and our possible experiences of them. We may, if we like, speak of the whole extent of past time as embodied in a transcendental object, but this can be understood, like the claim about the men in the moon, only in terms of an imagined series of experiences linking my present situation with some past or possible state. Such a mode of speech for referring to objects in the remote past is certainly clumsy, but it is also clear that our ordinary claims about 'the past' embody a similar, though perhaps less misleading, compression. Kant insists, however, that there is nothing improper about such a way of talking, so long as the restrictions on its use, and the dangers of its misuse, are clearly recognised. To use the term in such a way, at least in the effort to guide or encourage investigations into the past or into causal connections, is legitimate so long as the term is understood as an abbreviation and not as referring to a supersensible object.

The development of mathematics since Kant's day may have made some of his treatment of such conflicts outmoded. Yet it is in general true that philosophers and scientists are tempted to make mistakes through neglect of a distinction to which Kant points in this argument. Kant distinguishes between claims which may be made within some science, and claims which, though not made within the system, may nevertheless serve to direct enquiries in it. There is, for example, a difference between working on the assumption that p is true, and believing or claiming to know that p is true. A physicist or psychologist might work always on the assumption that everything has a physical explanation, but there is no compulsion for him actually to believe this to be true. Nor would success in providing such explanations by itself entitle him to claim that he knew it to be true. It is very natural for a scientist to believe such an assumption to be true, but such a belief has rather the status of a heuristic goal than of a constitutive truth. It expresses a chosen manner of enquiry rather than a general truth about method. It is, consequently, easy to generate fruitless arguments through failing to notice such differences. For disputes about the truth of such a claim are doomed to lapse into challenges either to produce an event which it would be impossible to explain physically, or, on the other side, to show that such explanations are available for every possible situation. Neither challenge can be met. An impasse in just such a conflict might, in Kant's time, have led the disputants towards the realm of intelligible objects. Few philosophers would nowadays consciously take refuge in such a realm, but to continue such an argument as though we had some means of settling it is to make a mistake of just the same kind.

It is worth while at this point to clear up one confusion that results from Kant's ambiguous use of the terms 'constitutive' and 'regulative'. In the Analytic of Principles Kant distinguishes the mathematical principles from the dynamical, by calling the former constitutive and the latter regulative (B 221–223, B 296). This naturally suggests the mistaken view that Kant regarded such a dynamical principle as the Second Analogy as a merely heuristic, regulative principle like those cited in the Dialectic. Mr. Warnock, for example, argued in this way (*Logic and Language*, Vol. 2, pp. 96–97):

> Kant found difficulties both in the claim that the alleged statement (that every event has a cause) was true, and also in the assertion that it was false; and accordingly suggested that it must be regarded as an injunction to extend the search for causes as far as possible, and to seek always to make more coherent and comprehensive our formulations of natural laws. Earlier, however, he had written as if the law of causation were a necessary truth.

In the passage to which Warnock refers to support his contention (B 526), Kant is discussing quite generally the whole Antinomy of Pure Reason. He says that the dialectical arguments in the Antinomy rest on the supposition that 'If the conditioned is given, the entire series of all its conditions is likewise given'; whereas Kant himself will admit only that 'If the conditioned is given, a regress in the series of conditions is set us as a task'. This general formulation of these dialectical arguments is not restricted to its causal interpretation, nor does Kant say anything in this passage to identify the regulative principle he favours with the principle of the Second Analogy. There is no textual support at all for War-nock's view. Nevertheless it is natural to read this principle as though it were about specifically causal conditions, and then to argue that since Kant regards this principle and that of the Second Analogy as 'regulative', it follows that the Second Analogy is supposed to be an injunction.

Such an argument is mistaken simply because Kant takes the trouble to distinguish between this dialectical principle and that of the Second Analogy, and also because he explicitly distinguishes the two senses of 'regulative' in which these two principles are said to be regulative. At B 537 Kant denies that the dialectical principle is a principle of possible experience, or of the under-standing; but the Second Analogy is a principle of this kind. At B 692 Kant states that the dynamical laws, such as the Second Analogy, are constitutive 'in respect of experience' in a sense in which the dialectical principles never could be. Kant, therefore, recognises the dual use of this contrast, and cannot mean to say that the principle of the Second Analogy is regulative in the way that the cosmological principle cited above is regulative. There is, therefore, on this argument no reason to hold that Kant believed the principle of the Second Analogy to be an injunction, or believed it to be neither true nor false because it was an injunction, or believed it to be an injunction because he found difficulties in the claim that the cosmological principle was neither true nor false (cf. Ch. 12, p. 198).

## (ii) CONCEPTS AND OBJECTS

The regulative Ideas in the Dialectic and the temptation to mis-use them provide some account of the occasions on which mistakes about an intelligible world may easily be made. On Kant's view it is also possible to provide a general account of the type of mistake involved in such dialectical inferences. This general account is given in such passages as the Amphiboly of Concepts of Reflection (B 316–349), the Postulates (B 265–287) and the Ideal (B 595–670). It is contained also in the many scattered passages in which Kant talks of the differences between 'things in general', 'things in themselves', and 'things as appearances'. In these passages Kant argues that the source of the trouble lies in the attempt to infer truths about objects from truths about concepts, or of a conceptual type. Such inferences are generally invalid, although Kant would presumably have admitted that some such inferences may be legitimate. This simple mistake is typified in a passage at B 302, where Kant claims: '. . . to substitute the logical possibility of the *concept* (namely that the concept does not contradict itself) for the transcendental possibility of *things* (namely that an object corresponds to the concept) can deceive and leave satisfied only the simple-minded.' Similar distinctions are made at B xxvi, note, and throughout the Postulates of Empirical Thought. Kant evidently supposes that we have certain concepts, particularly among our Ideas, from which alone we are inevitably tempted to infer the existence or possibility of a corresponding object. The best known example of such a concept is that dealt with in Kant's attack on the ontological argument (B 620–631), but for Kant the most general of such concepts is that of an object, which may be directly associated with the supposed inhabitants of a noumenal world.

In the Amphiboly (particularly B 335 f., and B 345–346) Kant gives examples of such mistaken inferences, taken allegedly from the views of the Leibnitz–Wolff philosophy. Kant argues in this section that such principles as the Identity of Indiscernibles, or that the real in things can never conflict, may be true conceptually, but are not necessarily true of actual objects. On Kant's view the Leibnitz–Wolff school made the mistake in these cases of arguing that since these claims are evidently not true of the world of our sensible experience, they must be true of an intelligible world beyond experience, of which our senses give us only a confused representation. It is not of prime importance to decide whether this is an accurate account of the Leibnitz–Wolff theory. What matters at present is only to see what sort of mistakes it is easy to make in this way. The general fault in all these claims is, according to Kant (B 337), that of supposing that if a distinction is not found in the concept of a thing in general, it is also not to be found in the things themselves.

One mistake of this kind can be seen to arise, on Kant's view, from the claim that realities never conflict (B 329, B 338–339 and note). Such a claim might be held on the basis of the view that strictly affirmative concepts cannot contradict each other. If such concepts were thought to reflect all and only the real items in the

72

world, then it might seem as though there could be no conflicts in the real world. For certainly a language which contained only such affirmative concepts would fail to contain, and so to reflect, any formal contradictions. Kant held that the inference from an absence of contradiction between concepts to an absence of conflicts in the world was invalid, since there are many such conflicts which cannot be expressed as contradictions. He explains that the argument strictly establishes only that 'a concept which includes only affirmation, includes no negation' (B 339, note), and this is a tautology about affirmation and negation, which certainly tells us nothing about conditions in the world. A much simpler, and therefore perhaps less tempting, example of a similar mistake would be that of someone who argued from the conceptual claim that 'Contradictions are impossibilities' to the material claim that contradictions never occur. In such a case what is an admitted truth about the concept of 'contradiction' is misconstrued as a truth about events in the world, of which it is in fact false. To argue from this evident falsity to the claim that contradictions never occur in some world of intelligible objects would be to make a mistake of the kind Kant exposed.

Kant believed that such mistakes were liable to occur in any context where our concepts have become abstract and apparently divorced from sensible reference. But such contexts are particularly likely to occur on the fringes of sciences, where the regulative Ideas are used or misused, or where the status of the science is considered. A good example of the latter context is given by Kant at B 313–314, where he rejects the view that Newtonian physics informs us not about things as appearances, but about things in themselves. What happens generally in such arguments is well described at B 345–346:

> Consequently what we do is to think something in general; and while on the one hand we determine it in sensible fashion, on the other hand we distinguish from this mode of intuiting it the universal object represented *in abstracto*. What we are then left with is a mode of determining the object by thought alone—a merely logical form without content, but which yet seems to us to be a mode in which the object exists in itself (*noumenon*) without regard to intuition, which is limited to our senses.

Such notions as that of a 'thing in general' form the bridge across which philosophers may carry admitted truths of a conceptual kind, until they become totally unrelated to any possible experience. Even our general notion of an object produces a similar temptation (B 306–307):

> The understanding, when it entitles an object in a (certain) relation phenomenon, at the same time forms, apart from that relation, a representation of an object in itself, and so comes to represent itself as also being able to form *concepts* of such objects . . . and so (it) is misled into treating the entirely *indeterminate* concept of an intelligible entity, namely of a something in general outside (apart from) our sensibility, as being a *determinate* concept of an entity that allows of being known in a certain manner by means of the understanding.

Kant places three general limits on all such procedures. One is to insist that to have a concept is no guarantee that the concept is not empty. He believes that there are numerous concepts which we indisputably 'have', which are nevertheless empty in various ways (e.g. 'fate' and 'fortune' (B 117), 'spirit' and 'God' (A 96), 'telepathy' (B 269–270), 'noumenon' (B 344)). Another is to insist that the division of 'things in general' into phenomena and noumena has to be understood only in a negative and not in a positive sense (B 307, B 311). Such a division is not, like an empirical distinction, between two genuine kinds of object, but only between phenomena, which are the things we ordinarily perceive and know about, and the empty (but not inconsistent) concept of a nonphenomenon. The final restriction is to say that concepts do not acquire an extension of their force, when they are freed from reference to sensible objects; on the contrary in such a situation concepts are apt to lose their meaning altogether. For concepts in general, even a priori concepts, can acquire a meaning only in relation to appearances (B 178, B 186, B 299).

It has been suggested (e.g. by Warnock in *Analysis*, Vol. 9, pp. 77–82) that Kant makes the mistake of 'illegitimately separating the application of concepts from having them', and this implies that his account of the dialectical mistakes is itself mistaken. For the account rests, as we have seen, on the belief that we have some concepts which nevertheless have no application, and are empty (cf. B 346–349). What tempts one to make this criticism of Kant are the claims that to have a concept just is to be able to apply (or use) an expression, and that the application (use) of an expression determines the sense of the concept so possessed. On these views any expression that is used at all must be used to express some concept, that is, have some function in our discourse. The concepts 'fate' and 'fortune', for example, are regarded by Kant as empty, and yet there is in our language and society an evident need to talk of good or bad luck. It may seem, therefore, that such concepts cannot be empty, since we do in fact make some use of them. But this does not rule out the possibility that such expressions may be misused, either because they are given no precise sense, or because they are given a sense which strictly has no application to the occasions on which they are used. Kant's criticism of the dialectical inferences thus rests only on the claims that just as concepts may be correctly applied, they may also be mis-applied, that they may be misused as well as used. Kant did not deny that the concept of a noumenon had a function in (philosophic) discourse; he insisted only that the function was not that of referring to an object (B 344), although some philosophers had believed that it did so refer.

Kant expressed this claim about the function of such a concept sometimes by saying that it had only a negative, and not a positive, use, that it could be given some sense through the notion of whatever was not phenomenal, a non-phenomenon, but must not be supposed to refer to any object. It has been argued that Kant's practice in this matter does not live up to such admirable precepts. Körner, for example (Penguin: *Kant*, p. 95), says that 'Kant's assertion that in the *Critique of Pure Reason* he uses the concept of a noumenon as a negative and limiting concept is thus incompatible with his actual use'. Körner goes on to say that although the *Critique* might be reconstructed to avoid this incompatibility, to do this would be to do more than merely interpret Kant's arguments. This argument rests on Kant's distinction at B 307 between the positive and negative uses of 'noumenon', and on Kant's sometimes saying or implying that things in themselves affect our senses. For Körner holds that this latter claim is a positive use of the notion. This is based on his account of the difference between the two uses of such a concept, which he explains by saying 'The concept of a noumenon is positive if its use, besides being governed by the rules governing "phenomenon" and "not", is also governed by other rules'. For on this score to talk of a noumenon as a cause is to treat the concept in a positive way.

But Körner's distinction between the positive and negative uses of the concept is not Kant's. All that Kant says is that if we understand by 'noumenon' an object of a non-sensible intuition, then we use the concept in a positive way; and if we understand by it only whatever is not an object of our sensible intuition, then we use it only in a negative way. One central difference between these versions of the concept is plainly that while the former implies that the concept names an object, the latter does not. The test for determining whether such a concept was being used positively or negatively does not therefore turn only on the properties ascribed to noumena. The test depends rather on whether in so describing such purported things it was to be understood that a certain type of object was being talked about.[1] It would then be possible to speak of noumena as affecting our senses, and still be using the concept in a merely negative way, as Kant uses it, for example, at B 344–345. For the reasons already given Kant would not have admitted that the concept of a noumenon was a concept of an object at all, but this does not prevent, and is not inconsistent with, attaching to the concept of noumena descriptions other than those of 'phenomenon' and 'not'. Once again, as in the case of the term 'transcendental object', there is no objection to saying things about it, so long as these are not misunderstood.

### (iii) THE 'OBJECT OF REPRESENTATIONS'

It was suggested earlier (Ch. 1, p. 17) that the passage at A 104–110, where Kant discusses the meaning of the phrase 'object of representations', might throw some light on Kant's term 'appearance'. For appearances are said to be both objects and representations. In this passage Kant does not say that appearances represent things in themselves, or intelligible objects, but only that they can be said to represent the transcendental object. Now that something has been said of the way in which Kant uses this phrase it is possible to begin to understand Kant's argument. The argument can usefully be divided into two halves, a preliminary part from A 104 ('At this point . . .') to A 106 ('. . . necessity of synthesis'), and a summary and conclusion from A 108 ('Now, also, we are in a position . . .') to the end of the whole section at A 100. What

---

[1] At B 342 Kant seems to use 'positive' and 'negative' in another way. The difference is apparent only, not real.

occurs between A 106 and A 108 (three paragraphs only) is of importance, but is too complex to be dealt with now. For present purposes the two identified passages are what matter.

In the opening section of the first passage Kant reiterates his view that appearances are representations and not things in themselves, and abruptly introduces the question 'What, then, do we mean by the term "object of representations" or "object corresponding to and distinct from our knowledge"?' To this question he answers simply that we can conceive such an object only as 'something in general = X'. This question, its mode of formulation, and the answer to it, are all couched in traditional terms. Since Kant speaks of appearances as representations he recognises that he is bound to explain what can be meant by the notion of an object of such representations. At the same time he concedes to a familiar sceptical argument, also rehearsed in his Logic (Ak., Vol. 9, pp. 49–50), that this question is apparently unanswerable. For we cannot identify such an object without representing it, and in that case we do not succeed in identifying an object independent of representations. Neither here, nor at any other point in this whole passage, does Kant try to answer the question by outlining any supposed causal relation between objects and our senses. It is clear that such a relation, and with it any general 'representative' theory of perception, such as Locke's, was not a candidate for the answer to the question.

Kant nevertheless does not abandon the question. Instead he considers why we have such a notion as that of an object at all. The answer now given is that such a notion derives from our ability to reach agreement in the application of concepts, and consequently from our ability to decide about the ascription of predicates.[1] Kant

[1] This is important in connection with Körner's criticism mentioned above. Körner emphasises that Kant does sometimes speak of noumena in the categorial terms of causality. Kant also says (B 149, B 344, B 522) that noumena can be regarded as non-spatio-temporal, and non-categorial. I cannot see how this is to be reconciled with the other modes of description, unless Kant held (as I think he did) that descriptions of noumena were a matter of indifference. Since there is no way in which such ascriptions could be tested, nothing is more natural than that contradictory predicates should be applied to the term, e.g. by different people. Such a situation is sharply contrasted, according to Kant, with that which obtains over phenomena. The whole basis of our idea of a phenomenal object is precisely that agreement and ability to decide about the ascription of predicates which is so hopelessly lacking in the intelligible world.

speaks of the 'unity that constitutes the concept of an object', and of the 'unity of rule' determining applications of concepts, and concludes (A 105): 'The concept of this unity is the representation of the object = X, which I think through the predicates above-mentioned of a triangle.' The same points about agreement in the application of concepts, and about the unity of conceptual rules required for our notion of an object in general, are repeated in the remainder of this passage, and in the *Prolegomena*, Sect. 18–20 (Ak., Vol. 4, pp. 297–302).

When Kant returns to the task of answering his question in the summary (A 108) the same points stand out again. To call something a representation is to suppose some object for it; appearances are not things in themselves, but they are the only things we are given immediately. If we regard them as representations, and say that they have an object, then such an object can be called a transcendental object. But to refer to such a thing is only a general way of expressing certain features of our experience. For the concept of such an object contains a way of expressing the idea of what confers objective reality on our empirical concepts. To speak of relation to this transcendental object is to speak of the objective reality of our empirical knowledge. These features of our experience, and this objective reality of our knowledge, depend at least partly on the rules which govern certain basic concepts in our language. They rest once again on what Kant earlier called that 'unity of rule' determining the application of concepts. Kant puts the point in this way (A 109):

> The pure concept of this transcendental object . . . is what alone can confer upon all our empirical concepts in general relation to an object, that is, objective reality. This concept cannot contain any determinate intuition, and therefore refers only to that unity which must be met with in any manifold of knowledge which stands in relation to an object. . . . Since this unity must be regarded as necessary a priori . . . the relation to a transcendental object, that is, the objective reality of our empirical knowledge rests on the transcendental law that all appearances, in so far as through them objects are to be given us, must stand under those a priori rules of synthetical unity whereby the inter-relating of these appearances in empirical intuition is alone possible.

The use made of the term 'transcendental object' in this passage can be understood through the similar use made of it at B 522–524 (see above pp. 68–69). There it was explained as a conceptual repository, or abbreviation, for certain ways of thinking about the past, or distant regions of space, or causal connections. Such an abbreviation, like the way of thinking it represents, sets a task for those who investigate the past, or space, or causal connections. But in the context of such scientific enquiries the philosophic interest of the term was limited to an account of its status and force. In the passage at A 104–110 Kant again uses the term as an abbreviation, but this time it represents certain ways of thinking about our experience or knowledge. In this case the philosophic interest lies not just in explaining the status of the notion, but actually in carrying out the task of investigation to which it points. Just as the term may set a task for scientists, so it may also set a task for philosophers. This task is that of explaining the ways of thinking which it abbreviates, that is, of accounting for that feature of our experience which can be called its 'objectivity' or 'objective reality'.

The reference to a transcendental object in the Deduction is thus not intended to represent a solution to Kant's problem about the meaning of the term 'object'. In particular it is not intended, as Prichard thought, to solve this question by relating our sensations to an imperceptible object beyond them. The term is only a cipher for expressing a philosophic task yet to be completed. The point of saying, as Kant curiously does, that the transcendental object = X, the unknown (cf. B 12–13), is to show that it presents us with an equation containing unknown terms, which it is a philosophic task to solve. The sense of the phrase 'the unknown' here is not a reference to any mysterious realm of intelligible objects, but refers only to the way in which we speak of an equation as containing so many unknowns. Kant does not believe that this term is in any way unknowable, or that the metaphorical equation is unsolvable. It is the task of the remainder of the Transcendental Deduction and the Analytic of Principles to solve it.

This helps to explain why Kant distinguished between the notions of a transcendental object and a noumenon at A 253, where he said: 'The object to which I relate appearance in general is the transcendental object, that is, the completely indeterminate thought of *something* in general. This cannot be entitled the noumenon; for I know nothing of what it (something in general) is in itself, and have no concept of it save as merely the object of a sensible intuition in general. . . .' The thought of an object in general is presupposed in all our empirical knowledge, and it is this thought that stimulates Kant's problem about the meaning of our notion of an object. This notion is precisely not the thought of any intelligible object, but only the idea of certain objective features of our knowledge and experience. The problem, then, is to say what exactly does confer objective reality on our experience, or again, what the notion of objective reality itself means. Kant, as we have seen, is prepared to answer such questions ultimately through the notions of conceptual rules, and agreement in the application of concepts.

The problem that Kant sets for himself in the Deduction yields another aspect of the general 'representation' problem for categories mentioned above (Ch. 4). That problem began from the difficulty of accounting for the use in our experience of certain very general concepts associated with the superior status of claims in such scientific systems as Newtonian mechanics. Kant wished to make clear how such concepts are attached to, and operate in, our ordinary empirical experience. Now he reaches the same task from a different starting-point. For the problem outlined at A 104–110 begins from the difficulty of accounting for a certain feature of our ordinary experience, namely, that it is 'objective'; that we speak of objects corresponding to, and yet distinct from, our knowledge; that we have public agreed criteria for the truth of factual statements. And the basis for an explanation of this feature of our experience has been suggested in the important influence of certain conceptual rules on our experience.

These two tasks are only two different aspects of the same enquiry. To show how categories operate in our experience is to reveal their special status, and to explain the objective features of our experience is, evidently, to appeal to the unifying function of certain conceptual rules (categories). The special status of categories is precisely shown in their responsibility for this feature of our experience, and their responsibility in this direction can be shown by an examination of the ways in which they operate in our experience. It has been suggested (Ch. 1, pp. 12–14, and Ch. 4, pp. 63–64) that the general way in which such concepts operate is by enabling us to discriminate between certain basic types of perceived thing. This is the problem outlined in the passage at B 235–

236. It is not an empirical task in psychology, but a conceptual enquiry into the relations between the categories and these basic discriminations.

This account of Kant's problem may seem very far from clear. Nothing has been done carefully to elucidate the notion, which sets the problem, namely that of an 'objective' feature of experience, or simply of an 'object'. A rough guide in more modern terms could be given by saying that Kant wishes to account for the fact that our experience is a common, publicly shareable one, that we are able to think and talk about commonly identifiable phenomena. Kant's problem would then arise because it is for him indisputable that this experience can be traced back ultimately to private or personal experiences. There is, on this view, a gap between the privacy of our experiences and the publicity of our experience, which it is Kant's task to bridge. This account can give no more than an illusory clarity to Kant's aim. For the terms in which it is now fashionable to state such an aim are themselves only dubiously clear. Moreover Kant's problem is just as much to analyse, or clarify, the sense of his notion of an 'object', or the modern notion of 'publicity', as it is to 'explain' them. The whole of the Analytic is engaged in this operation, so that it is not surprising that in the statement of the problem there should be terms whose sense is dubious. The problem indeed largely is to render the sense of such terms less dubious.

# 6

# THE TRANSCENDENTAL
# ANALYTIC

'Pure concepts of the understanding are thus a priori possible, and in relation to experience are indeed necessary' (A 130).

'This peculiarity of our understanding, that it can produce a priori unity of apperception solely by means of the categories, and only such and so many, is as little capable of further explanation as why we have just these and no other functions of judgment . . .' (B 145–146).

SO far Kant's problem in the Analytic, referred to generally as the 'representation' problem, has been briefly indicated without any account of the way in which Kant attacks it. But without some guide to the manner in which the different sections of the Analytic contribute to the solution of this problem Kant's argument may be lost in a maze of interesting, but often perplexing, detail. The most obvious guide to this whole argument is to be found in the different relations which each of the three main sections have to the categories. The arguments of the Metaphysical Deduction, Transcendental Deduction, and the Analytic of Principles certainly overlap in a number of ways, but it is helpful, even artificially, to separate them.

Kant's problem could be expressed in terms of an enquiry, of a transcendental and not empirical kind, into the ways in which we discriminate among the items presented to our senses. The force of the claim that this is a transcendental and not empirical enquiry appears partly in the investigation's being limited only to certain special concepts, and their influence on the discriminations we effect. For Kant is not concerned to investigate the discriminatory powers of all concepts, but only of those which have a special status in our experience. This claim is connected with another of the ways in which Kant's problem has been explained, namely, as an enquiry into the features of our experience which can be called 'objective'. On Kant's view it is just the particular concepts he is concerned with, which are in some way responsible for this feature of our experience. These same concepts have also a central position in the disciplines of Mathematics and the Natural Sciences. Kant's argument throughout the Analytic can be regarded as an attempt both to explain what is meant by ascribing a special status to these concepts, and to establish the ascription of such a status to them. The different sections in the whole argument can, therefore, be separated in terms of their different contributions towards the understanding of this status, and its ascription to these central concepts, the categories.

In the Metaphysical Deduction Kant identifies certain concepts as categories. But to say this is to raise at once a difficulty about the proper understanding of this passage. For this might be taken to mean that in the Metaphysical Deduction Kant shows that certain concepts have all the properties which are to be ascribed to categories. Such an account of the argument in this passage is bound to end in the complete dissatisfaction with it, which most commentators have registered. For if the argument were designed to establish finally that the chosen concepts are categories, it would certainly fail, and, at the same time, would have to be regarded as making the subsequent arguments of the Transcendental Deduction and the Analytic of Principles redundant. It is odd to regard the earlier passage as a failure because it does not perform successfully the tasks naturally allocated to the later sections, and it would be more economical to conclude not that the Metaphysical Deduction is a failure, but that it is not intended to perform these other tasks. The Metaphysical Deduction is an introductory argument and contains extensive claims about the properties of its selected concepts. But almost all of what is claimed to be true of categories in this passage refers for support to the Transcendental Deduction or Analytic of Principles. It would be better to say that in the Metaphysical Deduction certain concepts are initially, or tentatively, identified as categories, but that they are not yet proved to have all the properties which are ultimately ascribed to them. Its conclusion presents certain concepts rather as candidates for categorial status, and it is left to the later passages to show that these are successful candidates. Nevertheless it is clear that some properties are, however tentatively, ascribed to the chosen concepts on the basis of the arguments in this introductory section.

It would be natural, for example, to believe that the property of a priority is ascribed to categories in this passage. For Kant himself seems to say as much at B 159. Yet it would be just as natural to think that this elusive property is ascribed to categories on the basis of arguments in the Transcendental Deduction. For its preliminary sections (in B 13 and 14) suggest criteria for a priority which, it would be easy to think, the categories are shown to satisfy in the Transcendental Deduction. To complicate matters still more, it could certainly be argued that this same property is ascribed to the categories in the Analytic of Principles. For the proofs of the principles are designed to show how each category makes experience, or the objects of experience, possible; and this is the suggested test for a priority in Sect. 14 (B 124–126). This difficulty cannot perhaps be settled without considering each of these sections in detail, but it may be worth while to suggest one way in which it could be resolved. This is to regard the property of being a priori either as a complex property, the ascription of a part of which to the categories is supported by each section; or to regard it as a property ascribed to the categories on the basis of the arguments in all three sections. It is certainly true that the understanding and establishment of the special status ascribed to categories depends upon each of these sections. It would be wrong to think that the only place to which reference need be made to consider the claim that categories are a priori is the Metaphysical Deduction. Kant gives, in this section, some reason for saying that the selected concepts are a priori, and consequently some reason for admitting that they are categories. But these reasons cannot profitably be regarded as a proof of such claims.[1]

---

[1] The illusion that a proof is given in this passage, for example at B 102–106, is fostered by Kemp Smith's translation. For at B 105 where Kant says only: 'On this account they are called pure concepts of the understanding, which refer a priori to objects . . .' this is translated as 'On this account we are *entitled* to call these representations pure concepts of the understanding,

The Metaphysical Deduction can be regarded, therefore, as an effort to support, rather than to prove, the claim that the selected concepts have certain special properties. Kant provides an explanation of his method of selection, and some account of the relations between forms of judgment and categories. He provides also a number of claims about the merits and completeness of his classification, which have generally been regarded as exaggerated. To regard the whole section as a total failure, however, because of this would be to miss much that is valuable in it. One of the difficulties in attempting to understand this obscure passage is the pervasive temptation to load it with a force it certainly cannot bear. Kant himself encourages this in some of his claims, but it should be remembered that he speaks of the section in the unambitious terms of a 'clue to the categories', rather than in the ambitious terms of the establishment of certain concepts as categories.

The Transcendental Deduction can be represented as an argument about the categories, or rather categories, in general. In this it is chiefly distinguished from the detailed analysis of the categories, which appears in the Analytic of Principles. There are two central aspects of the argument in the earlier section, and both are concerned rather to explain or elucidate the notion of a category, than to establish that any particular concept is a category in the elucidated sense. Kant connects the notion of a category, through the terminology of 'transcendental apperception', with the ideas of 'objectivity' and 'personality'. Both of these connections can be seen in the arguments at A 104–110, A 119–123, and B 131–140, and both are associated with corresponding arguments in the Analytic of Principles. The arguments relating the idea of a category to that of an object reappear in the detailed proofs of the principles, where it is shown that each concept is related to a certain objective discrimination in our experience. The arguments relating categories to the notion of a person are much less obvious in the Analytic of Principles, but they reappear in the Refutation of Idealism (B 274–279) and in the 'General Note on the System of Principles' (B 288–294).

Both aspects of a category are designed to show that categories

---

and to regard them as applying a priori to objects . . .'. This may suggest, what Kant does not say, that the grounds for this entitlement have been already given in a proof of the a priority of the chosen concepts.

are in some way fundamental concepts in our experience. Kant's account of the term 'object' results in the claim that we can understand such a notion only in terms of the conceptual rules, which govern the way in which we discriminate items presented to the senses. The categories can be said to be responsible for the objective features of our experience, in this way, since they are the concepts which embody these linguistic rules. But since the argument in the Transcendental Deduction is an explanation of the notion of a category, and not an argument about any particular concepts, it would be a mistake to think that it has yet been shown that the concepts chosen in the Metaphysical Deduction are categories, in this sense. It is true that some few references are made to these concepts, and moreover that there is a natural tendency to think that the claims made in the Transcendental Deduction for categories are true of the chosen concepts. But this is another of the complicating overlaps in the whole argument, which it is better to disentangle. What Kant claims to have shown in the Transcendental Deduction is only that some concepts must be fundamental in these ways, and not that any particular concepts are fundamental in this way, or must be so.

These are neither the only features of the Transcendental Deduction, nor the only features which reappear in the Analytic of Principles. Kant provides in the earlier section an account of imagination (A 100–102, A 123–125, B 150–152), which corresponds to the later argument of the Schematism (B 176–187). He provides also an account of the restrictions placed on the categories, that they have a significant employment only in application to appearances (B 146–150), and this reappears later in the argument in the section on Phenomena and Noumena (B 294–315). Finally, Kant provides in the Transcendental Deduction some examples of the ways in which categories bear on our discrimination of appearances (B 162–163), which ought properly to have appeared in the Analytic of Principles. This does not exhaust the points of contact between the two sections, but it can serve to show the way in which Kant's arguments sprawl over the Analytic, and sometimes to places where they do not strictly belong.

The Transcendental Deduction is sometimes thought to have a close connection with Kant's idea of the sciences, particularly mathematics and physics. When, at the end of the argument (A 126–129, B 159–165) he speaks of 'prescribing laws to nature', it may seem as though he is referring to that procedure in which scientists formulate and test their hypotheses.[1] There is, of course, no doubt that Kant intends to explain certain features of scientific enquiry, and particularly the special authority which claims in the sciences seem to possess. But it would be wrong to think that this is all that can be meant by 'prescribing laws to nature', or to think that in the Transcendental Deduction Kant is primarily engaged in what we should call 'philosophy of science'. The arguments of the Transcendental Deduction are not restricted to this scientific context, and to talk of prescribing laws to nature is for Kant a metaphorical way of expressing a complex relation between categories and the whole range of our experience. It is plain that Kant's account of the laws which we might be said to prescribe to nature points not to the particular empirical laws which scientists might formulate, but rather to certain basic, conceptual laws, on which these empirical claims are supposed to rest. But these conceptual laws operate even in our ordinary experience, and not only in the context of a science. The examples which Kant gives in the Transcendental Deduction of the operation of categories (B 162–163) are designed to show their influence in quite unscientific contexts, in which there is no reference to the formulation of any scientific hypothesis. For these reasons, to give an account of the Transcendental Deduction in purely scientific terms is to present only one side of the whole argument.

It would be natural to say that even if Kant's argument in the Transcendental Deduction is not directly or exclusively related to scientific claims, the argument in the Analytic of Principles is. All the principles formulated and proved in this latter section, with the possible exception of the Postulates, are closely connected with certain principles in mathematics or natural science. Yet even in this section it would not be true to say that Kant is interested only in the scientific implications of these principles. At B 201–202 Kant seems to indicate that the principles have a wider scope than this:

> But it should be noted that we are as little concerned in the one case with the principles of mathematics, as in the other with the

---

[1] An account of the Analytic along these lines is given in Martin: *Kant's Metaphysics and Theory of Science*, particularly Ch. III, pp. 90–98.

principles of general physical dynamics. We treat only of the principles of pure understanding in their relation to inner sense (all differences among the given representations being ignored). It is through these principles of the pure understanding that the special principles of mathematics and dynamics become possible.

Earlier in the same section (B 197–198) Kant expresses the same point in another way: 'That there should be principles at all is entirely due to the understanding. Not only is it the faculty of rules in respect of that which happens, but is itself the source of principles in accordance with which everything that can be presented to us as an object must conform to rules.' For the contrast between the two sides of understanding appears to be that between its operations in a scientific context, and the more basic operations it reveals in the whole of our experience of objects.

This general argument in the Analytic of Principles is the consequence of the account given in the Transcendental Deduction of the term 'object'. When Kant claims that everything that can be presented as an object must conform to certain rules, he is echoing the claim that categories are responsible for the objective features of our experience. This claim is expressed elsewhere (B 125–126, A 111, B 197) by saying that the categories, or conditions of a possible experience, are also conditions of the possibility of objects of experience. It is in this general way that the Analytic of Principles completes the argument of the Transcendental Deduction, by showing for each category that it genuinely is a condition of this kind.

What it means to be a condition of the possibility of objects of experience is, in part, explained in the Transcendental Deduction. It can be understood in the light of what has been said already of Kant's aim, and in the light also of Kant's procedure in the proofs of the principles. Kant speaks of what is presented to the senses as an undifferentiated manifold, indeterminate or nondescript until it is conceived to be of some definite kind. This sets Kant the problem of explaining how we are enabled to differentiate between the distinguishable items in our experience. On this score the principles are intended to reveal the power of each category to make certain discriminations possible in our experience. Kant hopes to show how categories are involved in these discriminations, by showing the ways in which they operate to distinguish one kind of appearance from another.

The general procedure in proving the principles is to connect each category with a certain temporal discrimination. But it is clearer to understand what Kant could mean by an 'object', or an 'objective feature of experience', by referring to certain concepts which mediate between the categories and these temporal notions. Such mediating concepts occur in our ordinary experience, and are supposed to contain a reference both to a category and to a temporal feature. They include such concepts as that of a class, number, magnitude, degree, object, property, alteration, state, and event. Kant indicates the relation between a category 'cause' and such a mediating concept 'event', in a specific case, at B 816:

> In the Transcendental Analytic, for instance, we derived the principle that everything which happens has a cause, from the condition under which alone a concept of happening in general is objectively possible—namely by showing that the determination of an event in time, and therefore the event as belonging to experience, would be impossible save as standing under such a dynamical rule.

What the category, and its associated principle, make possible in such a case is the discrimination of such an 'object' as an event. Kant claims to be able to show in similar ways that all the categories are responsible for such objective features of our experience. It is also in this way that he intends to reveal finally the importance and special status of the concepts selected in the Metaphysical Deduction as candidate categories.

The general relations between all three sections of the Analytic can be briefly summarised. In the Metaphysical Deduction Kant identifies certain concepts, in a non-committal way, as candidates for categorial status. These identifications are supported by arguments designed to show that the method of selection picks out certain concepts which are basic in our language. In the Transcendental Deduction Kant argues, without special reference to the chosen concepts, that a category is a concept responsible in some way for the objective features of our experience. This argument is no more than an attempt to elucidate the meanings of such terms as 'object' and 'category'. Nothing is said in this section to show that the concepts chosen in the Metaphysical Deduction are categories. It is argued only that some categories are necessary for our experience, and not that any particular concepts are necessary in this way. It is, finally, the task of the Analytic of Principles to tie these threads together, by showing in detail how the concepts selected in the Metaphysical Deduction satisfy the requirements for categorial status which were elucidated in the Transcendental Deduction. It is in the Analytic of Principles that Kant shows how each particular concept makes possible the objects of experience. Thus it is only at the end of the whole Analytic that one is strictly entitled to call the chosen concepts categories, and to understand by this that they enjoy all the properties that Kant ascribes to categories.

# 7
# CATEGORIES
# AND JUDGMENTS

'It is to synthesis, therefore, that we must first look to determine the origin of our knowledge' (B 103).

'To put all this in a nutshell, it is first necessary to remind the reader that we are here not talking of the origin of experience, but of what is in it . . .' (*Prol.*, Sect. 21a. Ak., Vol. 4, p. 304).

IT is obvious enough that in the Metaphysical Deduction Kant identifies certain concepts as categories, and something has been already said about the non-committal nature of this claim (Ch. 6). If it is held that in the Metaphysical Deduction Kant finally establishes that his chosen concepts have all the properties that categories are supposed to have, then the argument will seem inevitably defective. But if the chosen concepts are regarded instead as candidates for categorial status, then the argument has at least some hope of success. In this case the whole passage is designed to give grounds for, and explanations of, the list of candidate categories which terminates it. Unfortunately neither the grounds nor the explanations are at all clearly expressed. Throughout the section Kant contrives, even more successfully than usual, to condense his argument to the point of assertion. This means that much of the discussion can be only guided, and not dictated, by Kant's own words. There are two points at which the discussion will deviate from Kant's own exposition. Appeals will sometimes be made to the later arguments of the Schematism, and the passages which introduce the Analytic of Principles (B 169–202). The reason for this is that the later passage contains further elaboration of the links between categories, judgments, and the concepts of space and time. More importantly Kant's order of exposition in the Metaphysical Deduction will not be followed in the discussion. Of the two central passages to be considered, B 92–95 and B 102–104, the latter will be discussed first. For these reasons it may be useful to give a brief outline of the arguments in these passages as Kant states them.

In the introductory passage at B 91–92 Kant indicates in general terms that he intends to collect, or classify, concepts in his effort to isolate what he calls (B 89) the elements of pure understanding. He says: 'When we call a faculty of knowledge into play, then as the occasioning circumstances differ, various concepts stand forth and make the faculty known, and allow of being collected with more or less completeness.' This argument serves to explain what is to be meant by claims about the faculty of understanding, or about the elements of understanding. Such claims are to be understood as testable, to be established or rejected, by reference to the classification of concepts. Kant insists that such a classification should be 'systematic', and 'proceed according to a single principle', so that the concepts classified can be 'connected with each other according to one concept or idea' (B 92).

The search for a system of classification appears to be conducted in the next section on 'The Logical Employment of the Understanding' (B 92–95). And, indeed, the conclusion to this section seems to point to the discovery of the required systematic principle (B 94): 'The functions of the understanding can therefore be discovered if we can give an exhaustive statement of the functions of unity in judgment.' This is to say, apparently, that after a search for the required principle Kant succeeds in stating it. The principle is simply that the classification of concepts should proceed by listing forms of judgment. That this is what Kant means is borne out by a passage at B 106, where he says: 'This division is developed systematically from a common principle, namely, the faculty of judgment (which is the same as the faculty of thought).'

It has not always been thought so easy to identify the principle on which Kant relies to make his procedure systematic. And it may be that some such complex set of inter-relations between the forms of judgment, as that investigated by Klaus Reich,[1] lies con-

---

[1] K. Reich: *Die Vollständigkeit der Kantischen Urteilstafel.* Kant does not seem to distinguish at all carefully between being systematic and being com-

cealed behind the apparent simplicity of Kant's own exposition. Kant certainly makes no explicit appeal to such an elaboration in this passage, but seems to hold that to classify forms of judgment is to proceed systematically. Kant's execution of the systematic plan leans heavily on accepted classifications of judgments in formal logic. Unfortunately neither formal logic, nor anything else, can justify the claim that every form of judgment has been listed by Kant. The most that can be said of the list is that it may be comprehensive. Nevertheless Kant's choice of judgment-forms as the basis of his classification of concepts is important, and will be discussed later.

The remaining arguments in the Metaphysical Deduction deal with the transition from the table of judgments to that of categories. In the first section (B 102–104) Kant discusses the differences between general and transcendental logic, and the associated difference between analysis and synthesis. In the second part (B 104–105) he gives a brief account of the relation between the two tables. The argument in this passage is particularly obscure, but is evidently supposed (cf. B 105) to provide some ground for regarding the chosen concepts as a priori, and some ground for using the table of judgments as a guide to the chosen concepts. Clearly both of these claims need to be considered. In the following account the argument from B 102–104 will be considered first, and the passages from B 92–95 and B 104–105 will be discussed afterwards.

### (i) ANALYSIS AND SYNTHESIS

Kant's argument in the passage at B 102–104 proceeds along these lines. General logic and its analytic activities should be distinguished from transcendental logic and synthesis. Indeed the former discipline rests on the latter, so that analysis can be said to presuppose synthesis (cf. B 133–134 and note). For this reason it is to transcendental logic and synthesis that we must look for the 'first origins of knowledge' (B 103). Kant also represents the difference between these disciplines as that between bringing different representations to concepts (analysis), and bringing the

plete, but Reich is concerned rather with the claim that Kant's classification of judgments is complete, than that it is systematic. It may be that while Kant's programme of classification is systematic, his execution of the programme is not complete.

pure synthesis of representations to concepts (synthesis). General and transcendental logic are thus to be distinguished not only in terms of their, analytic or synthetic, procedures, but also in terms of their empirical or a priori materials. Transcendental logic has at its disposal the transcendental content of space and time, but general logic abstracts from all content of knowledge and requires items to be given, perhaps empirically, as its material for investigation (B 102).

What Kant means by an analytic procedure in general logic can be explained in this way. If we suppose a set of items named and described in various ways, then it is an analytic procedure to arrange the concepts used as names or descriptions in a logical order. It may be possible, in this way, to clarify the concepts, or even to enlarge them by grouping the items under other more general headings based on the descriptions already given. Analytic procedures therefore presuppose some set of discriminations in a language, which it is a task of general logic to analyse, order, or clarify. That certain items are supposed already named and described reflects Kant's view that analysis requires certain ideas to be given. This supposition is quite neutral as to the existence of any objects in our experience, which satisfy the descriptions. This is one way in which general logic may mislead, by tempting philosophers to think that analytic claims about concepts always reflect truths about objects[1] (cf. Ch. 5, pp. 71–76).

When Kant says, therefore, that general logic looks to some other source for its data, or that it abstracts from all content of knowledge, or that no concepts can first arise by way of analysis, he is arguing that analytic procedures always presuppose certain concepts, or certain discriminations in a language. It follows from this that analysis cannot provide a complete account of language, since it must always presuppose certain concepts, which would then be omitted from the explanation. If, for example, an analytic procedure were used to explain the way in which a language is learned, then Kant's argument shows that such an explanation

[1] Cf. the Amphiboly generally (B 316–349) and B 325 particularly. Kant's point in this latter passage is that we may elaborate logical relations between concepts, without saying whether the concepts are empty or not; that is, whether any phenomena satisfy them. General logic is thus non-committal about the application of concepts, but transcendental logic is not. This is connected with another of Kant's claims (B 174–175) that transcendental philosophy can specify a priori the instances in which categories are applied.

would be incomplete. For analysis can show only how certain concepts depend logically upon other concepts, and these latter must in the end be assumed to have been given, or already learned. But a complete account of the way in which a language is learned would have to explain how a concept is learned, when no prior concepts are presupposed. Analysis would, for this reason, always be left with some unexplained concepts on its hands, and would therefore fall short of a complete explanation. It is for this reason that analysis indicates the need for some further kind of explanation, to which Kant gives the name 'synthesis'. Kant's claims that analysis presupposes synthesis should thus be understood as a denial that analysis can provide a complete account of language. If analytic methods are supposed to show how languages are learned, then they yield only partial explanations; if they are used to show the logical dependence of concepts in a language, then they cannot explain or exhibit the dependence of every concept.

It is not altogether easy to see what conclusions should be drawn from this account of analysis and synthesis. It may seem trivial to say that in order to analyse concepts, there must be concepts to be analysed; or to say that when a child first learns or understands a concept it must have gone through a process of synthesis, and not analysis; or to say that the statement ' "Red" is a colour' depends in some way upon the statement 'That is red' (B 133, note). Yet it is not easy to see how such claims bear on Kant's account of categories. It would be naive, for example, to suppose that when Kant claims that categories embody a pure synthesis, which is presupposed in analytic procedures, he means to say that concepts like 'cause' or 'substance' or 'necessity' are among the first that a child learns. (Cf. Berkeley's criticism of Locke: *Principles*, Introduction, Sect. 14.)

Kant's argument contains a radical criticism of such an empiricist theory of language as Locke provided. And if it were shown that such an empiricist account is defective, then it would be natural to say that not all concepts in a language are open to such empirical explanation. Kant certainly believed that an empiricist theory such as Locke's could not explain the status of categories, and uncompromisingly rejected any such account of them (B 117–118). Moreover, it is clear from the conclusion to the argument at B 102–104 that the distinction between analysis and synthesis is supposed to give some ground for saying that the categories are non-empirical or a priori (B 105, and cf. B 158). Kant's claim, therefore, that some concepts are a priori may be understood, and perhaps justified, if it can be shown that Locke's account of language is incomplete. To put this in less committal terms, Kant might show that Locke's account is incomplete, and that it requires a reference to categories for its completion.

It is easy to understand Locke's programme as an analysis of complex concepts into simpler. When Locke outlines the way in which we might acquire a complex concept, he can generally be understood as explaining how such a concept depends upon simpler concepts. The concept of a type of material object, for example, might be shown to depend upon the simpler concepts of a certain colour or shape or feel. If this were all that Locke intended, then it could be said that his account of concepts, because analytic in this way, is inevitably incomplete. For all his analyses rest ultimately on the identification of certain simple concepts, which are thus presupposed in every explanation. But this is to admit that his account is incomplete, since, although it may explain how complex concepts depend on simple concepts, it cannot give an analysis of the simple concepts themselves. It might be said that simple concepts are just those which do not depend on any other concepts. Or again, if Locke's account is expressed in terms of our learning languages, then it may succeed in showing how complex concepts are, or could be, learned, once certain simple concepts are already understood. But it cannot in the same way tell us how these simple concepts are learned, since there are no other concepts from which to learn them. If such an account were to cover all the concepts in a language, then it would require completion of a kind to which Kant points when he speaks of synthesis.

It is natural to defend Locke by saying that he also admitted the need for some further explanation of the way in which we learn even the simple concepts. On Locke's view even a simple concept, such as 'red', can be analysed, not into simpler concepts, but into particular ideas from which the concept 'red' may be abstracted. Locke apparently supposed that his account of the simple concepts could be completed by appealing to the doctrine of abstraction to explain their origin or dependence. This defence of Locke helps to reveal the extent of Kant's deviation from such

ANALYSIS AND SYNTHESIS

an empiricist programme. For it is clear that the kind of completion which Kant envisaged for analysis is radically unlike that which Locke produced. While Locke tried to break out of the framework of concepts, by appealing to entities supposed to be simpler than any concept, Kant appeals to other concepts in the language, and these of the most abstract and general kind. Locke pursues the things he regards as most particular and most sensible, while Kant looks to those which are the most general and most intelligible.

There have been many criticisms of the doctrine of abstraction,[1] and its limitations can be only briefly indicated here. It is in the inadequacies of the doctrine that Kant's deviation from it may best be seen. Because the doctrine purports to break out of the framework of concepts, it is primarily a claim about learning, and not about the logical dependence of concepts. If it is treated in the latter way, then it gives rise to circularities of the kind that Locke's own explanations seem sometimes to commit. Locke claims, for example (*Essay*: Bk. II, Ch. xiii, Sect. 4), that our ideas of 'certain stated lengths, such as are a foot, or yard, etc.' can explain how we 'frame to ourselves the ideas of "long", "square", "feet", "yards", etc.'. But to say that the concept 'long' or 'foot' depends on our concepts of stated lengths, such as a foot or yard, is to commit a circularity. Such an account can avoid triviality only by supposing that there is some process in which we learn the concept 'long' from our perception of certain lengths. It would be very imprudent to deny that there was any such process, and yet Locke gives very little reason to suppose that it is of the kind he describes.

The main support for Locke's description of this process comes from an analogy with the analysis of concepts. Because it is possible to learn a complex concept by attending to the simpler concepts, on which it logically depends, Locke supposes that we must also learn the simplest concepts by attending to, and abstracting from, the simple experiences in which the concept is exemplified. But it is all very well to say that we must learn what 'red' means in a way like that in which we could learn what 'colour' means, once we already understand 'red'. It is quite another matter to produce evidence of a sort to support the use of such an analogy. Locke produces no such evidence, and this is in general what is wrong

[1] Most recently, and very violently, in Geach: *Mental Acts*, pp. 18–44.

97

with his doctrine. For it is properly a claim in empirical psychology, and yet it rests on an a priori assumption. On the evidence that we all ordinarily have about learning there is quite as much reason for denying as for affirming the use of the analogy. For the process to which the analogy is applied is admitted to be radically unlike that from which it derives. There is no a priori reason for supposing that the analogy can or should be carried over into such a different context.

Even if these arguments reveal defects in Locke's final account of language, they do not yet show that Kant's account is any better. Kant certainly avoids some of the objections that can be raised against Locke. Although Kant, for example, speaks of the 'origins' of our knowledge on occasion, he plainly is talking of the dependence of concepts, and not of their learning. It may, however, still be unclear that Kant could be justified in arguing from these defects in Locke to the conclusion that there are a priori concepts. Certainly the mere fact that Locke's analysis of concepts is incomplete, in the way that any such analytic account would be, does not mean that his simple concepts are a priori. Nobody would say that the concept 'red' is a priori, even though it has to be presupposed in his account of the dependence of concepts. For whatever is the process by which such a concept is learned, most people have a conviction or prejudice that it is learned somehow from the perception of particular red items.

This conviction shows the extent to which the contrast between empirical and a priori even now is attached to a hypothesis about the learning of concepts. But since Kant is not offering an account of the ways in which concepts may be learned, this contrast ought to be given some other sense in the field of concept dependence. What evidently tempts Kant to say that the categories are a priori is that they are associated with concepts on which even Locke's simple concepts depend. If there were such concepts, then it would be natural to conclude both that such a dependence is unlike that exploited in empiricist analyses, and that the concepts themselves are not of a type standardly regarded as empirical. It makes no sense to speak of a priori concepts if the idea of an empirical concept is unexplained. If Locke's simple concepts are standard examples of empirical concepts, then Kant has some reason to say that any concepts of a different kind which are presupposed in such simple concepts can be regarded as non-empirical. It may be that the labels 'empirical' and 'a priori' are no longer acceptable in philosophy,[1] so that it would be preferable to use Kant's own contrast between 'sensible' and 'intelligible' concepts (cf. Ch. 4, p. 53). For Kant holds the view that concepts may be classed in these ways, according to their relation to perception. But whatever labels are used for this purpose Kant's argument is that certain concepts can be identified, on which even the empirically simple sensible concepts depend. How these concepts may be identified can be better considered in Kant's other arguments.

### (ii) CONCEPTS AND JUDGMENTS

The kind of completion that Kant envisaged for an analytic account of language is two-fold. At the first stage it gives a ground for selecting certain concepts as basic in our language, and so indicates those concepts on which even the simple concepts of empirical analysis depend. This first stage in the argument is carried through in the passage on 'The Logical Employment of the Understanding' (B 92–95). At the second stage Kant connects the identified forms of judgment with the concepts he calls categories. This argument is given in the brief passage from B 104–105. It is in this second stage of the argument that Kant finally indicates the connection between the analysis of judgment-forms and the synthesis involved in the categories.

### (a) B 92–95

Kant provides several clues to the argument supporting his decision to classify forms of judgment as a guide to the categories. He says, for example, that the only use which understanding can make of concepts is to judge by means of them (B 93), and that all acts of the understanding can be traced back to[2] judgments (B 94). In another passage in *The Mistaken Subtlety of the Four*

---

[1] Some philosophers would say that this contrast can be understood only in terms of the distinction between synthetic and analytic. (Cf. Ayer: *Language, Truth and Logic*, pp. 16 ff.) But this latter contrast is of no use to Kant in the present context, since no sense has been given to the idea of analytic or synthetic concepts.

[2] Kemp Smith translates 'zurückführen' as 'reduce', which may mislead in the light of the modern philosophical use of 'reduction'. 'Trace back' is less misleading.

*Syllogistic Figures* (Ak., Vol. 2, pp. 58–59) Kant also argues that distinct concepts presuppose judgments. What needs to be done is to consider the ways in which it is correct to say that concepts presuppose, or can be traced back to, judgments. For in this argument can be found not only the basis of Kant's decision to classify forms of judgment, but also the ground for claiming that even simple concepts depend in some way upon other concepts in a language.

It would be natural to understand Kant to mean that concepts can be shown to have a relation to assertions, or judgments, which the latter do not have to them. And it is not difficult to see that simple concepts require forms of judgment, if they are to be understood. This rests on the obvious truth that in order to be used intelligibly, concepts need the sort of completion that judgment forms provide. Even the notion of a concept itself points to this need, for it involves the notion of something conceived to be of a certain kind, or in a certain relation. Such an account of concepts indicates at once the idea of a form of judgment in which the concepts may figure, and this is implicit in Kant's account of a concept as a possible predicate. Most, and perhaps all, of our term classifications, such as 'name', 'predicate', 'description', refer back to operations of the judging kind, such as naming, predicating, or describing.

But if it is true that concepts require a reference to forms of judgment for their completion, it is also true that the forms of judgment themselves require particular concepts for their completion. The idea of someone's understanding what a concept is without having a notion of what it is to predicate something seems impossible; but it is no more impossible than that of someone's having a notion of what it is to predicate something without the least idea of what a predicate or concept is. The notion of a judgment, on which our discrimination between judgment forms and concepts rests, has a necessary reference to both of these elements and does not suggest, still less establish, any priority on the part of either. If Kant had meant to rely on any such asymmetry in the dependence between judgment-forms and concepts, then his argument would be inadequate. But there is no sign, in the passage from B 92–95, that he is relying on such a claimed asymmetry. He is nevertheless plainly relying on the view that concepts of all types have a reference to forms of judgment, even though a similar relation holds also in the opposite relation. Some further reason, however, seems to be needed to support Kant's decision to classify forms of judgment.

One answer to this difficulty would be to say that Kant regards the classification of judgments as a way of classifying simpler concepts in the language. On such a view a classification of judgments is not opposed to a classification of concepts, it is rather that the former is a comprehensive example of the latter. When Kant says that he chooses to appeal to a classification of judgments, because it is in judgments that all concepts have their use, he suggests that only a classification of judgments can be comprehensive, or cover all the simpler concepts in a language. And this suggestion is supported by the truth that classifications of judgments in logic are not independent of the simpler concepts which may complete a given verbal form. The classification in traditional logic of the universal affirmative form 'All S is P' is dependent upon the distinction between predicates which apply distributively through a class, and those which apply only collectively to the class. The two propositions 'All Texans outnumber the citizens of any other state in America' and 'All Texans are taller than the citizens of any other state in America' do not both exemplify this logical form, however similar their verbal structure may be. If this relation between judgment and concept classifications is generally true, then there would be some reason for saying that the classification of judgments covers or comprehends that of the simpler concepts which complete forms of judgment.

Kant has, however, another argument at his disposal, which is based on the criticism of Locke already discussed. It is that if all concepts have a reference to judgments, or to forms of judgment, then even such 'simple' concepts as those on which Locke based his analysis of language also have such a reference. For this purpose it does not matter that the dependence between judgment-forms and concepts is entirely symmetrical. All that Kant needs to say is that there are certain features of a language on which even the simplest concepts depend, even though it is also quite true that, in another direction, these same features depend on the simpler concepts. Kant evidently has the belief that even though simple concepts, such as 'red', acquire their meaning primarily through their relation to certain sensible experiences, they also owe a part of their meaning to something else. This additional feature could be indicated by saying that the ways in which a concept may figure in judgments partly determine our understanding of it. A concept like 'red', for example, has its meaning not only in terms of our perception of red items in experience, but also in terms of the framework of judgment in which it figures, or has its use. We say that 'red' names a property, for example, so that part of what we understand by it relates to our ideas of a property, or of property-ascription, in ordinary discourse. Again, the notion of a property is logically connected with that of an individual to which a property may be ascribed. Our understanding of 'red', therefore, also depends in part upon our notions of an individual, and upon categorical forms of judgment in which ascriptions of properties to individuals are standardly expressed (cf. The discussion of substance. Ch. 10, pp. 163–164). To speak of forms of judgment in this way is quite plausibly to speak of a linguistic framework into which every concept, even a simple concept, fits, and to which every concept owes a part of its sense.

If this account can be accepted, then Kant has gone a considerable way towards explaining and justifying his preference for forms of judgment. It is not that forms of judgment are prior to simpler concepts, but rather that the latter depend in some way upon the former for a part of their sense, and also that a classification of the former is in some way comprehensive of the latter. It is clear, moreover, that this dependence is not of the kind considered in such an empiricist account of language as Locke's. If the characteristic idea of dependence in empiricism is that in which complex concepts depend on simpler concepts for the criteria of their application, then the dependence of simple concepts on forms of judgment is plainly not of this kind. Kant has, therefore, some reason for saying that this dependence points in a non-empirical direction away from the standard empirical, or sensible, concepts to others which deserve by contrast the labels 'non-empirical' or 'intelligible' concepts.

Kant's picture of language is, in this way, designed not to re-allocate priorities, which Locke had misplaced, but rather to rectify a distortion which results from Locke's over-emphasis on simple sensible concepts. Kant admitted that Locke's account of language was acceptable on the sensible side, but regarded it as defective in failing properly to accommodate any other. Locke's picture of the structure of language is that of a pile of bricks, each course of which is supported by a larger number of smaller bricks underneath it. The operations by which such a pile is erected leave apparently no particular trace. Kant's picture, by contrast, is more like that of a balance, in which sensible concepts on one side are balanced by intelligible concepts on the other. Locke's account of dependence is in one direction, that of complex concepts on simpler concepts; Kant's is an account of interdependence, that of sensible and intelligible concepts on each other.

Nothing has been very precisely said about the concepts, on which even the simplest are supposed to depend. All that has been suggested so far is that if there are such concepts, then they can be called non-empirical, and can be found in our classifications of judgment-forms. But the arguments considered so far are intended to do no more than explain the belief that such a classification of judgment-forms can be regarded as a clue to the categories (B 91, chapter heading). A clearer idea of Kant's use of such a clue can be gained through the transition from the table of judgments to that of categories.

## (b) B 104–105

The same function which gives unity to the various representations in a judgment, also gives unity to the mere synthesis of various representations in an intuition; and this unity in its most general expression we entitle the pure concept of the understanding. The same understanding, through the same operations, by which, in concepts, by means of analytical unity, it produced the logical form of a judgment, also introduces a transcendental content into its representations, by means of the synthetic unity of the manifold in intuition in general.

It has been suggested already that this brief passage contains an explanation of the relations between the two tables, of judgment-forms and categories. This explanation has two parts, one in each of the two sentences. The first is designed quite generally to connect the unities of function, revealed in the analytic classification of judgment-forms, with what is called 'unity of synthesis in intuition'. The second qualifies this general connection by speaking of the introduction of a 'transcendental content' into the representations of the understanding. Since categories, or pure concepts of understanding, are concepts expressing, or representing, the mentioned synthetic unity, it is clear that they must be also connected both with the analytic unity of judgment-forms and with the transcendental content.

The general connection between forms of judgment and categories is that they both share a reference to, or both derive from, the same function. Part of the force of this claim is that whatever unities, or functions of unity, are present in judgments, are also present or preserved in our manner of synthesising what we intuit. This means that if we analyse or classify the functions of unity in judgment, then our intuitive syntheses can be identified or expressed in terms of such functions. That the same unities expressed in judgments are preserved in our intuitive syntheses should not be regarded as a psychological discovery or coincidence. It is rather that Kant is explaining how we should understand and identify what he calls an intuitive synthesis. Just as his proposal to classify concepts at B 95 can be taken as an explanation of what is meant by claims about the faculty of understanding, so the claimed connection between analysis and synthesis can be taken to elucidate what is meant by 'synthetic unity in intuition'. Kant claims that in order to identify such synthetic unities, it is possible to appeal to the analytic classification of judgment-forms. It is clear that analysis and synthesis are not intended to be identical, but that the latter can be identified in terms of the former.

This connection may be illustrated by considering how forms of judgment are related to our perception, or to our understanding of what we perceive. If we say, for example, that one unity expressed in judgments involves the notion of an individual's having a property, then we may say also that one way in which we understand our perceptual experiences will be in terms of such a relation. We normally express judgments about what we perceive in terms of the ascription of properties to individuals. It follows therefore that one way in which we synthesise, or understand, what is presented to us intuitively is in terms of individuals and properties. To say that there is some common element in our analytic classifications and our intuitive syntheses is to say that the latter can be identified in terms of, but not with, our forms of judgment.

It is true that our experience generally can be identified in terms of the concepts in our language. Kant's restricted claim that synthetic unities can be identified in terms of judgment-forms

CONCEPTS AND JUDGMENTS

indicates in part his own direction of interest,[1] in part the conviction that judgment-forms have a special importance in the
language. Up to this point Kant's argument could be represented
as justifying the claim that forms of judgment are central in our
language. At this point it is argued that such forms of judgment
may be regarded as guides to certain concepts central in our
experience. For forms of judgment reveal certain general discriminations through which we understand what we intuit or
perceive. To say that our ways of synthesising what we intuit may
be identified in terms of our forms of judgment is to say that these
forms of judgment are guides to the concepts which express or
represent these ways. Such concepts are the categories.

It is important to insist that the forms of judgment are, on this
view, not identical with the categories, but only guides to them.
If this proviso is not made, then Kant may be thought to hold that
categories and forms of judgment are identical, so that it could be
objected to him that a certain judgment-form does not always express the appropriate categorial proposition. Körner, for example
(*Kant*, p. 55), says that '. . . the category embodied in the
given and any other hypothetical judgment is that of causality'.
But there are many hypothetical judgments of which it would be
quite wrong to say that they embodied a notion of causality, as we
ordinarily understand it. To say that for Kant the categories simply
are forms of judgment would perhaps be to guarantee the transition from one table to the other. But it invites the criticism that
Kant failed to notice the variety of uses to which a given judgment-form might be put.

Kant expresses the relation between the two tables, or between
the two kinds of unity, not in terms of identity, but in terms of
their common origin. But to say that they both share a reference
to some basic function is not to say that they are identical, but
only that they are intimately related in the way suggested above.
Kant often indicates that a given category contains something
more than a mere logical form (B 128–129, B 186–187), in the way,
for example, that the notion of a substance is more than that of a
logical subject. It is, however, also true that on occasion Kant
speaks of 'pure categories', divorced from their sensible reference

[1] To say, for example, that transcendental logic teaches how to bring not
representations, but the pure synthesis of representations to concepts (B 104)
is to indicate an interest in complex rather than simple concepts.

to space and time as 'mere logical forms' (B 175). But Kant could not have failed to notice that not all judgments of a given form express claims about categories, for he himself gives examples of judgments which have certain forms but are explicitly supposed not to contain any category. Such judgments are called 'judgments of perception' in the *Prolegomena* (Ak., Vol. 4, pp. 297–299: Sect. 18–19). It is clear from all this that Kant would not have agreed without qualification that categories and judgment-forms are the same. But it is also clear that some of the difficulty arises from an ambiguity in the notion of a category. This ambiguity is resolved in the second sentence of Kant's explanation at B 104–105.

In Kant's second sentence it is indicated that the categories are related to space and time, as well as to forms of judgment. The 'transcendental content' at B 104 is the 'manifold of a priori sensibility' (space and time) supposed to be at the disposal of transcendental logic. This link between categories, judgment-forms, and space and time could be made to yield a general rule for extracting the appropriate category from a given form of judgment. For the addition of certain spatio-temporal concepts to the forms of judgment provides a schematic outline of the various categorial claims. But it is more important to notice the analysis of categories, which such a connection indicates. It suggests that the categories, as we ordinarily understand them, can be analysed into a sensible (spatio-temporal) and an intelligible component. This leads directly to Kant's distinction between 'pure' and 'schematised' categories. The pure categories have no reference to space or time, so that the ordinary concepts of 'cause' or 'substance', for example, are not pure but schematised categories. The term 'category' is in this way ambiguous, since it refers sometimes to a concept with, and sometimes to a concept without, any spatio-temporal content. Since the 'intelligible' component is derived from the logical classification of judgment-forms, the pure categories might, but the schematised categories could not, be said to be identical with forms of judgment.

Kant has, therefore, some ground for saying that pure categories, divorced from any sensible reference, are mere logical forms. But the sense in which this is true is compatible with the claim that a given judgment-form does not always express a claim of the appropriate categorial type. Kant would not, then, be committed to the view that all hypothetical judgments embody the category of causality. For our ordinary concept of a cause is that of a schematised category, which is certainly not identical with a mere form of judgment. The classification of hypothetical (or conditional) judgments nevertheless indicates the general notion of a condition, which is involved in the ordinary concept of a cause. Such a classification of judgments points to an intelligible component of the schematised category, and it is generally in this way that the classification of judgment-forms is a guide to the categories. Schematised categories are not identical with any logical classification or any forms of judgment, but they contain a reference to an intelligible concept, which can be extracted from the classification of judgment-forms. These intelligible, or pure, concepts are themselves identical with certain logical terms employed in the classification of judgment-forms, but even these terms are not identical with any verbal forms of expression. They are rather labels which show what such verbal forms standardly express.

Kant indicates, in the Schematism and elsewhere in the Principles, the analyses that might be given of the schematised categories. He is himself reluctant to talk of defining the categories (B 108–109, A 241–242), and does not devote much space or care to the elaboration of the analyses. Consequently it would be a mistake to put too much stress on them, or to regard them as more important than a schematic elucidation of these concepts, which are properly considered only in the proofs of the principles themselves. The schematised category of extensive magnitude, for example, has a reference to the intelligible concept of homogeneity, or of a class in general, which is standardly expressed in quantitative judgments. Kant's argument is that the addition or measurement of spatio-temporal units, and the notion of number itself, presuppose the general concept of a class. Intensive magnitude is supposed to have a reference to the general notion of a scale, applied to the content of a spatio-temporal instant.[1] The concept

---

[1] The logical classification of qualitative judgments may seem only dubiously connected to the idea of a scale. Ryle, for example, calls the classification of 'infinite' judgments a fraud. Yet there is an analogy between the halfway position of the predicate '. . . is immortal' between the predicates '. . . is mortal' and '. . . is not mortal', and the notions of presence, absence, and half-presence, or 'on', 'off', and 'half-on'. '. . . is immortal' occupies this 'halfway' position because it applies to objects which share the property of being alive with those which are mortal, and the property of not dying with those which, because they are not alive, are not mortal.

'cause' refers to the intelligible idea of a sufficient or necessary condition, with the notion of temporal priority; and the concept 'substance' refers to the idea of an individual, or logical subject, with that of persistence in space. The concepts of modality are intended to contrast the logical notions of possibility, necessity, and actuality with their material counterparts. Kant's central interest in the Principles is to show how these concepts operate, and are related, in our experience; it is not to provide detailed analyses or definitions of the categories. For the purposes of the argument in the Metaphysical Deduction, however, it is enough to show that there is some relation between the concepts we ordinarily understand by the categories, and the classification of judgment-forms.[1]

The argument in the Metaphysical Deduction may be represented in two general ways, either as a series of strong, committal, claims, or else as a set of weaker, and less committal, theses. That the listed concepts are categories, that they are a priori, that the list is complete, and that these conclusions have been conclusively established in the passage, these form the stronger theses. That the listed concepts are only candidates for categorial status, that there is some reason to call them 'a priori', and that some grounds have been given to explain the procedure for selecting the candidates, these form the weaker set of claims. Kant himself sometimes seems to favour the strong claims, and so invites the more severe criticism. But if the argument is measured by such standards, then it will certainly appear as a total failure, and much that is important in the argument may be missed. Moreover, to represent the passage in this way is to leave nothing for the later arguments in the Transcendental Deduction and Analytic of Principles to do. It is, consequently, better to emphasise the weaker theses, which are more plausible, and no less important, than the stronger.

The argument in the Metaphysical Deduction may be repre-

---

[1] One useful conclusion can be drawn from Kant's ambiguous notion of a category. Kant insists that his principles are synthetic, not analytic, and that his proofs are not dogmatic, not from concepts alone (B 23, B 263–264). Yet his arguments appear to be what philosophers nowadays call 'conceptual'. This can be resolved by noticing that the principles connect concepts with intuitions, not concepts with concepts. The pure categories contain no reference to space and time, and so any proposition which relates these cannot be analytic, on Kant's view. This does not, however, prevent us from regarding his arguments as of a conceptual kind. (Cf. Prichard's mistaken argument, *Kant's Theory of Knowledge*, p. 269.)

sented as a step from the claim that certain features are central in our language to the conclusion that certain concepts are central in our experience. Kant gives reasons for supposing that forms of judgment embody certain features of our language which influence our understanding even of the simplest empirical, or sensible, concepts. But it is not a logical step from this claim to the conclusion that the categories are central in our experience, and this conclusion cannot be taken to have been finally established in the Metaphysical Deduction. The step is supported in the passage by the argument that intuitive syntheses can be identified in terms of our judgment-forms, but this is a quite general point about language and experience, which still needs elaboration and support in the Analytic of Principles. In this later passage Kant shows how the chosen concepts operate in our experience, and can reveal the central position of these concepts in our experience only at this stage. The Metaphysical Deduction has, in this respect, justified the choice of a certain starting-point, and of a certain direction of interest, but it should not be confused with the ultimate destination.

In a similar way the Metaphysical Deduction can be made to yield an analysis of the categories, but this does not make the further analyses in the Transcendental Deduction or Analytic of Principles superfluous. Indeed the hints contained in the earlier passage can be understood only by referring to the later elaborations of them. These later passages are, therefore, required for the completion of arguments only begun in the Metaphysical Deduction. The Transcendental Deduction, for example, completes the elucidation of the concept 'category' which is begun in the transition from features of language to features of experience. The Analytic of Principles completes the connections between categories and intuitions, and purports to show that the categories are concepts central in our experience, and therefore with a special status in it.

# 8

# THE TRANSCENDENTAL
# DEDUCTION

---

'To the synthesis of cause and effect there belongs a dignity which cannot be empirically expressed . . .' (B 124).

### (i) INTRODUCTION

ANY short account of the Transcendental Deduction such as this must fail to do justice (even in the stern sense) to Kant's argument. This is not only because the argument branches profusely in so many different directions, but also because Kant provided rather different versions of it in the two editions of the *Critique*, in the *Prolegomena*, and in the *Metaphysical Foundations of the Natural Sciences*. It is, for these reasons, hard to say simply, but truthfully, what is the central issue in the argument, and impossible to cater for all its ramifications. Kant nevertheless provided a short general summary of his aim (B 116–129), saying that he intends to justify our use of certain concepts, or to establish their objective validity. Unfortunately this way of expressing his task is apt to be misunderstood, unless some qualifications are added to it.

Kant himself makes some of these qualifications clear. He insists, as we have seen (Ch. 1), that his task should be understood not as an empirical but as a transcendental enquiry into our concepts or mental powers (B 117–119, A 97). It is natural to read this rejection of Locke's procedure as a repudiation of any central interest in questions of empirical psychology, although many philosophers would claim that the argument in the Deduction is objectionably psychological. This conflict has been considered already (in Ch. 1), and there is no further point in any general attempt to settle it. In one way the conflict is unsettlable; the truth is that Kant deals with both logical and psychological terms. He speaks of such things as recognition and consciousness, as well as of such other things as concepts and linguistic rules; indeed on his view all these notions are intimately related. But the account given of even the psychological terms is not of an empirical so much as of a conceptual kind. It is, as Kant himself often puts it, an account of the status or 'dignity' attaching to certain concepts. This is certainly part of the force of claiming to conduct a transcendental enquiry.

When Kant speaks of establishing the objective validity of certain concepts, or of justifying their use, it is easy nowadays to think that he wishes to establish that certain terms have a correct use in our discourse, or to establish what that correct use is. Yet Kant certainly means to do neither of these things in the Transcendental Deduction. It is quite apparent that the central arguments (A 95–130, B 129–144) show no interest whatever in any particular concepts, but deal with categories in general, or with the general notion of a category. Nothing in these passages can be understood as an analysis of the concepts listed as categories in the Metaphysical Deduction, nor is any attempt made to show that there are certain standard occasions on which such concepts would be correctly used. Yet it is tempting to believe that Kant should be conducting such an enquiry into the correct use of these concepts if his aim is to justify their use. If Kant is thought to be properly engaged on a task of this kind, then the whole of the Transcendental Deduction must seem a pointless if not mistaken enterprise.

Kant does not merely not perform this kind of enquiry in the Deduction, but actually rejects it. What he calls an 'empirical illustration' of the categories' use (B 123, B 126–127) would be an attempt to solve the problem in this way, and is evidently regarded by Kant as of no use to him. Again in the *Prolegomena* (Ak., Vol. 4, pp. 258 ff.) Kant makes it clear that his argument against Hume over the concept of 'cause' and categories in general cannot be settled by any appeal to the 'ordinary use' of these terms. Kant's phrase for such an appeal is 'Die Berufung auf den gemeinen Menschenverstand' (literally 'The appeal to common human understanding'), but the force of such an appeal, like the appeal to ordinary language, is initially to establish that a certain term has a correct use in some field of discourse. Kant does not regard such an appeal as generally mistaken, but only as inapplicable to his enquiry. Hume's critics, for example, are censured for having missed the point when they tried to refute Hume by appealing to the use or usefulness of the disputed concept. The point at issue for Kant is not whether such a concept is 'correct, usable, or even indispensable for natural science' (*Prol.*, Ak., Vol. 4, p. 258), but rather whether it can be said to have a special status or dignity, to which Kant generally gives the label 'a priori'.[1]

It would be wrong, therefore, to think that the Transcendental Deduction must be defective simply because it does not appeal to our ordinary discourse in the attempt to justify the use of certain concepts. It is clear from what Kant says that he is not asking a question to which such an appeal could provide an answer. The main reason for this is that the ascription of a special status to a concept could not be established only by showing that a term has a correct use, or even only by showing what that correct use is. In this way Kant's problem about status presupposes that the disputed terms have a correct empirical use, concern with which would presumably count as a 'question of fact' rather than as a 'question of law' (B 116) where Kant's main interest lies. Nevertheless it is reasonable to object that features of a term's use (in the widest sense) must have some bearing even on the projected ascription of a certain status. It was suggested earlier (Ch. 5, p. 75) that to show terms like 'fate' and 'fortune' to be fraudulent or empty would be to examine ways in which they may be misused. Consequently there is some reason to believe that Kant's goal cannot be reached without some enquiry into the use of the concepts concerned.

This argument is quite correct, though it is not a criticism of the Transcendental Deduction. Kant would have admitted that if the notion of 'use' is construed as widely as possible, then features of the use of concepts are relevant to the ascription of a special status.

---

[1] It is difficult to avoid prejudices about this label, but it is chosen here to stand non-committally for whatever special features Kant believes the categories to have. It is better not to jump to conclusions about it, but to understand it strictly only in connection with the passages in which the ascription of this special status to categories is supported, i.e. the Transcendental Deduction, and the Analytic of Principles.

It was admitted earlier (Ch. 5, pp. 80–81) that Kant's general problem about categories was ultimately to be solved by showing how these concepts operate in connection with our experience. But Kant's appeal to such features of these concepts is made not in the Transcendental Deduction, but in the Analytic of Principles. Some philosophers would be inclined to say that this shows the Deduction to be superfluous (cf. Weldon: *Kant's Critique of Pure Reason*, 2nd ed., p. 160), but this is a mistake. For in order that such features of the use of concepts should be shown to be relevant to the ascription of a special status to them, something needs to be said of what the special status is or amounts to. Until something has been said to elucidate such an ascription there is no guide to the type of features needed to establish that categories are of this special kind. It is in the Transcendental Deduction that Kant shows the relevance of such features by providing a general account of this status, and of the notion of a category.

It has already been hinted that the argument of the Deduction provides a general account of categories rather than of *the* categories. This is perhaps the most important qualification to be made to Kant's expression of his problem. The evidence for it lies less in any explicit claim on Kant's part, than in his manner of tackling the problem. It is quite obvious that in the central arguments of this passage Kant does not rely on any appeal to particular categories. Sometimes, it is true, Kant illustrates his theme by referring to a category (e.g. that of 'cause' at A 111–112), and sometimes he provides an analysis of particular categories briefly (e.g. of 'cause' and 'quantity' at B 162–163), which should be regarded as an anticipation of the arguments in the Analytic of Principles. But these rare descents to particularity are illustrations of what is a quite general theme about categories. At the start of the Deduction (A 95) Kant refers to 'pure a priori concepts, *if such exist* . . .', as though he envisages an argument about the function of categories, whichever they may turn out to be for us. Again in the crucial arguments from B 129–144 Kant makes no effort to specify or mention particular concepts, or to argue from discovered features of the concepts listed as categories in the Metaphysical Deduction. The argument is about categories in general, and the conclusion is expressed quite generally in the last sentence of Sect. 20 (B 143):

Consequently the manifold in a given intuition is necessarily subject to categories.[1]

This point has been obscured both by Kant's failure to insist on it, and also by the inevitable supposition that if *the* categories have been correctly listed in the Metaphysical Deduction, then even a general argument about categories must apply to the chosen concepts. This latter supposition appears even in Kant's over-concise argument in Sect. 20 (B 143-144), but it would be a mistake to imagine that Kant has at this point finally proved that the selected concepts are categories. If this were so, there would then be no point in providing the arguments in the Analytic of Principles. For it is in this last passage that Kant tries to prove that the chosen concepts have features which justify their being called categories. If this account is admitted, then it yields a satisfactory general picture both of the relation between the Transcendental Deduction and the Analytic of Principles, and of the internal structure of the Deduction itself. For this account supports the view mentioned above (Ch. 6, pp. 89-90) that in the Transcendental Deduction there is provided an analysis of 'objective validity' and of 'category' which is essential for the claim in the Analytic of Principles that the concepts chosen in the Metaphysical Deduction are objectively valid, or are categories. In the Metaphysical Deduction certain concepts are chosen as candidates for a priority; in the Transcendental Deduction this notion and other associated notions are elucidated; and in the Analytic of Principles it is finally shown that the candidate categories are successful candidates.

The internal structure of the Transcendental Deduction is, on this account, designed not to prove any concepts to be categories, or to be objectively valid, but to explain the notions of a category or of objective validity. Kant himself says at the end of the Deduction (A) (A 128): 'More was not required in the Transcendental Deduction of the categories . . . than to make comprehensible the objective validity of (its) pure a priori concepts.[2]. . . ' Kant tries to explain quite generally what it is to be objectively

[1] Kemp Smith translates this as '. . . necessarily subject to *the* categories', although no definite article appears in the text.

[2] Kemp Smith cuts Kant's sentence into two, and thereby slightly distorts the force of the claim that this comprehensibility is the limited aim of the argument.

valid, what kind of concept a category is, and why there have to be categories of one sort or another. Kant is, of course, not in doubt that our categories are the concepts listed in the Metaphysi cal Deduction. But the argument of the Transcendental Deduction is wrongly understood to show why we must have these. The Deduction shows that we must have categories, but not that we must have the ones we do have. Kant's analysis of these central terms is contained in the difficult notion of apperception, which points both to the notions of a personal and a conceptual unity. The core of the Deduction can be examined by concentrating on these twin ideas within the framework of argument just outlined.

Associated with Kant's ascription of a special status to categories there is a series of distinctions which derive from this status. The existence of these distinctions in our experience is part of the empirical basis for Kant's general representation problem (cf. Ch. 4, pp. 60 ff. and Ch. 5, pp. 80 ff.). For Kant believed that such ordinarily accepted distinctions required validation by means of the special status of categories. Some of these distinctions are between different kinds of judgment, for example, those between empirical and a priori generalisations (B 3–6), or between judgments of perception and judgments of experience (*Prol.*, Ak., Vol. 4, pp. 297–299). Others involve more vaguely a distinction between the kinds of support we have for making judgments, for example, those between a 'mere association of ideas' and their 'necessary unity' (cf. A 100–102, A 121–122), or between subjective and objective unity (B 141–142), or between persuasion and conviction (B 848–849). These distinctions are related to each other and also to the special status of the categories. Indeed in the *Prolegomena* Kant largely replaces his account of apperception by an analysis of the distinction between judgments of perception and judgments of experience. The argument in the Transcendental Deduction can therefore be further elucidated by considering these conventional distinctions, and the claim that their existence rests in some way on the categories.

In particular this subsidiary classification of judgments and the licences on which their assertion rests can help to show how Kant's defence against Hume is organised. Kant regards Hume's analysis of the concept 'cause' as reducing causal relations to the level of a 'subjective necessity' (B 168) or a 'mere association of ideas'. Hume is thus represented as having obliterated, or cast doubt on the validity of, the mentioned contrasts between what is subjective and what objective, what is a mere association of ideas and what a genuine connection between objects (cf. B 127–128). Kant treats these distinctions as self-evident facts, so that his task can be represented as that of preserving what is commonly believed against the subtle but misleading attacks of a sceptic such as Hume. Kant points out that generalisations based only on an enumeration of observed positive instances are of an inferior kind to those found in mathematics or physics. He argues that the mere association of ideas can license only a weak assertion of the form 'If I support a body, I feel an impression of weight', whereas ordinarily we recognise a right to assert something stronger than this when we say 'The body is heavy' (B 142). Such facts as these are enough to dispute Hume's supposed obliteration of these accepted contrasts (cf. B 128), but they are Kant's initial data for investigation and not his conclusions. They point to a means of refuting Hume by examining the force of and justification for such distinctions, but they do not by themselves constitute a refutation. To think that they did would be to commit Beattie's mistake (*Prol.*, Ak., Vol. 4, p. 258, and above pp. 111–112).

Kant's attempts to obtain a sympathetic hearing for his suit against Hume, by appealing initially to such commonly accepted distinctions, has not been generally successful. One reason for this lies, no doubt, in the rather simple view ascribed to Hume, but a more important one lies in the labels Kant attaches to these distinctions. It may seem reasonable to admit that we can legitimately assert that the body is heavy, and not merely that if I lift it I feel an impression of weight. But it may seem just as reasonable to deny that this distinction can properly be marked by the contrast between a mere association of ideas and a necessary connection. It is natural to feel that the statement 'The body is heavy' expresses neither a mere association of ideas nor a necessary connection between objects. When Kant speaks of the necessary connection involved in causal relations he appears to be inflating the notion of a cause to a pressure from which Hume had rightly deflated it.

Yet this is a mistaken view of Kant, who certainly did not think of himself as denying all that Hume had said, and did not subscribe to the view that the necessity of 'objective' statements meant that these statements were necessarily true (cf. B 141–142).

In particular Kant's effort to reinstate the 'dignity' of the causal relation was not meant to restore the situation as it had been before Hume's criticism. On Kant's view Hume had been right to deny that particular causal laws could be known a priori (A 127–128, B 165), but had gone too far in suggesting that such laws should be regarded as a mere association of ideas (*Prol.*, Ak., Vol. 4, pp. 257 ff.). Kant regarded himself in this way as rectifying a distortion which resulted from Hume's otherwise correct, but incomplete, analysis of the 'cause'. This distortion appears in the claim that Hume obliterated the conventional distinctions outlined above, and reduced objective truths such as causal laws to subjective associations of ideas. The incompleteness appears in the belief that Hume failed to see a feature of the concept 'cause' which gave to causal laws a dignity which raised their status above that of associations or conjunctions of ideas, without making them necessarily true (cf. B 794–795). This conviction, that there are features of such concepts as that of 'cause', which Hume failed to notice, should not be swept aside merely because Kant expresses it in terms of necessity and a priority. For what these terms mean can be understood only by examining the Deduction and Analytic of Principles where they are elucidated and their ascription to categories supported.

## (ii) APPERCEPTION

It has been suggested above that one central argument in the Transcendental Deduction provides an analysis of the notion of apperception. In this section some preliminary points will be made about it, within the general framework of argument, before it is properly discussed in the next chapter. Kant's introduction of the concept differs in the two editions of the *Critique*. In the first edition the term 'apperception' appears at the end of Kant's account of the three-fold synthesis, but in the second edition there is no introductory appeal to this doctrine (B 129–133). Something has been already said of the opening arguments in the first edition (Ch. 1, pp. 12–17), and it is enough here simply to restate and explain the general framework of Kant's procedure. Once apperception is introduced the arguments in which it figures do not differ essentially in the two editions.

Kant's opening argument in the first edition has two crucial steps. First it is supposed that the ability to apprehend (reproduce and recognise) is required for, or involved in, knowledge of empirical truths. Second it is supposed that such an ability is required also for knowledge even of a non-empirical kind. The first of these steps is made in the elaboration of the terms 'apprehension', 'reproduction', and 'recognition', and the second in Kant's persistent inference from empirical to transcendental claims. The term 'apperception' is introduced to stand for a complex condition governing even the transcendental operation of these abilities (A 106–107: 'This original . . . transcendental apperception'. Cf. B 150). The central argument of the Deduction is an elucidation of this condition. In the second edition Kant wastes no time on the moves from an empirical to a transcendental account of the three-fold synthesis. He points instead to one basic condition of all empirical knowledge, personal consciousness, and argues from an empirical to a transcendental account of that (B 130–133). That this argument is also present in the first edition, although it is concealed behind the detail of the three-fold synthesis, can be seen from the concise summary of the argument at A 117, note. For there the introduction of transcendental consciousness or apperception follows the pattern of the second edition. In both versions the same general features remain. There is first an insistence on the view that knowledge involves essentially the ability to judge (synthesise or combine); and second a move from what is true empirically of our knowledge to what is true transcendentally of it.

Something should be said to unravel part of these two points. It is a mistake to think of the three-fold synthesis as a description of the steps by which we originally learn empirical truths. There are not, strictly, three successive syntheses, but one synthesis, that of apprehension,[1] which breaks down or unfolds into three distinguishable but inseparable elements. If we admit 'apprehension' as the name of a general ability to discriminate between, name and describe what is presented to our senses, then the other synthetic abilities are part of what is already involved in such an achievement. Apprehension involves the ability to reproduce (remember)

---

[1] Kant very likely was not wholly consistent in this. But such passages as that at A 102, where he discloses the intimate connection between apprehension and reproduction, and that at B 160–162, where apprehension clearly covers the other abilities, make it certain that in one of the ways in which Kant used these terms they do have this 'telescopic' relation.

and recognise (identify) what we perceive, and is not a first step in our mental lives to be succeeded by reproduction and recognition. It is exercised in such operations as that of counting, which requires us to remember what has gone on so far (how many we have already counted (A 102)), and to continue in accordance with a rule for counting things of this kind rather than that (recognising what we are counting (A 103)).[1] That we cannot know truths of such an empirical kind without perceiving, without remembering, or without recognising discriminations between different kinds of thing, may seem to be a trivial claim, but it is certainly not false.

Kant's second step from an empirical to a transcendental account of synthesis, or consciousness, is more difficult to explain and to accept. Some passages (e.g. A 100, A 102, and B 135) in which Kant effects this transition appear to involve ambiguity and even mistakes. For Kant seems to conclude that there is an a priori or non-empirical synthesis on the basis of his examination of empirical apprehension. This involves a move not only from an empirical to a transcendental account of synthesis, but also from an account of empirical to an account of a priori synthesis, so that the term 'non-empirical' seems to be ambiguous. For it indicates both a non-empirical, that is, transcendental enquiry, and also a non-empirical, that is, a priori synthesis. This ambiguity may seem to point to an elementary mistake in the argument. For the argument could be represented as a move from the claim that a synthesis is necessary for empirical knowledge to the claim that there is a necessary synthesis, and therefore that there is a non-empirical or a priori synthesis. Such an argument would be fallacious. It would be like arguing that since, in order to make a cake, a mixing of ingredients is necessary, there must be, somehow, a necessary, that is, non-empirical or a priori mixing, over and above the conventional procedure.

This fallacious argument certainly misrepresents Kant's argument at this point. He is not arguing to the existence of a priori knowledge or synthesis, but rather presupposing that there is such knowledge, and arguing that it must involve abilities of the kind contained in apprehension. Kant explains in the introduction to

[1] This example can illustrate what may seem to be a defective unclarity in the distinguished abilities, but what is really a reflection of their intimate connection. For certainly remembering how many we have already counted involves remembering how many things of this kind have been counted so far.

the argument that the whole Deduction presupposes rather than proves the existence of a priori knowledge (B 120–121). This is borne out by the suggestion made earlier that Kant's central aim in the Deduction is to clarify rather than establish such a claim. The fallacy disappears as soon as it is made clear that Kant is not arguing towards such a claim, but presupposing its truth. The ambiguity in 'non-empirical' can be resolved by saying that Kant means to conduct a transcendental enquiry into the general conditions of all our knowledge (cf. B 401–402), and also that he calls it transcendental partly because it is designed to explain the possibility of even a priori knowledge, as in mathematics (cf. B 25, B 40, B 80–81).

The central negative lesson of these arguments from empirical to transcendental claims can also be learned from the account given already (Ch. 3) of this basic distinction. In distinguishing between empirical and transcendental syntheses, or between empirical and transcendental consciousness, Kant does not mean to point to two separate syntheses or two types of consciousness. Just as the answer to the transcendental question about the objects of perception did not serve to distinguish properly between two kinds of object, so the arguments from empirical to transcendental in this new context do not constitute a move from empirical objects to transcendental objects. There are not two identifiable syntheses or types of consciousness, but only two ways of talking, empirically or transcendentally, about synthesis or consciousness. Certainly when Kant speaks of a transcendental consciousness he invites the dangerous assumption that this names an identifiable thing, both like and unlike its empirical correlate. Yet Kant also made considerable efforts to avoid such misleading interpretations. In the Paralogisms, for example, he insists rigorously on the limits to be set to the notion of a transcendental consciousness or apperception, and exposes the mistakes which result from the naive view that such a term names an object correlative to that of an empirical consciousness.

The term 'apperception' is given a dual, if not ambiguous, sense in the Deduction. It is elucidated through the notions of consciousness and personal identity, as well as through those of objective judgment and conceptual rules. Kant very rarely tries to distinguish these two aspects of apperception. Even terms which appear to us to fall naturally on one side of this division, such as 'concept', are explained by means of terms which appear to fall equally naturally on the other side, such as 'consciousness'. At A 103, for example, Kant says: 'The concept of a number is nothing but the consciousness of this unity of synthesis.' Again, in the footnote to B 133, where Kant speaks of different ways in which a concept, such as 'red' may be understood, these logical distinctions are expressed in the clumsy and unfamiliar terminology of 'analytic and synthetic unity of consciousness'. To speak of consciousness was evidently for Kant one way of speaking about concepts. Thus when he elaborates the synthesis of recognition in concepts he appeals not only to the functions which concepts have, but also to the notion of self-consciousness. Apperception is the common anchorage in which these two appeals, to personal and to conceptual unity, are moored.

As a result of this duality Kant's use of such terms as 'unity (or identity) of apperception', or 'unity (or identity) of consciousness' is unclear. When Kant speaks of the 'thoroughgoing identity of the apperception of the manifold' or of 'the identity of consciousness in (i.e. throughout) these representations' (B 133), it is not clear whether he is referring to the identity of a person apperceiving different ideas, or to a person's apperceiving identical ideas. Consequently such phrases seem sometimes to refer to a claimed unity or identity in concepts or language, and sometimes to a claimed unity or identity of the person. Often both elements are undeniably present, for example, at B 139: 'The transcendental unity of apperception is that unity through which all the manifold given in an intuition is united in the concept of an object.' Here it is tempting to understand the unity through which the manifold is united in terms of a certain unity of person; and yet it is obvious that the same unity might be understood, in the light of what follows, to be a certain unity of language in accordance with which we name and describe what is presented to our senses.

There is no doubt that the arguments involving apperception turn on both these types of unity or identity. One part of what Kant wishes to say is that identity of self-consciousness is a condition of our having any knowledge whatever; and another part is that it is a condition of our having any knowledge whatever that there should be a certain unity of synthesis or language. The first part of this argument is developed in the references to Hume's account of personal identity (B 134), in the link between this and our ability to conceive ideas (B 131–133, A 117, note, etc.), and in the insistence on the limitations of a non-intuitive intelligence (B 135, B 138–139). The second part is developed in terms of the function of conceptual rules (A 104–110), the features of objective judgment (B 140–143),[1] and in all the places where Kant appeals to classifications of judgments (*Prol.*, Ak., Vol. 4, pp. 297–299).

It would be natural to regard the two aspects of apperception as the result of a confusion on Kant's part about the concept. But, at least initially, it must be said that Kant develops these two aspects in a parallel way, and fails sharply to distinguish them, not because he was confused about his term, but because he wished in the end to insist on the intimate connection between the two aspects. This intimacy is expressed in a number of passages, of which the most clear occur at A 108 and B 135. In the first of these Kant says:

> The original and necessary consciousness of the identity of the self *is thus at the same time* a consciousness of an equally necessary unity of the synthesis of all appearances according to concepts, that is, according to rules which not only make them reproducible necessarily, but also in so doing determine an object for their intuition, that is, the concept of something wherein they are necessarily connected.

In this passage consciousness of personal identity is equated to consciousness of a certain conceptual unity. The same point emerges from the second passage:

> I am conscious of the self as identical in respect of the manifold of representations that are given to me in an intuition. . . . This amounts to saying that I am conscious to myself a priori of a necessary synthesis of representations—to be entitled the original synthetic unity of apperception—under which all representations given to me must stand, but under which they have also be be brought by means of a synthesis.

Similar claims are made again at B 135 ('The principle . . . cannot be thought') and A 129 ('Now to assert . . . has been developed').

[1] Anyone who prefers to see Frege, rather than Hegel or any nineteenth century Idealist, as Kant's spiritual successor may legitimately point to a striking similarity between what Kant says at B 140 and what Frege says at greater length of the distinction between sense, reference, and associated idea. (Cf. *Translations from the Philosophical Writings of Gottlob Frege*, ed. Geach and Black, pp. 59–60.)

These passages make it clear that Kant distinguished between the two kinds of unity involved in apperceptions, but wished nevertheless to insist on a close connection between them. Like the aspects of the three-fold synthesis, the two aspects of apperception are distinct but inseparable. If there is a duality in the notion of apperception it is not simply the result of a confusion.

### (iii) APPERCEPTION, CATEGORIES, AND OBJECTIVE VALIDITY

So far the argument in the Transcendental Deduction has been represented as an enquiry into the status of categories, rather than into their use, as involving a classification of judgments and the licences on which their assertion rests, and as an analysis of 'apperception'. It may not be at all clear how these different parts of the argument bear on the central theme, namely the elucidation of the notion of a category and of the special status to be ascribed to categories. In this section something will be said to indicate how these parts contribute to the central theme, so that certain claims made in the argument can be picked out for discussion in the following chapter.

Both the analysis of apperception and that of judgments in the *Prolegomena* emphasise the importance of concepts or language in our experience. Apperception, for example, is introduced as a complex condition of our knowledge, which can be broken down into the notions of a personal and conceptual unity. It follows from this analysis that these identified unities are also to be regarded as conditions of our knowledge or experience. If the conceptual side of the argument is considered, then the analysis of apperception yields the claim that concepts, or language, are in some way essential to our experience or knowledge. This claim, in turn, suggests the views that what 'language' refers to in this case is some set of basic concepts in our language, and that these concepts will be categories. Such a line of argument elucidates the notion of a category by explaining it as a concept in some way essential to our experience. The argument points to the possibility of identifying a nucleus of concepts basic in our language which would be natural candidates for categorial status. This possibility has been already realised in the argument of the Metaphysical Deduction, though this represents the chosen concepts as candidates for this status, and not yet as successful candidates.

Even in the argument of the Transcendental Deduction Kant is not proving any concepts to be categories (in the strongest sense of 'category'). He is merely elucidating the claim that categories are (to be understood to be) conditions of our knowledge and experience, and arguing therefore that categorial concepts, whichever they are, will be objectively valid or a priori, in so far as they are conditions of experience. The statements 'Categories are objectively valid' or 'Categories are of a special status' are in this way conceptual claims which purport to elucidate the notions of a category and of objective validity. The notion of a category is thus introduced to signify a concept of this special kind. This conclusion does not extend so far as the specification, still less the proof, of any particular concepts as categories. Kant has not, in this argument, shown that Hume was wrong about the concept 'cause'; all he has shown is that Hume would have been wrong about the concept if 'cause' genuinely is a category for us.

This outline of argument ought to seem suspect. Kant's procedure appears to be that of establishing that categories are objectively valid, or have a special status, by defining them so that they can be said to have these very properties. In this way Kant seems to provide an example to anticipate Russell's remark about the advantages of theft over honest toil. Nothing seems to be easier than to provide a series of definitions of such terms as 'apperception', 'category', or 'objectively valid' which produce the required conclusion. This is not, of course, anything like the whole story. Even if the notion of a category is introduced and understood in this way, it still has to be shown that there are concepts of this kind. And as a prior condition of showing this more has to be said to explain the sense of the terms 'condition of experience' and 'objective validity' than is contained in the definitions. There is in this way a structure of substantial argument lying behind and supporting the façade of definitions. Kant has to show that we should accept these definitions, and to do this is more difficult than merely to produce them.

At least the definitions point clearly enough to the arguments that need to be further examined. Something needs to be said of the argument that concepts or language are in some way essential to our experience. If Kant were to establish this, then the definition of a category as a concept of this kind could be accepted. Something needs also to be said of the other argument that a personal unity is in some way essential to our experience. For this claim completes the analysis of apperception, and is, as we have seen, intimately linked with the notion of a conceptual unity.[1] Finally something needs to be said of the analysis of judgments, and of the way in which it points to and supports the adoption of the crucial definitions. In the next chapter these three items will be separately examined.

---

[1] It will have been noticed that this side of the analysis has not figured prominently in the general account of categories given so far. There are good reasons, and one good excuse, for this. The reasons are that Kant's treatment of personality is given only incompletely in the Transcendental Deduction. It needs for completion an examination of the Analytic of Principles and of the Paralogisms. It is, therefore, for the moment better to give it less attention than is to be given to the notion of a conceptual unity, so that it can be properly treated in a later chapter (Ch. 11). The excuse is that Kant said (in *The Metaphysical Foundations of the Natural Sciences*), after he had written the second edition Deduction, that the argument could be developed more economically solely from the notion of an objective judgment, as though the conceptual side of the argument were of more importance.

# 9

# THE TRANSCENDENTAL
# DEDUCTION *(continued)*

'For appearances can certainly be given in intuition independently of functions of the understanding' (B 122).

'Consequently the manifold in a given intuition is necessarily subject to categories' (B 143).

THE path to be followed here has been already marked out in the previous chapter. What has in general to be done is to examine those arguments which elucidate the notion of apperception, and so make the notion of a category intelligible. Kant employs a tentative distinction between an empirical and a transcendental treatment of his problem (in A), and it is useful to follow this procedure. In this way Kant's highly general problem about the conditions for a possible experience can be introduced in the simpler terms of what is admittedly true of our experience. The argument involves an account of the linguistic unity indicated in the idea of apperception; of the personal unity connected with the same idea; and of Kant's classification of judgments.

## (i) LANGUAGE AND EXPERIENCE

Kant's opening argument in the second edition account of apperception indicates at once its dual reference both to persons and concepts. The point is expressed with a somewhat baffling economy at B 131: 'It must be possible for the "I think" to accompany all my representations; for otherwise something would be represented in me, which could not be thought at all, and that is equivalent to saying that the representation would be impossible, or at least nothing to me.'[1] Such a claim reflects the simple facts that we express our claims to knowledge in judgments, and that for this it is required both that there should be persons to make such claims, and concepts in which to express them. But although these facts are reflected in Kant's argument, his point is more than merely that such facts obtain in our experience. What he says is that representations or appearances would be impossible, or nothing for us, if we could not conceive them. This is to claim that conceivability, or describability, or the ability to judge whatever is presented to the senses, is a necessary feature of our experience, and not only that persons or concepts are necessary features of judgment. The main point is that there is some kind of necessity in the feature of our experience that what is presented to the senses is, or should be, describable; and this would be only inadequately expressed by saying that as a matter of fact we do describe what we perceive.

It has been pointed out already (Ch. 4, pp. 57 ff.) that Kant regards as logically possible a situation in which our senses are presented with appearances, even though we lack the resources of understanding, and so are unable to describe or say what we thus perceive. Yet he now wishes to claim that appearances, or representations, would be impossible, or nothing for us, if we could not describe or conceive them. The solution suggested to this paradox was to say that while it is not logically impossible to imagine such a situation, in which we cannot describe what we perceive, there is a peculiarity in it, which sets a limit to our understanding of it. Kant's aim must be to say that the describability of our experiences is a sufficiently important part of our experience to make it misleading to suppose that it is only a fact about our experience. Its necessity is not that in which it is logically impossible to conceive its absence, but only that in which the effort to conceive such a situation sets a limit to our understanding of the notion of experience itself. If it were true that our use of language to conceive experiences sets a limit to our understanding of such a situation, then there would be a ground for Kant's belief that this feature is necessary in, or for,

---

[1] Similar claims are made elsewhere in the Deduction, e.g. A 111: 'The appearances might . . . as good as nothing', and A 117, note: 'All representations have a necessary relation . . . admission of their non-existence.'

that experience. Not every feature of our experience has a similar power. There is no serious difficulty in imagining, for example, that all our visual experiences are monochromatic, or even that there are no visual experiences. Not only is it possible to name situations of this kind, but it is also possible to give ourselves a very clear picture of what it would be like to be in them.

There is no straightforward logical impossibility in a situation where some creature is supposed to perceive, but to be unable to describe what it perceives. There are many familiar situations of this kind, in which the fact that the creature itself has no means of describing its own experiences does not prevent our describing and understanding them. Absence of a language, or of linguistic behaviour, from a given situation does not, in particular, prevent us from ascribing perceptual experiences to the creatures in it. We often give descriptions for their experiences, which presume a deep penetration into the creature's life, when, for example, we ascribe feelings or wishes, moods or intelligence to a dumb animal. Sometimes, no doubt, these descriptions go too far, and sometimes they are not to be taken seriously, but there is no practical limit to the extent or admitted success of our efforts to understand situations of this kind. If linguistic behaviour is absent, then other forms of behaviour, or other analogies with human organisation, have to be relied upon.[1]

It will be seen, nevertheless, that although there is no empirical, or practical, limit to the analogies we might draw between such situations and our own, there is another kind of limit implicit in such efforts. It is possible for us to understand such situations, so far as we can, only because we can interpret them in terms of our own situation. If we were unable to interpret them in these terms we would fail to understand them. And to interpret such situations in this way is to describe or conceive them in terms whose primary application is to our own experience. Thus one limit placed on our attempt to understand any situations different from our own arises because our understanding depends upon the ways in which we

[1] Some philosophers seem to deny that such efforts to understand these situations ever made sense. Hampshire (*Thought and Action*, pp. 141–142), for example, says: 'No sense could be given to a question about the beliefs of beings who possess no language in which to express them. . . .' The truth is that, however puzzling it may be, we do talk in these ways. The puzzles arising from these procedures, moreover, are more likely to be resolved by considering how they are possible, than by denying that they are.

understand or conceive our own situation. This remains true whether the contrast is that between human beings and dumb animals; between human beings who do, and those who do not, speak a language; between human beings who speak different natural languages; or between those who speak the same natural language. It is true even of the same man at different times in his life. It would be impossible to understand any other experience if we could not understand our own; and we could not understand our own if we could not conceive or describe our experiences.

Since we can in general envisage situations from which language is absent, we can envisage, and even express, the possibility that we might be creatures in such a situation. But the limitations which such a situation imposes upon our understanding effectively prevent us from having any idea of what such a situation would be like. We would be, in such a predicament, unlike that in which our vision became monochromatic, shut off from one condition requisite for our understanding. Just as we can express the possibility that there are no languages only because we have a language in which to express such a claim, so we can envisage, and describe, situations of this kind only because we are not in them. Just as it would be absurd to *say* 'There are no languages', so it would be absurd to *say* 'I am in a position, where description is impossible'. It is, of course, true that we speak of indescribable experiences, but in the licentious way in which we also speak of puzzling events as 'inexplicable', or of doubtful chances as 'impossible'. The interest in such situations is not at present the empirical one of determining current limits to the analogies that we might draw in trying to understand them. Their interest lies in the fact that through them we can indicate the way in which our language and concepts are essential to our experience. It would not be too much to say that it is in terms of our language that we may define our experience itself, and identify and describe our experiences. Without such an ability to express, describe, or conceive what we experience, our experiences would be nothing for us.

Kant's claim that ideas would be nothing for us, if we could not conceive them, points at once to the general notion of a category. If our language, unlike our polychromatic vision, is a feature essential to our experience, then it is natural to suppose that there are concepts in the language which share this property. The language we have can itself be outlined, or identified, by means of the central concepts in it, and if such concepts could be selected, then they would have the property of setting a limit to our understanding. If our language in general sets a limit to our understanding of the notion of experience, then the kind of language it is will also set a limit to the kind of experience it is possible for us to understand. The concepts which are, in this way, basic or central in our language, and so share this limiting property with it, will then be categories. This is certainly to give a very general and uninformative account of categories, since nothing is said in the Transcendental Deduction to distinguish such concepts from others which are not basic to our language. Kant has already selected his categories in the Metaphysical Deduction, and given some account of their principle of selection, but such a specification is not at issue in the Transcendental Deduction. It is nevertheless clear that the sense in which Kant uses the term 'basic' of his chosen concepts is radically different from that sense in which empiricists or atomists would speak of basic concepts in language.

These arguments fall short of Kant's aim in the Deduction in two main ways. They neither explain the function of concepts in our experience, nor indicate the special role of categories among concepts. This argument designed to show the importance of language in our experience only prepares the way for Kant's account of categories, and does not complete it. Kant intends still to argue that there is some connection between our language, its concepts, and the idea of an objective experience. Concepts both exhibit and are responsible for what may be called objective features of our experience. The notion of a category is that of a concept responsible in some way for the objectivity of our experience.

Kant illustrates the notion of objectivity in several different ways. In the passage at A 104 he speaks of an 'object of representations', or of an 'object distinct from and corresponding to my knowledge'. Elsewhere (*Prol.*, Sect. 18, Ak., Vol. 4, pp. 297–298; B 140–142, B 848) he speaks of the contrast between judgments that we intend everybody to accept, and those which reflect merely my own impressions, or subjective associations. In still other places (A 110–111, B 132–133, *Prol.*, Sect. 20) he contrasts a general 'experience' or 'consciousness' with particular experiences, or a particular conciousness. It is not difficult to exemplify these contrasts in our experience, or to see how they are connected. We ordinarily distinguish between our experiences of objects, and the objects of which they are experiences. We easily differentiate between judgments which are, and those which are not, intended to hold true for anyone. We recognise the difference between the experiences which belong to some particular person, and an experience in general which he shares with others. If we take some particular type of experience, say, of a material object, then it is easy to detect connections between these contrasts. To distinguish my experience of a material object from the material object itself is to indicate also the difference between statements about the experience, and statements about the object. I do not generally expect or intend that the former statements should be true for anyone else, but I generally intend that the latter statements should be, whether they are or not. In this latter distinction, too, is contained the idea of a general type of experience, of material objects, which I share with others, to be contrasted with the particular experiences I or others might have of any such object.

Such accounts of Kant's general contrast between what is subjective and what is objective are not incorrect—Kant gives them himself—but they are subject to a number of qualifications. They are useful as a means of introducing the idea of objectivity in terms of admitted features of our experience, but they are only empirical illustrations of what is a transcendental argument. It should be remembered, therefore, that these empirical contrasts do no more than introduce the account of objectivity; that they can be exemplified in our experience shows that they are only empirical counterparts of a connected, but different, transcendental distinction. The same proviso arises, too, from Kant's belief that although these situations exhibit the objective features to be examined, their function is to indicate the special concepts, categories, which are responsible for these features. Kant's interest is not in the empirical concepts which exhibit objective features, but in the connection between such features and categories. Finally it should be understood that when Kant speaks of objects in this context, he does not mean physical objects. To speak of physical, or material, objects is indeed one way of speaking objectively, but it is not the only way. Such a mode of discourse does not exhaust our objective discriminations between appearances, and it is this vocabulary in general with which Kant is concerned. It is true, in the end, that Kant ascribes a pre-eminence to the objects of outer sense, among all those that we discriminate in experience, and that physical objects are included among those presented to us by outer sense; but this pre-eminence is not involved in the arguments of the Transcendental Deduction.

Kant's accounts of the objective features of our experience appeal immediately to the functions which concepts have (cf. A 104–105, A 110–111, *Prol.*, Sect. 18). It has been already mentioned (Ch. 5, pp. 77–78) that Kant's analysis of the term 'object of representations' issues in a recognition of the unifying function of concepts. The idea of an object can, on this view, be understood and explained only in terms of the unity of conceptual rules, which determine or describe the manifold in one definite way or another. The idea of an object points to that of agreement in the application of concepts (A 104, *Prol.*, Sect. 18), and the notion of a concept itself contains that of the possibility of agreement in so describing or determining what we perceive.

The idea of an object distinct from my experiences is, in this way, the idea of something that can be conceived as independent of those experiences, but not independently of them. Kant did not believe that objects totally independent of any experience could be identified by us, or that we could identify such objects independently of experiences, even though he conceded that we might emptily conceive such objects as non-phenomena. Hence when Kant comes to speak of the relation of objects to appearances (A 111), he speaks of objects in, or for, appearances ('*zu* den Erscheinungen'), and not, for example, of independent things causally related to appearances. Objects and appearances are thus not different things, but reflect the intimate relation discussed above between phenomena and appearances (Ch. 4). The only way in which to understand the notion of an object in, or for, appearances is through the notion of a concept's application in some particular experience. Such a notion reflects the relation which we conventionally express by speaking about the experience 'of' something, where what was experienced could be experienced by other people, or by the same person on different occasions, that is, through different experiences. Objects are, in this way, related to particular experiences, since without such experiences we could not apply any concept (cf. B 147–149), but their important feature is that they can be identified in different particular experiences. One sense in which we speak of objects as independent of experiences is that in which it can be said that they are not tied to any particular experience, but must be related to some particular experiences. An objective description is, therefore, one which while dependent for its sense on particular experiences, does not name any such experience uniquely.

In this way the idea of something distinct from my experience is related to that of agreement in the application of concepts, and to the generalising function which concepts essentially have. Whatever is described in terms which can be applied to other particular experiences can be regarded as an object. To say this is only to say that what is called an objective feature of experience can be exhibited only through the generalising function of concepts, which makes it possible to rank different particular experiences under a common title. More accurately, such objective features can be exhibited only through the generalising function of concepts, which *is* that of ranking different particular experiences under a common title. If such agreement in the application of descriptions were impossible, then our language would consist of names referring uniquely to particular experiences. Such terms would resemble those logically proper names ideally associated with particular sense-data, in Russell's logical atomism. (In *Logic and Knowledge* (ed. Marsh), p. 198: '. . . all the names that it would use would be private to that speaker . . .'.) Kant indicates several times (e.g. A 99, A 103, B 134–135) that such names would have no unifying function, and would not therefore contain the possibility of objective discourse. An experience under such conditions, like any other in which the generalising function of concepts was absent, would be nothing for us, less even than a dream (A 112).

Kant's analysis of 'object' follows directly from his account of the importance of language in our experience, for it leans heavily on what we understand to be the function of concepts. But Kant is not content merely to explain objects in terms of the generalising function of concepts. Although even empirical concepts exhibit these objective features, Kant regards the appeal to such concepts as inadequate. The main purpose of such an analysis is to indicate the special concepts called categories, which can be said to be responsible, in some way, for these objective features. It should not be thought that this responsibility is primarily causal, in the way in which a clutch's responsibility for successful transmission is. It would be a mistake to think of categories as entities (perhaps on a confused physiological model) which produce an objective language in such a mechanical way. It would be even more of a mistake to think that categories might serve to explain the possibility of communication between people. There is a temptation to think of categories, in this way, as a basic 'form of experience' implanted in our brains, which might explain the possibility of our understanding each other. Kant's argument, viewed as a hypothesis of this sort, explains nothing. To suppose that we all have, at least potentially, the same categorial form inside us is rather a part of what is meant by supposing that we can communicate, and does not explain it. Kant's claims are on a conceptual and not empirical level; they are analyses of what is meant by terms like 'object' or 'concept', and not hypotheses about the mechanism of our brains.

Consequently when Kant implies that categories are concepts responsible for objective features of our experience, this should be taken to mean only that certain concepts with a special status can be selected to stand as the prime exhibitors of objectivity. Kant argues (in the Analytic of Principles) that the candidate categories have such a special status, and this argument supports the claim that they are responsible for objective features of our experience, in a way in which empirical concepts are not. For the present it is better to regard a category simply as that of a fundamental concept in our experience, and therefore as playing a fundamental part in our discriminations of objects in that experience. It was suggested above that not every concept can be regarded as setting a limit to our understanding of experience itself. Such concepts as those of colours, which reflect the fact that our vision is polychromatic, might have no application without much disturbing our experience. Kant's ascription of responsibility for the objective features of our experience to the concepts called categories is a belief in the existence of concepts which do set limits to what we understand by experience itself.

Kant's account of agreement in the application of descriptions has no special concern with the fact that we are a community of people speaking the same language. To speak of the possibility of agreement in the application of descriptions is to make no particular reference to the ways in which empirically this possibility is realised. It is only to give an account of what is meant by a concept; and the indicated generalising function of concepts might be just as evident in a world populated by one person as it is in the present situation. It is, nevertheless, natural to illustrate such an account by referring to communication between different speakers, but such illustrations are not by any means necessary. Kant himself uses such illustrations, on occasion (cf. B 140–141), but in general he is concerned with the abilities of individuals rather than with their public manifestations. Kant is, in this way, firmly in the Cartesian tradition, in which knowledge is explained as belonging essentially to an individual. He is nevertheless equally firmly opposed to the same tradition, in which all knowledge is explained as inferred from knowledge of that individual, that is, of his mental states. There is, therefore, no special value in illustrating Kant's thesis in terms of a community of speakers. The idea of such a community is only that of an ability common to its members to understand others' experience in terms of their own.

In a similar way Kant's contrast between objective and subjective has little directly to do with our empirical distinction between what is private, personal, or belonging to an individual, and what is public, impersonal, and shared between different people. This is the reason for saying earlier (Ch. 5, p. 81, and above pp. 130–131) that such distinctions can give only an illusory clarity to Kant's aim. Since it is possible for me to characterise my experiences without overt reference to external objects the field of discourse in which I speak solely of such experiences is just as objective as that in which I speak of external objects. The ordinary distinction between what is private and what is public corresponds only to Kant's empirical contrast (A 378–379) between inner and outer sense, and both inner and outer experience, in fact, satisfy the test for being objective. The transcendental distinction between what is subjective and what is objective may correspond to the empirical contrast between my inner experiences and the outer objects of which they are on occasion the experiences, but these distinctions are not equivalent. It is true that Kant uses this empirical contrast to illustrate his transcendental argument, as we have seen (p. 130 above); but there is a good reason for this, which will be discussed later. There is, too, a connection between the categories and these empirical contrasts between inner and outer objects. For in the end Kant wishes to say that the categories are responsible, in some way, for this empirical contrast.

## (ii) CATEGORIES AND PERSONALITY

Kant's account of the connection between categories and personality, like that of categories themselves, is given in an entirely general and abstract way in the Transcendental Deduction. It requires for its completion a reference to the later arguments of the Paralogisms and Refutation of Idealism (see Ch. 11), but something must be said of it as it appears in the Transcendental Deduction. The argument rests on Kant's claim that what he calls 'empirical apperception' or 'empirical consciousness' is not enough to account for our notion of personality or personal identity. Such an empirical consciousness is said to be 'diverse', and 'unrelated to the notion of subject identity' (B 133). This can be taken to mean that empirical awareness is of diverse objects, and not of any one object which could count as a, or my, personality. It is easy to think that no awareness of any outer object (even of my own body) will qualify as a candidate for awareness of a personality; and also that no candidate from among the things in inner experience, of which I may on occasion be empirically conscious, will be a successful candidate. To be aware of any physical object, or of any particular inner condition, is to presuppose a personality which is conscious of these things. Empirical awareness of such types of object cannot, therefore, be of that identical personality presupposed in the ascription of inner states to me. Views of this kind have often been stated by philosophers. Hume, for example, expressed the same problem in a concise way (*Treatise*, Bk. 1, Sect. VI): 'It must be some one impression that gives rise to every real idea. But self, or person, is not any one impression, but that to which our several impressions and ideas are supposed to have a reference.' These difficulties have led philosophers to claim that the idea of a personality, in this required sense, is a myth or inexplicable,[1] or to elaborate the use of such a term as 'I'. Kant is led by such an argument to introduce the notion of transcendental

[1] Reid said: Our conviction of personal identity 'needs no aid of philosophy to strengthen it; and no philosophy can weaken it without first producing some degree of insanity.'

apperception, or transcendental identity of consciousness, as that notion of personality which is presupposed in our empirical awareness. Once this notion has been introduced Kant's interest is to analyse its force, or, what comes to the same thing, to examine its connection with the notion of a category.

Kant frequently claims that personality, in the required sense, indicates the necessity of a certain synthesis of ideas. At B 134, for example, he says: 'The thought that the representations given in intuition one and all belong to me is therefore equivalent to the thought that I unite them in one self-consciousness, or can at least so unite them; and although this thought is not itself the consciousness of the synthesis of representations, it presupposes the possibility of that synthesis.' Elsewhere (B 135: 'I am conscious of . . . a synthesis', or B 138: 'Although . . . "I think"') Kant explains that although efforts to express the requirement of personal identity issue in analytic truths, yet they point to the claim that such a requirement itself rests on the possibility of a synthesis of some kind. To say that I remain the same throughout all the ideas of which I am conscious is to utter a tautology, and yet to speak of myself at all is to presuppose the possibility of a synthesis of all my ideas. Since this synthesis is, on Kant's view, that involved in the categories, the argument amounts to saying that the required notion of personality can be accounted for in terms of this categorial synthesis.

Kant cannot mean that we become aware of our persons in the required sense, whenever we produce a judgment, or a synthesis of ideas. To be aware of such a procedure would be just as much a part of empirical consciousness as to be aware of a pain or a sunset. Nor will it do to think that Kant is indicating a very important judgment, involving the categories, which might in some way make us non-empirically aware of our transcendental ego. Such a claim involves insuperable difficulties in identifying such a judgment, and the personality it is supposed to reveal. Kant's point can, however, be understood in terms of the analysis given so far of a category. If categories are taken to be a set of conceptual rules which determine certain fundamental ways in which we conceive our experience, then Kant is claiming that such a set of rules must govern also our recognition of personality. His argument is, then, that just as such categorial rules are required for objective discriminations in general, so this same condition holds for our discrimination of persons. Without the possibility of some such categorial synthesis, or without the ability to objectify experience by means of concepts, it would be impossible for us to have an idea of personality, in the required sense. Part of what Kant means is that an analysis of personality is an analysis of the conceptual conditions in which it is possible to discriminate persons in our experience.

Since this account of the connection between categories and personality follows directly from the account given already of categories, it may seem a disappointing conclusion to reach. Yet it suggests a more informative account of this connection. What Kant calls a basic synthesis or combination (B 132–133) is that by which experiences or ideas are ascribed to me. It is, therefore, natural to suppose that categories enable us to achieve this basic discrimination in a more particular way than merely by being conditions of any objective description of experience. For the notion of a person, in the required sense, is that of something to which inner experiences are empirically ascribed. But this concept can be understood and explained only in terms of a contrast between what is an inner experience, ascribable to me, and what is not. Our discrimination of persons, in this way, rests upon our ability to distinguish between experiences ascribed to me, and experienced objects, which are not ascribed to me.[1] If the categories are responsible for all discriminations in our experience, then they will also be responsible for this basic discrimination between myself and other things. To say that categories are responsible for this discrimination is to say that they are responsible for the empirical contrast between inner and outer objects. It is in somewhat this way that the thought of representations belonging to me presupposes the possibility of a synthesis, namely that which governs our ordinary contrast between inner and outer, private and public, objects.

This particular view follows quite naturally from the argument of the Transcendental Deduction, although, for the reasons given above, this account of the relation between categories and personality is not specifically stated in the Deduction. Ascription

---

[1] This should not be taken to mean that no experienced objects are ascribed to me. Some experienced objects, in this Kantian sense, are experiences, and so are ascribed to me; and at least one outer object, namely my body, is also said to be mine.

of such a view to Kant is, however, supported by a passage at B 400–401, as well as in the argument of the Refutation of Idealism. At B 400–401 Kant says of transcendental apperception: 'Meanwhile, however free it be of empirical admixture . . . it yet enables us to distinguish through the nature of our faculty of representation two kinds of objects. "I" as thinking being, am an object of inner sense, and am called "soul". That which is an object of the outer senses is called "body".' It is, therefore, quite plausible to understand Kant to mean that categories are related to the required notion of personality, because they govern our discrimination between what is inner and what is outer, and so make possible the empirical ascription of experiences to me. This points to a more detailed way in which it might be shown that categories are responsible for objective features of our experience, by arguing that they are responsible for this basic distinction between that to which experiences are ascribed, and that which, outwardly, they are experiences of.

Much of the force of this account of personality is lost because it refers to arguments that appear only later in the Analytic of Principles and Paralogisms. It is in the Paralogisms, for example, that Kant reveals limits in the concept of transcendental apperception, or transcendental consciousness, which it would otherwise be natural to suppose that he himself had overstepped. Even in the Deduction, however, Kant hints that this notion is not so straightforward as it may appear to be. At A 117, note, for example, he says of the idea 'I' (transcendental consciousness): 'Whether this representation is clear (empirical consciousness) or obscure, or even whether it actually occurs, does not here concern us. But the possibility of the logical form of all knowledge is necessarily conditioned by relation to this apperception as a faculty.' The suggestion implicit in this passage is that the notion of consciousness is straightforward only in an empirical context, in which the 'required' sense of 'personality' is presupposed and not explained. The philosophic notion of a person is, for this reason, obscure, and can be said to set a problem. Kant makes it clear later (in the Paralogisms, cf. Ch. 11) that this problem may be misconceived, and so give rise to difficulties that are not genuine. For the notion of a transcendental consciousness may be mistaken for a concept which names some identifiable object, and may therefore stimulate attempts to identify such an object, which must end in failure. On Kant's view such a concept does not have the straightforward empirical function of naming any identifiable object; it is, rather, a way of talking about the conditions in which we are able to discriminate and name objects in our ordinary experience. To talk of a transcendental personality is, in this way, not to talk of any object apart from that which we regard empirically as a person, it is only a different way of talking about such an object, and of a problem about the ways in which we can discriminate such an object in our experience.

(iii) TRANSCENDENTAL DISTINCTIONS AND<br>EMPIRICAL ILLUSTRATIONS

Kant attempts to illustrate his argument in the Transcendental Deduction by appealing to certain classifications of judgments. In The *Prolegomena* he distinguishes between judgments of perception and judgments of experience; in the Deduction he contrasts objective judgments with expressions of subjective association; and later in the *Critique* (B 848) he draws an associated distinction between persuasion and conviction. These distinctions are plainly intended to reflect the ordinary contrast between what is subjective, or private, and what is objective, and public. Yet the distinctions themselves, and the ways in which Kant explains them, have often been thought objectionable, and in conflict with the central argument of the Deduction.[1] There certainly are differences between saying that the room is warm and that air is elastic; or between saying that a body is heavy, and that if I lift it, I will have an impression of weight; or between saying that when the sun shines on the stone, it gets warm, and that the sun warms the stone. Yet it may be doubted whether these differences all amount to the same thing, or whether they really mark the distinctions Kant supposes them to mark.

There are two apparent conflicts between Kant's arguments in this part of the *Prolegomena* (Sect. 18–19), and those in the *Critique* itself. The first can be put by saying that while in the *Prolegomena* the relation between categories and judgments appears to be simple, in the *Critique* it appears to be complex. In the *Prolegomena*

---

[1] Kemp Smith (*Commentary*, pp. 288–289) says, for example, of the contrast between judgments of perception and judgments of experience, that it is 'entirely worthless' and that 'it cuts at the very root of Kant's critical teaching'.

the difference in status between judgments of perception and judgments of experience is ascribed to the presence in the latter, and absence from the former, of a reference to a category. But the argument in the Transcendental Deduction claims that in the absence of categories no experience would be possible. If judgments of perception have no reference to a category, then it should not, strictly, be possible to express them at all. Again, it is not difficult to see that this linguistic contrast, between subjective and objective judgments, does not match what has been so far said of the notion of an object. It has been suggested that every concept exhibits objective features, but if this is so, then even judgments of perception could be said to be objective.[1]

The second conflict arises from the suggestion in the *Prolegomena* that objective judgments are necessarily true, although in the *Critique* this view is rejected (cf. B 141). Again, the examples in the *Prolegomena* of objective judgments all have a general form, although this is not so in the *Critique*. It is tempting, therefore, to think that Kant has confused the generality, or scope, of a claim with its necessity, or status, and so has committed himself to the absurd view that any judgment expressed in general terms is true, and even necessarily so (cf. R. Robinson: *Mind*, July 1958, pp. 291–295). Even if Kant is not thought to be committed in this way, it may seem plausible to interpret him as saying that the only authority for making general claims arises when those claims are necessarily true. In this way Kant's disagreement with Hume could be represented by saying that Hume wrongly supposed that particular causal laws were never necessarily true. This account of the disagreement, however, runs quite counter to what Kant himself says of it in the *Critique*, and is not even properly supported in the *Prolegomena*.

The first conflict is only apparent and not genuine. For the simple relation between categories and judgments indicated in the *Prolegomena* is compatible, and indeed connected, with the complex relation between them indicated in the *Critique*. The ground for this compatibility, and connection, is that the linguistic contrasts are empirical illustrations of a transcendental argument. It was suggested earlier (pp. 130–131) that the distinction between

[1] This difficulty is reflected also in Kant's argument at B, Sect. 19 (B 141–142) where all judgments are, strictly, objective, even though it is apparently possible to formulate a subjective judgment.

what is inner and what is outer is only empirical, for Kant, and since the linguistic contrasts reflect this same distinction, they share the same status. To admit that there are in our experience both judgments of perception and judgments of experience, as Kant supposes, is already to concede that the contrast between them is of an empirical and not transcendental kind (cf. Ch. 3, pp. 40–42). Just as the empirical illustrations of a transcendental argument in perception were shown to be inadequate, so these empirical linguistic illustrations of a transcendental account of categories will also be inadequate. For these reasons the empirical relation between categories and judgments of experience corresponds, but is not equivalent, to the transcendental relation between categories and all judgments.

The connection between the empirical and the corresponding transcendental distinction can be illustrated from Kant's examples. The empirical contrast is partly that between judgments which directly express categorial claims, and those which do not. 'The sun warms the stone' is a claim ascribing a causal property to the sun, and 'Air is elastic' is objective when based on a knowledge of the causal conditions in which air expands.[1] By contrast, to say that the room is warm, or wormwood nasty, is not to express a categorial claim, but to record a relation between something and my sense experience. It would be true to say, transcendentally, that this relation could not be stated without presupposing the discriminations which the categories effect, but empirically such judgments of perception express neither categorial nor objective claims. Again, the relation between a person and a room expressed in the judgment 'The room is warm' may be suitable for a causal enquiry, but I can express it on the basis of my feelings, without knowing how it should be explained. Kant argues that one way of showing the difference between these types of judgment is that while a claim like 'The room is warm' is not intended as a candidate for general acceptance, claims about causal connections are so intended, whether they are generally accepted or not.

The point of appealing to these contrasts is to show that ordinarily we make claims of a status superior to those which

---

[1] Kant does not classify these judgments as they may be made in any context. 'Air is elastic' is, for example, a judgment of perception in some contexts, but a judgment of experience in others. Part of what distinguishes these contexts is the reference in the latter to certain causal connections.

reflect a subjective association of ideas. Such empirical linguistic contrasts set Kant the problem of accounting for this superiority, and this problem could perhaps be solved by showing that the superior judgments are more closely related than the others to the categories. If it could be shown that the categories have a special status in our experience, then it would be natural to conclude that the empirical use of these concepts shares in that special status. The transcendental argument that the categories make experience possible would, therefore, help to explain the difference in status we ordinarily recognise between categorial and non-categorial claims. It is partly in this way that the simple empirical relation between categories and judgments of experience presupposes the complex transcendental relation between categories and all judgments.

Once Kant has presented these contrasts in the *Prolegomena*, he attempts to explain and analyse them; and it is this analysis which may appear to confuse generality and necessity. Kant does not express his views about 'necessary universal validity' in this passage with perfect clarity, but there is evidence that he does not mean to say that judgments of experience, or objective judgments are necessarily true. Even in the *Prolegomena* (Sect. 22, note) Kant notices the difficulty of saying that empirical judgments of experience are also necessary, though there is no difficulty in saying that we regard them as objective. This shows that for Kant the necessity of such judgments is compatible with their being empirically true, or false. Again, in the *Critique* (B 141) Kant explains that the necessity of objective judgments does not attach to the relation between subject and predicate, so that it could not be properly expressed by saying that something necessarily has a property, or that the judgment is necessarily true. It is important, too, that in the *Prolegomena* Kant speaks rather of the intention that a claim should be generally accepted than of its actual acceptance (Sect. 18: 'All our judgments . . . and intend the judgment to be valid . . .'. Sect. 19: '. . . and hence are not intended . . .'). The distinction between subjective and objective judgments lies partly in our intentions in asserting them, regardless of whether they are true or false. And this suggests that Kant's notion of necessity or objectivity is not simply that of necessary truth.

The most striking rejections of this view, however, come from Kant's account of his disagreement with Hume. It has been suggested already that Kant did not dispute Hume's view that particular causal laws are not a priori, or necessarily true. This is made clear in the *Prolegomena* (Ak., Vol. 4, p. 258; and Sect. 27), and also in the *Critique* (B 793–794). Kant wished to argue, negatively, that such causal laws cannot be subjective associations of ideas, and positively, that their objective status was justified. The justification for their status lay, on Kant's view, in the special status of the categories which they contained. It is not, for example, that causal laws are necessarily true but that they can be said to be objective, and can be distinguished from associations of ideas, because they are intimately related to *the* causal law, which is necessarily true. Particular causal laws share in the status of *the* causal law in accordance with which they are formulated, and which makes them possible. The idea of *the* causal law can be made clearer in the light of Kant's claims that categories embody fundamental conceptual truths, and that empirical concepts cannot by themselves explain the objectivity of our experience. For this rejection of empirical concepts rests partly on the view that their sense is determined by these fundamental non-empirical truths, at least in part.[1] *The* causal law will, then, be such a conceptual truth, introducing the concept of a cause into our experience or governing its operation in that experience (cf. Ch. 10).

If the distinctions between judgments are classed together in one general contrast between subjective and objective judgments, then this must be a complex distinction, reflecting a number of different but connected criteria. It reflects, for example, the difference of status between judgments which express, and those which do not express, categorial claims; it reflects the difference also between general claims and particular claims; between claims intended as candidates for general acceptance, and those which are not so intended; and between claims about public objects and those about particular experiences. The paradigm case of an objective judgment would be a general categorial claim about a physical object, which is intended as a claim for general acceptance. The standard case of a subjective judgment would be a particular claim about some particular sense experience, not expressing a categorial claim, and not intended as a candidate for general acceptance.

---

[1] Kant often speaks in this way of categories as providing for any concept a determinate sense, apart from the ideas which different people may associate with a word (cf. A 100–101, B 140, B 143, *Prol.*, Sect. 20).

It would be right to query the suggestion that claims about a particular sense experience are not intended for general acceptance. They are not, necessarily, true of other people, but they are often true for others, and are intended to be. This reflects again the difficulty that even empirically subjective judgments are transcendentally objective. To say of something that it is transcendentally objective is to say that it can be conceived independently of any particular experience, but not independently of every experience. Even personal experiences are, therefore, transcendentally objective, since such things as pains are conceived independently of any particular pain experience. It is for this reason that a claim about my pain can be true for others, or for myself at another time, even though it is not true of them. But particular claims about personal experiences are empirically subjective, for they are not true independently of any particular experience; if they are true at all, they are true of a particular experience. Categorial claims, however, expressing for example a causal connection are not, in this way, dependent for their truth on any particular experience, and so are empirically, as well as transcendentally, objective. The empirical distinctions between objective and subjective judgments reflect the relative distinctions between claims true of public and claims true of private objects, or between impersonal and personal claims. These distinctions are exemplified in our experience and so are empirical; but all these judgments are objective transcendentally.

It follows from what has been said of the empirical contrast between what is objective and what is subjective, that any corresponding transcendental contrast cannot be exemplified in our experience. This is only to re-state the claim, admitted above, that all concepts, even those of an empirical kind, exhibit objective features. Categories are distinguished from other concepts not because they alone exhibit such features, but because they alone are the fundamental concepts responsible for these features. But if every concept exhibits this characteristic, then the whole of our experience, in so far as we can conceive it, must be objective in a transcendental sense, so that what is transcendentally subjective cannot be exemplified in it. The idea of what is transcendentally subjective would be that of an experience without any reference to the ways in which it might be conceived or described. We may form some idea of what is, in this way, transcendentally subjective, just as we may form some idea of a transcendentally external cause of appearances, but to speak in either of these ways is not wholly comprehensible. For we could not understand what such an experience would be like without appealing to the concepts, through which we ordinarily describe our experience; and to do this would be to take advantage of what are specifically objective features of that experience.

It would be easy to think of what is transcendentally subjective in a thoroughly metaphysical or mystical way; the notion certainly has something in common with what Wittgenstein said of the subjective limits of the world.[1] There is, however, no need to speak of it in these mystical terms, and Kant would not have done so without making certain important provisos. The concept of a transcendental, or intelligible, object may be regarded, on Kant's view, as that of a limit placed upon our knowledge, and it is quite natural to think of what is transcendentally subjective in the same way. The very notion of a transcendental concept is that of a limit which should not be overstepped. What is transcendentally objective, in this limiting sense, is something which cannot be experienced, that is, an intelligible object, or non-phenomenon. To think of such a concept as the name of a genuine object would be to misconceive it, for properly it expresses only a metaphysical reflection of the claim that our knowledge is restricted to phenomena, or objects of a possible experience. The notion of a transcendental object may be used in this metaphysical way, so long as the obvious dangers of hypostatisation are avoided, but it has a still more acceptable sense as an abbreviation for the fundamental concepts in our language (cf. Ch. 5, p. 78 f.). The metaphysical idea of a transcendental object is only that of an object of the understanding, without any reference to the senses. But the idea of an object of the understanding has no meaning apart from the fundamental concepts in the language.

In a similar way the notion of what is transcendentally subjective may be given a mistaken metaphysical sense, as well as a limiting sense, which reflect certain simple but essential features of our experience. The notion of a transcendental subject or person is the exact counterpart of the misconceived idea of a transcendental

[1] *Tractatus Logico-philosophicus*, 5.6 ff. Cf. Stenius: *Wittgenstein's Tractatus*, pp. 220–222.

object. But if what is transcendentally subjective is not misconceived in this way, then it may be understood to express a limit placed upon our knowledge. Just as a transcendental object may be understood to reflect the claim that our knowledge is restricted to what can be experienced, so what is transcendentally subjective reflects the claim that our knowledge is restricted to what can be conceived. For to speak of what is transcendentally subjective, that is, of an experience without any reference to a way in which it might be conceived, is to speak emptily. This limit is nevertheless based upon the fact that experiencing, or sense-perception, is just as fundamental in our experience as are our concepts. These transcendental or metaphysical notions are simply reflections of the empirical contrast between perceiving and conceiving, or between experiences and the ways in which they are discriminated. They are reflections of the view that both of these features are in some way essential to our experience, so that to speak of either without the other is to speak emptily, or to point to limits in our experience. But these reflections have often been distorted by philosophers, who have sometimes been misled into accounting for the objects which such transcendental notions may seem to name.[1]

This account of what is transcendentally subjective may help finally to explain what can be meant by transcendental Idealism. For to speak of what is transcendentally ideal is to speak of what is transcendentally subjective. This latter notion reflects the claim that experiencing or sense-perception are essential in our experience, or that our knowledge is based ultimately upon personal experiences. This may seem inevitably to lead to an Idealism in which it is held that all our knowledge is of experiences. The doctrine of transcendental Idealism may be seen as an attempt to show why this inference is mistaken, or in what way it can be made satisfactory. For Kant's objection to this step would be to say that if the conclusion is to be accepted, then the term 'experiences' in it must be understood not in an empirical, but in a transcendental sense. For empirically experiences or ideas are specifically contrasted with external objects, of which, on occasion, they may be the experiences. If, therefore, we are to say that our know-

[1] It is perhaps worth considering whether the modern introduction of the term 'sense-datum' was not an attempt to characterise what is, in this way, transcendentally subjective and so indescribable.

ledge is always of experiences, then this term must be given a special, extra-ordinary, sense in which it is permissible to say that a physical object may be an experience. But to speak of our knowledge as restricted to experiences in this transcendental sense is only to insist on the importance of experiencing in our knowledge, and not to draw any limit to the descriptions of experienced objects we might empirically give. Transcendental Idealism holds, then, that all our knowledge is based upon experiences, and that we have no knowledge of anything that cannot be experienced, but that this is compatible with our empirical discriminations of what we experience into inner or outer objects. To put it in another way, the force of transcendental Idealism is only to suppose that we have experiences, and that these play an essential part in our knowledge.[1]

[1] In this way transcendental Idealism reflects a (negative and unexceptionable) part of what was intended by some phenomenalists, namely that to speak of sense-data amounted only to admitting that we do perceive things, that we have perceptual experiences on which our knowledge is based. (*Foundations of Empirical Knowledge*, p. 116.)

# 10

# THE FIRST AND SECOND
# ANALOGIES

'For this concept (cause) makes strict demand that something, A, should be such that something else, B, follows from it necessarily, and in accordance with an absolutely universal rule' (B 124).

'If, therefore, wax, which was formerly hard, melts, I can know a priori that *something* must have preceded, upon which the melting followed according to a fixed law, although a priori . . . I could not determine . . . either the cause from the effect, or the effect from the cause' (B 704).

THERE are many different ways in which Kant's argument in the Analogies may be presented. They are all nevertheless directed towards revealing the connection between the categories of relation and certain time discriminations. In the first two Analogies, to be considered here, Kant deals with a range of inter-connected concepts, such as 'substance', 'cause', 'alteration', 'change', 'persistence', 'succession', 'state', 'event', and others. There is no single way of correctly depicting these relations between such concepts, although, no doubt, there are many incorrect ways of so doing. Kant may be understood as analysing the schematised categories of 'cause' or 'substance', or as indicating how the pure concepts associated with these categories operate in our spatio-temporal experience, or again, as analysing what is involved in our conventional discriminations between alterations, states, or events. The aim common to these different approaches to the argument is that of showing how the categories are required for, or make possible, certain discriminations in our experience.

There is, of course, a trivial way in which any concept makes some discriminations possible. The concept 'cause', for example, embodies a discrimination between what is a cause and what is an effect. Kant's account of the way in which categories operate in our experience is not always, or obviously, trivial in this way. For the general discrimination effected by the categories is that between certain kinds of temporal relation, and the connection between the categories and time is not obvious. It has also been suggested that the categories are responsible, in some way, for the basic discrimination between what is inner and what is outer in our experience, and this responsibility is certainly not obvious. Even if Kant's claims for the categories were true, they would not all be trivially true.

Kant's ultimate aims in this investigation are similarly various. The close connection between the Analogies, and what Kant calls the laws of 'general physical dynamics' (B 202) makes it plain that the argument is intended to explain the status of these scientific laws. Yet it is also clear from the passages at B 197–198 and B 201–202 (Ch. 6, pp. 113) that Kant is not in the *Critique* concerned primarily with these scientific laws; such a concern is shown rather in the *Metaphysical Foundations of the Natural Sciences* (Ak., Vol. 4, pp. 465–567). Kant certainly intends to suggest that such scientific laws presuppose his a priori principles, and so share, in some degree, their special status. But the categories and their principles operate no less even in our ordinary experience, and Kant intends to establish their status by showing how they govern that experience as well as the laws of physics. The categories and their principles are responsible for our discrimination of such temporal phenomena as duration and succession, and these belong as much to our ordinary experience as to science.

There are two features of the argument in the Analytic of Principles which should be mentioned before discussing the Analogies. For they serve to locate the Analogies in the structure of the Analytic of Principles, and so may justify the emphasis which is here placed on these two principles. First is Kant's distinction between mathematical and dynamical principles which indicates a certain superiority of the Analogies over other principles. Second is an apparent conflict in Kant's treatment of space and time in the Analytic of Principles. Both points suggest that Kant's order of exposition in this whole section is misleading, and might be reversed in the interest of clarity. The second point indicates a difficulty in Kant's account of space and time, which can be resolved properly only later in the discussion of personality (Ch. 11).

The distinction between mathematical and dynamical principles is made at B 199–202, and elaborated elsewhere (e.g. B 218–219, B 220, B 692). The distinction, in conformity with the arguments of the Axiom and Anticipation, limits the application of these mathematical principles primarily to intuition and sensation. The dynamical principles, and especially the Analogies, are by contrast concerned with the existence of appearances, and, as Kant says (B 218–219), 'constitute the essential in any knowledge of objects of the senses, that is, in experience as distinguished from mere intuition or sensation of the senses'. In this way Kant indicates a certain superiority of the Analogies over the mathematical principles, not in the status of their evidence, but in their relation to experience.[1] This superiority can be made clear from the kind of discriminations properly associated with these different principles. The two mathematical principles are supposed to justify the ascription of numerical magnitudes (extensive or intensive) to appearances primarily as intuitions or sensations, and are, strictly, non-committal about the objects of intuition or sensation, to which they may also be applied. The restriction placed on these principles is not that they can be applied only to intuitions or sensations, but that they do not themselves specify what the objects of intuition or sensation may be. They justify the ascription of magnitudes to such objects, however they may be conceived. The Analogies, on the other hand, are associated with discriminations between the objects of intuition or sensation, and so are presupposed in the application even of the mathematical principles to such objects. It is in this way that the Analogies have a certain pre-eminence among the principles, which Kant himself acknowledges (cf. *Prol.*, Ch. 26, Ak., Vol. 4, pp. 309–310).

This distinction suggests that the order of exposition in the Analytic of Principles might usefully have been reversed. If Kant had dealt with the Analogies before the mathematical principles,

[1] This is compatible with the claim that the mathematical principles are constitutive and the dynamical principles regulative, which seems to mean that while the former justify the ascription of properties, the latter justify rather claims about relations.

for example, it would have been clearer that even the ascription of magnitude to such objects as a house (B 160-161), or to the illuminative power of the sun and moon (B 221) depends in part on the discriminations effected in the Analogies. But there is also some reason for arguing that the whole of the Analytic of Principles is back to front. The main reason for such a view is the difference of emphasis which Kant variously places on space or on time in his argument. At the start of the section, in the Schematism, all the emphasis is placed upon time, but at the end of the argument it is the spatial features of our experience which are emphasised (B 288-294, B 274-279). In Kant's own exposition this final emphasis on space is apt to be forgotten or overlooked, and it might have been better to explain this apparent conflict before considering the proofs of any of the principles. The argument would then have begun with the 'General Note on the System of the Principles' (B 288), together with the Schematism, proceeded with the dynamical principles, and concluded with the mathematical.

This difficulty over space and time can be resolved by saying that Kant thinks of the temporal discriminations effected by the categories in their application to spatial objects. In this way he can claim both that categories are responsible for certain time relations, and also that these discriminations have their basic application to spatial phenomena. The discrimination of duration and succession, which are dealt with in the Analogies, have their primary application to the duration of spatial objects, and the succession of their states. This shows once again the importance of the Analogies, for it is on them that this primary application of such terms rests. It helps also to explain why Kant chooses to illustrate his argument in the Second Analogy by referring to spatial objects, such as a house and ship. But there is a serious difficulty in this explanation. For Kant has not so far given any reason for accepting his view that such time discriminations are primarily of objects in space. The reasons for this view are given in the Refutation of Idealism (B 274-279), and in the Paralogisms. They are of some importance, as Kant recognised (B 293-294), for his account of personality, and will be considered later. Kant's argument in the Analogies can be understood without presupposing these reasons, but it may be preferred to recognise this presupposition, with the reservation that it has yet to be validated.

## (i) THE ANALOGIES

Just as it can be argued that the Analytic of Principles as a whole is the wrong way round, so it can be argued that the Analogies themselves are presented in a misleading way. It is not so much that they are presented in the wrong order, as that their arguments should not be separated in the artificial way in which Kant has separated them. The temporal relations of succession, simultaneity, and duration are intimately related and properly involved in each of the Analogies. To treat the separate sections as though they each dealt exclusively with only one of these relations is to obscure the argument, and to duplicate parts of it unnecessarily. Kant himself suggests in the First Analogy (B 226: 'And simultaneity . . . no time relation') that duration, which is treated in this section, is dependent upon the discrimination of succession, which is properly treated only in the Second Analogy. It is also clear from Kant's re-statement of the First Analogy at the start of the Second that this latter argument also refers back to the category of substance, and may therefore be represented also as containing a proof of its principle. Both arguments are similar, too, not only because they involve the intimately connected notions of duration and succession, but also because they proceed by analysing the similar concepts of 'alteration' and 'event' ('Alteration' at B 230: 'The correct understanding of the concept of alteration . . .'; 'Event' at B 236: 'Let us now proceed. . . . That something happens . . .'). Since both analyses are of the same, or a very similar, concept (cf. B 291), it is unnecessary to separate them, and better to concentrate on the Second Analogy, which contains the central argument, and to consider the First Analogy only afterwards.

It is sometimes claimed that Kant's argument in the Second Analogy contains several different proofs of the principle (cf. Kemp Smith: *Commentary*, p. 363 f.). But Kant's method of discussing the principles generally is to provide a variety of comment upon an initial proof. Since his task can be understood in different ways, and his conclusions have implications in different contexts, it is not unnatural to find some variation in his arguments. The Second Analogy may, for example, be understood as an analysis of the concept 'event', or as an account of the way in which the category 'cause' operates in our experience. Or again, the argument may be treated on a transcendental level, at which no reference

153

need be made to empirical science (cf. B 232), but it can also be regarded as the establishment of a principle relevant to scientific procedures. In these different contexts it is not surprising that Kant's point should appear in different forms, but there is no strong reason for thinking that the later passages in the Second Analogy conflict with the initial proof given at B 232–239. It is on this argument that attention will be concentrated.

In this passage Kant repeats the conclusions of the First Analogy ('The preceding principle . . . pass to the proof'), outlines the task he has set for himself ('I perceive . . . rule of apprehension'), and finally completes the set task ('Let us now proceed . . . what determines the event'), namely that of explaining the conditions in which we may discriminate a time order in phenomena. Kant assumes for this purpose that it is possible to recognise different states or properties of the same object at different times. He argues that even if it is possible to recognise different states of the same object, this is not the same as recognising an order of such states in time. His problem is, therefore, to explain what more is required to complete such a discrimination of a time order. The view that our recognition of succession can be explained completely by the successive perception of states in an object is rejected (B 233: 'For time cannot be perceived in itself . . .'). Kant similarly rejects the view that an objective time order is one which belongs properly to noumena, or intelligible objects (B 236: 'Now immediately . . .'). The question whether there is an object in appearances is the question whether what we perceive stands under a conceptual rule, which distinguishes it from every other apprehension (B 236: 'Since truth . . . necessary rule of apprehension'). In this way a genuine problem about the objects in, or of, appearances is simply a question about the possibility of a discrimination in what we perceive between one kind of thing and another. Kant is not interested, at this point, in establishing that we do discriminate a time order in appearances, but in the more complex problem of elucidating the conditions in which such a discrimination is possible. In the Second Analogy Kant tries to settle his problem about our discrimination of succession by analysing the notion of an event, in which our idea of a time order is embodied (B 236: 'Let us now proceed . . . That something happens . . .').

The analysis of an event has two parts. Kant first says that for something to happen a given object must be supposed to have two different characteristics, or states. To apprehend an event is to perceive first one state of an object, and then another state of the same object (B 237: 'Every apprehension . . .'). This is evidently to rely on the argument of the First Analogy, but to accept that our discrimination between things and their properties is necessary for our recognition of events is to show how the category 'substance' operates in our experience. For the concept of substance governs our distinction between things which remain to be identified throughout their alterations, and the features in respect of which they alter. Although this discrimination is necessary for our recognition of events, Kant argues that it is not sufficient. For this condition is satisfied even in cases, like that of our successive apprehension of a house's roof and basement, where no event is involved at all. What distinguishes the apprehension of such a non-event from our apprehension of an event, such as a ship's sailing downstream, is that in the latter case the constituent states of the object are regarded as irreversible. An event is an ordered relation of two states of the same object. As Kant says (B 238): 'But in the perception of an event, there is always a rule that makes the order in which the perceptions follow upon one another (in the apprehension of *this* appearance) a necessary order.' The necessity in such a case is the logical necessity that to apprehend a ship's sailing downstream is, necessarily, to apprehend an event in which the ship's position downstream followed its position upstream. The order of *this* event is a necessary order, not because it is impossible for ships to sail upstream, but because if the constituent states had been reversed the event apprehended would have been a different event. It would have been the event of a ship's sailing upstream. Kant's concluding argument is that if this is what we mean by an event, then it presupposes the notion of a reason or ground for the constituent states of an object being in such a determinate order. But the notion of such a reason or ground for one state's succeeding another is that of a cause. If this concluding step were correct, then Kant would have shown that the concept of 'cause' is required for our recognition of an event. To show that the category has such a function is to reveal its central position in our experience, for the recognition of events is that of a time order in phenomena.

The force of this argument may be measured by some of the

common objections made against Kant. Prichard, for example, argued (op. cit., pp. 294–295) that Kant's problem simply does not arise, because we apprehend the time order of events immediately. While Kant rejected the view that our discrimination of a time order could be explained simply in terms of our perception, Prichard evidently held that it could be accounted for in this way. Prichard's view has, apparently, much to recommend it. There is no doubt that ordinarily we tell the order of events in time through having perceived them. The claim that Jones beat Smith in the hundred yards is normally based upon the perception of Jones crossing the finishing line, followed by that of Smith crossing it. Prichard would say that in such standard cases the recognition of the order of these events is based simply on the perception of the way things happened.

There is one initial difficulty in this objection. It is that Prichard speaks of the order of events, whereas Kant speaks of the order of states that go to make up an event. Prichard seems to misconstrue Kant in this way because he insists that events are immediately apprehended, so that, for him, there are genuine questions only about the order of events, and not about the order of states in an event.[1] But whether or not Prichard is right to say that there is no process by which we apprehend an event, it remains true that we may identify and distinguish events in terms of the orders of two states in the same object. That water has frozen or ice melted are different events based upon different orders of the same states of solidity and fluidity in water. There is no reason why questions should not be raised about the order of states in an event, any more than there is a reason why questions should not be raised about the order of two distinct events. Kant has, in any case, an adequate ground for choosing to consider the order of states rather than the order of events. Since he intends to explain the conditions in which it is possible to discriminate events in our experience, it would be pointless to analyse complex events, such as 'Jones winning the race from Smith', which them-

[1] Hume tends also to make the same assumption that questions of a time order are questions of the order of events, and not, as Kant supposes, questions of the order of states in an event. Hume says, for example (*Enquiry*, Sect. IV, Pt. I, 25): Every effect is a distinct event from its cause; as though it were proper to speak of a causal relation only between events. His examples are usually of this complex kind (cf. *Enquiry*, Sect. IV, Pt. I, pp. 29–30 (ed. Selby-Bigge).

selves depend upon simpler events. We naturally name and describe many complex events, for example the Derby, which are
themselves made up of other events, but in order to analyse the
notion of an event Kant has naturally chosen to consider the
simplest events on which the discrimination of more complex
events depends. Such simple events depend not upon any other
events, but only upon the order of states in an object. Kant has
every reason for supposing that the time order of events presupposes the time order of states that make up an event. We could
not speak of the order of events, unless we already recognised the
simpler order of states in an event.

Once this initial difficulty is resolved Prichard's objection can
be amended so that it becomes relevant. It would then be objected
to Kant that we simply perceive the order of states that make up
an event. Kant does not, of course, deny that our recognition of
the order of states in an object is based upon our perception of
these states. He argues only that such perception is not enough to
yield a discrimination of events. It would be natural to think that
Kant relies at this point on the fact that our perception is not
always reliable, or that we sometimes mistake apparent events for
actual events. But Kant does not appeal to such facts as these. It
is not that from an event A–B's apparently taking place we may
mistakenly suppose that an event A–B actually has taken place. It
is rather that having perceived state A and then state B it is not
always appropriate to speak of an event at all, whether apparent
or real. When we perceive first the roof and then the basement of
a house, we perceive in succession two states of the same object,
but nobody would normally say, at Kant points out (B 235), that
this is to perceive an event. When, on the other hand, we perceive
a ship in one position and then in another position downstream,
we can describe what was perceived as the event of a ship's moving
downstream. This is so, whether the ship actually has moved or not.

Kant is interested, therefore, not in the inference from 'The
event A–B appeared to take place' to 'The event A–B really took
place', but in the prior inference from 'I perceived A and then
perceived B' to 'I perceived the *event* A–B'. The priority of the
latter inference rests on the obvious truth that while the premiss
of the former already presupposes the vocabulary of events, the
premiss of the latter does not. Kant argues that because there are
some descriptions of perceived states in the same object which do

not yield event-descriptions, the latter inference is not valid. He concludes from this that the perception of states in an object is not enough to discriminate between events and non-events. But if such successive perception does not serve to distinguish events from other kinds of phenomena, then Kant's problem about the further conditions required for such discrimination is not, as Prichard thought, a pseudo-problem.

Kant's argument has often been construed as an attempt to justify inferences from the way things appear to happen to the way in which they actually happen. In the light of what has been said so far this cannot be wholly right. Even to believe that an event appeared to take place is already to presuppose the concept of an event, the possession and sense of which Kant is trying to explain. For Kant attempts to explain how it is possible for us to describe events, whether in the tentative terms of apparent or the committal terms of their actual occurrence. The explanation of the conditions in which we may describe events is, in this way, designed to cover even cases in which we may mis-describe them. What encourages the belief that Kant is concerned with inferences from apparent to actual events is his talking of the transition from subjective to objective succession. For this inevitably suggests the contrast between apparent and real succession. But although this latter contrast can be said to be involved in Kant's account, his use of it is to indicate not a difference between recognition and mis-recognition of an event, but one between discrimination and non-discrimination of an event. It is possible to mis-recognise an event only if it is possible already to discriminate between events and other kinds of phenomena; for I could not be said to have mistaken something for an event unless I already knew what 'event' means. The inference from 'I perceived A and then perceived B' to 'I perceived the event A–B' effects a transition from state-descriptions to event-descriptions, and not one from a qualified to an unqualified claim about events. Again Kant's interest in this inference is quite neutral as to the distinction between appearance and reality; he could just as well have used the inference from 'I seemed to perceive A and then seemed to perceive B' to 'I seemed to perceive the event A–B'. What distinguishes an actual event from a perceived succession of actual states in an object also distinguishes an apparent event from a perceived succession of apparent states in an object. Such an inference, and the transition it makes from state-descriptions to event-descriptions, involves a question about the meaning of the concept 'event', which is presupposed in questions of the criteria for distinguishing real from apparent events. Kant would say that these latter questions, like all problems about illusions, are empirical only and not transcendental (cf. Ch. 1, p. 16, note).

Both premiss and conclusion in Kant's inference have subjective and objective features. Both report perceptions, and so might be said to be subjective, and both describe what is perceived in different but equally objective terms. Kant regards the premiss as subjective because it records a succession only in perception and not in what was perceived. The conclusion records a succession necessarily, not because it is guaranteed to be true, but because to claim an event's occurrence is to claim, necessarily, a certain time order in what was perceived. It may be objected that to speak of perceiving one thing and then another is already to presuppose discrimination of an event in perceiving. But Kant's premiss is not intended to presuppose any such discrimination, and could less misleadingly be expressed as 'I perceive A' followed by 'I perceive B'. In this way, even though there is a succession in the perception of A and B, it is not expressed in the perceptual reports themselves. Kant speaks of the perception of states and events, in his analysis, because he believed that discrimination of objects in experience is always based upon perception. He held also that the discrimination of an object can be understood only in terms of our descriptions of what is perceived. This is what the notion of an object is explained to mean, in the Transcendental Deduction (Ch. 9). In order, therefore, to achieve any objective discrimination, something must have been perceived, although we can understand such perception only in terms of some already presupposed descriptions. The premiss in Kant's inference from state to event-descriptions satisfies both of these conditions, for it reports perceptions, which are themselves described in terms of states of an object without reference to succession. Kant illustrates the premiss by referring to our perception of physical objects, because he believes that the Analogies have their primary application to outer objects. But since what we perceive may be an inner or an outer object, Kant's analysis of an event could be understood to apply to objects of either sense.

Failure to understand Kant's argument in this way has led to two criticisms of his illustrative examples. Both are designed to show that even in the perception of a house it is not true, as Kant implies, that there are no events at all. The usual objection (cf. Schopenhauer *Werke*, Frauenstädt, Vol. I, p. 86) is to say that if I perceive successively the roof and basement of a house, an event will have taken place because my eyes are supposed to have moved. Kant does not, of course, need to deny this, but only that such an event can be inferred from the given description of what was perceived. It would ordinarily be agreed that in perceiving a house in this way I have not perceived an event, even though there may have been many other events in the situation, which I might have described if I had directed my attention to them. Since Kant is analysing the concept of an event by showing the relation between state-descriptions and event-descriptions, he is perfectly entitled to choose some particular state-descriptions and to ask of them whether they yield event-descriptions. That we might give descriptions of other states of an object in such a situation has no more direct relevance to Kant's argument than the fact that we might, when seeing a ship move downstream, refrain from remarking on it.

The other objection would be to say that even from the claim that I perceived a house's roof and then its basement, it is possible to infer that I perceived an event. Admittedly the events in question are not normally believed to take place, and yet it is possible to find such descriptions. It might be inferred, for example, that in such a situation I perceived an event which could be described by saying that the house's roof turned into a basement, or that the house turned upside down. But the fact that it is possible to give such descriptions does not count against the claim that it is not always possible to give them. To give such descriptions in such a case would still be to contrast them with the situation in which the same states were perceived, although there was no such event. Kant has chosen, for the purposes of his analysis, to contrast a standard example of an event with a standard example of a non-event, but he could, with some loss of clarity, have chosen such non-standard examples as these. So long, however, as there is some contrast between events and non-events, however these are exemplified, the same problem about differentiating between them will still arise. Kant's problem of differentiation is that of saying what we mean when we speak of events, or use event-descriptions; his method of resolving the problem is to analyse the contrast between cases where we would and cases where we would not speak of events.

The objections considered so far have all been directed against the analysis which Kant gives of an event, and the step from this analysis to the notion of a cause has yet to be considered. Kant himself suggests an argument to support his view of the relations between the two concepts at B 239. He there considers the question: What would it be like if we could not conceive a ground or reason for one state's being determined to follow another? On Kant's view the answer to such a question could be only that we would, on such a supposition, be unable to discriminate events in our experience, and so would fail to have any conception of a determinate time order in phenomena. For if we were unable to conceive the idea of something determining the order of states in an object, then we would be unable to conceive the idea of their being in a determinate order. The analysis of an event has shown that perception of different states in an object is not enough to discriminate events from non-events. What distinguishes one from the other is that events are regarded as ordered in a determinate way in time. What we mean by 'event' is such a determinate temporal order of two states in the same object. But the idea of a determinate order between two states presupposes that of something which determines it; and this idea of a determinant or reason for such an order is that of a cause. The notion of a determinate order clearly has some reference to that of a determinant; indeed to express such a relation between the concepts of event and cause may seem just as tautological as to say that substance persists (B 227). Kant has, therefore, some ground for saying that the concept of a cause is required for our discrimination of a time order in phenomena.

Kant is, of course, required to suppose neither that we have to know the cause of an event before we can say that it has taken place, nor that there is just one causal factor in all the events we perceive. It would clearly be absurd to imagine that we must know the cause of something's happening before we can say that it has happened. Ordinarily we enquire into the specific causes of something only when we know that a certain event has taken place. Kant's argument is entirely compatible with this empirical relation of events and their causes; for his argument is only that the concept of an event presupposes that of a cause in general, and not

that a particular recognition of an event requires us to have discovered the particular cause. To recognise an event is to presuppose that some causal factor is present, but not to presuppose any
particular causal factor. In this way the argument says and presupposes nothing about what we count in experience as a cause, and
so is not committed to any view about the limits in the number of
causes that we might recognise. The relation between the notions of
a cause and an event is simply of a conceptual kind, and needs to be
supplemented empirically in order to yield any particular causal law.[1]

It might be admitted that Kant can support his claim that concepts like 'substance' and 'cause' occupy a central position in our
experience, and even that they have a special status in that experience. Yet it may still be doubted whether their centrality is
enough to establish that they are a priori, or that their status could
properly be described as non-empirical. It might be admitted that
such categories are, in the ways indicated, fundamental concepts
in our experience, and yet denied that they can be said to be
independent of experience. In large part such a problem about the
label with which to mark admitted features of such concepts is of
no value. The term 'a priori' does not have so clear a sense that
it can be understood independently of the properties which such
concepts are admitted to have. But Kant's idea of the contrast
between what is empirical and what is a priori derives from his
philosophical predecessors, particularly Locke and Hume. Something may be gained, therefore, from a brief account of the
differences between Kant's treatment of these concepts, and the
treatment of them which these empiricist philosophers gave.

Kant's account of the concept 'substance' is directed towards
showing how this concept is connected with our discriminations
of changes, events, and duration. To claim that the concept of an
event presupposes our discrimination between individuals and
their properties, or their states, is already to suppose that the
category of substance is required for our recognition of an event.

[1] The fact that we may employ our empirical knowledge of particular
causal laws in order to check the time order of phenomena is important for
Kant's argument in the Postulates, but not especially for that of the Second
Analogy. It could be used in this latter context to stress the usefulness, even
indispensability, of the concept in its empirical or scientific employment, but
this is in any case assumed in the argument, and not at issue between Kant
and Hume (cf. *Prol.*, Introd., Ak., Vol. 4, pp. 257 ff.).

In a similar way the recognition of an alteration or change in our experience is dependent upon a distinction between what remains the same throughout changes, and the features in respect of which it changes. Kant assigns the two words 'alteration' ('Veränderung') and 'change' ('Wechsel') to the different ways in which we think of individuals and properties as changing. These terms do not normally convey such a distinction, but there is no doubt that we ordinarily think of change in terms of such a distinction. It is also true that our conventional ways of expressing temporal duration reflect these distinctions. We speak of the time that elapsed between two events, or between the changes which some object has endured. On Kant's view such modes of speech indicate the operation in our experience of the category of substance. For they either express or presuppose the contrast between an individual and its properties, or between individual and generic identity which is embodied in the pure concept. They show also the importance in our experience of such a category, by showing that it is required for, or presupposed in, our discrimination of temporal duration.

Locke also held that the concept of substance was important, even necessary, in our experience, but he seemed unable to explain its origin in empirical terms. The reason for this apparent failure can be simply explained. For Locke's programme involved the claim that all complex concepts can be analysed ultimately in terms of simple sensible properties. But the complex concept of substance is that of something in which properties inhere, and hence cannot itself be reduced to a collection of properties. In this way Locke appears to have held the three conflicting views:

(i) That the concept of substance is necessary to stand for what properties inhere in.
(ii) That substances are logically different from properties.
(iii) That the only way to analyse complex concepts is in terms of simple sensible properties.

Locke could have avoided his difficulty only by denying either (i) or (ii) or (iii). Berkeley, somewhat ambiguously, preserved the empiricist principle (iii), by denying both (i) and (ii). Kant, on the other hand, admitted both (i) and (ii), but denied (iii), arguing that if this is what an empiricist analysis means, then there must be some other analysis of a non-empirical kind to account for such concepts as that of substance.

Locke's failure can be regarded, in this way, as an inevitable consequence of his programme, and so as showing a radical defect in such an empiricist analysis. It was suggested earlier (Ch. 7, pp. 101–103) that Locke's account of the concepts in our language was inadequate, because it did not accommodate certain concepts, on which the sense even of the simplest empirical concepts depends. The category of substance, or more accurately, that of individual and property, is an example of such a concept. Even simple sensible concepts presuppose a certain linguistic framework, in terms of which they are used and understood. The notions of an individual and a property, and of the ascription of properties to individuals, are a part of that framework. Since they are of a type basically different from the simple concepts, which presuppose them, it is not unnatural to call them non-empirical. At least to understand what can be meant by saying that they are non-empirical it is possible to point to such differences.

Locke's difficulty arose because, in speaking of simple sensible properties, he was already committed to the correlative notion of something to which these properties could be ascribed. But his programme of reducing complex concepts to such simple sensible properties refused official recognition to the other half of the categorial classification. Although he was, therefore, forced on one side to recognise the importance of the concept 'substance', he was forced on the other side to admit that he could not explain why it is important. Kant not only recognised its importance, but also believed that he could explain it. For the adoption of the way of thinking embodied in the category is, on his view, a necessary condition of our discrimination of such temporal phenomena as duration and succession. This gives a point to the suggestion that such a category sets a limit to our understanding of experience, for we have no idea of what it would be like to be without such temporal discriminations.

In a somewhat similar way it is true that Hume recognised the importance, and even necessity, of the concept 'cause', but did not adequately explain these features. Kant was right to say that the issue between himself and Hume over this concept was not that of its usefulness or indispensability. But Hume concluded from the claim that particular causal laws are not necessarily true, that the necessity of causes was only that of an unavoidable propensity to think in such terms. To speak in this way of the basis of our causal enquiries as a mere subjective necessity is objectionable. For it does not explain the importance of such causal laws in our experience, and even suggests that there is no real basis for our belief in them (B 168). Such a view as Hume's also obliterates the ordinary distinction between an objective claim, such as a statement of a causal connection, and a subjective association of ideas. Kant did not try to refute Hume only by appealing to this ordinary distinction. He attempted instead to reinstate it, by explaining why the concept 'cause' was important. His additional step beyond Hume was to show what kind of importance, and what kind of necessity, can be said to belong to the concept.

Kant's principal charge against Hume is, therefore, that he drew the wrong conclusions from the true premiss that particular causal laws are not necessarily true. Hume argued from this that the only necessity which can belong to the concept 'cause' is subjective, but he should have inferred instead that particular causal laws presuppose *the* causal law, which is a necessary and not a contingent truth. The point is stated at B 793–794: 'Hume was therefore in error in inferring from the contingency of our determinations in accordance with the law, the contingency of the law itself.' Particular causal laws are thus contingently true and so falsifiable for both Kant and Hume. Our knowledge of such laws depends upon our knowledge of regularities in phenomena, and we may mistake or misread them. That the heat of the sun will melt wax is something that cannot be known a priori, and such a claim is neither self guaranteeing nor necessarily true. But such empirical laws presuppose the causal law, which is not itself contingent, since it expresses a conceptual truth which is a pre-condition of the formulation or discovery of particular causal laws. The causal law is, in this way, what Wittgenstein called the 'form of a law' (*Tractatus*, 6.32)[1] and does not itself express any causal relation between particular phenomena. It is rather a conceptual

---

[1] Kant does not, however, formulate the causal law in the way that Wittgenstein did ('There are natural laws', *Tractatus* 6.36), but as a necessary relation between the concepts 'cause' and 'event'. This relation is often carelessly expressed as 'Every event has a cause', although Kant usually formulates it as 'Every event presupposes a cause' (B 240, B 263–264, B 289). Perhaps the least misleading formulation would be 'The concept "event" presupposes that of "cause"'. It is important to note these variations, since otherwise it is easy to confuse the principle of the Second Analogy with others such as the cosmological principle of totality (cf. Ch. 5, pp. 70–71; Ch. 12, pp. 198–200).

truth which determines the sense of the concepts 'cause' and 'event', and may be regarded as introducing the concept 'cause' into our experience, or as expressing its function in that experience. The necessity of causes is, therefore, a reflection of the fundamental part which this concept plays in our experience, for without it the discrimination of an event, and of an objective time order, would not be possible. In the Transcendental Deduction Kant argues that there are certain fundamental conceptual truths in our experience; in the Second Analogy he supports the claim that the causal law is such a fundamental truth. The central position of this law explains the importance of the concept 'cause' in our experience in a way in which Hume did not explain it. It shows also that the causal law is not a contingent but a conceptual truth, and so necessary in a non-subjective way. Apart from such claims the question whether the concept 'cause' is a priori or empirical has no particular value.

Kant's reinstatement of the empirical contrast between subjective and objective judgments (cf. Ch. 9 (iii)) may be regarded as a doctrine about our entitlement to make objective claims. The question which Kant asks about objective judgments is not: How do we know that (or when) they are true? but rather: Under what conditions can we be entitled to assert them? Kant evidently thought of Hume as having questioned our right to assert objective claims, by having degraded causal laws to the level of subjective associations. Kant's intention is negatively to resist any such empiricist restrictions on what we have a right to assert; and positively to justify our right to assert objective judgments. Kant may be regarded as arguing that our right to assert objective judgments is just as effective as our right to assert subjective claims, and that this right rests in both cases upon the existence of categories and their associated principles.

It is easy for empiricists to doubt whether we have a right to assert objective claims, since these are general and impersonal, while the evidence available to our senses is particular and personal. Kant's negative intention is to reject such an empiricist doubt, for the ideal on which it is based, that of a language which expresses only and exactly the content of our sensible experience is, on Kant's view, mistaken. In his terms such an ideal is the impossible one of understanding or describing what is transcendentally subjective (cf. Ch. 9, pp. 145–148); his rejection of it is a special case of the view that a private language is impossible. On Kant's view experience is possible only if it is transcendentally objective, or, only if it is possible to conceive or describe our experiences. But if it is possible to describe them, then it is possible for the description to be exemplified in another experience, and so possible for a judgment to be generally accepted as true, and intended to be so accepted. Kant's positive intention is to say that it is under such a condition that we have a right to assert any judgment. Since this holds just as much for empirically objective judgments, which are true of experience generally, as for empirically subjective judgments, which are true only of a particular experience, we have, on this condition, as much of a right to assert the former as the latter. This condition is satisfied by the existence of categories, and of the fundamental conceptual truths in which they figure.

## 11

# PERSONALITY

---

'We can assign no other basis for this teaching than the simple, and in itself completely empty representation "I"' (B 404).

'. . . the simple "I" in the representation to which all thought relates, has its own importance. For apperception is something real' (B 419).

SOME account of the notion of personality has already been given in the discussion of apperception (Ch. 9, pp. 136–140). But it was emphasised there that Kant's treatment of the concept cannot be understood apart from the later arguments of the Paralogisms and Refutation of Idealism. In this chapter something is to be finally said of this theoretical and personal aspect of apperception. Kant has both a negative, or critical, account of the limits to be placed upon this personal sense of 'apperception', and also a more positive theory of the relation between categories and personality. These two accounts exhaust Kant's theoretical interest in personality, but the same notion is involved also in the transition from theoretical to practical philosophy in the Third Antinomy (cf. B 430–431). It was suggested earlier (Ch. 2) that Kant's commitment to noumena cannot be assessed until this transitional passage has been considered. The accounts of personality and of noumenal objects can therefore be completed by a discussion of this transitional argument in the next, and final, chapter.

## (i) INNER SENSE AND APPERCEPTION

In the Transcendental Deduction (B 152–157) Kant provides a general explanation of the contrast between apperception and inner sense. He says, for example (B 154):

Apperception and its synthetic unity is, indeed, very far from being identical with inner sense. The former, as the source of all combination, applies to the manifold of intuition in general, and in the guise of the categories, prior to all sensible intuition, to objects in general. Inner sense, on the other hand, contains the mere form of intuition, but without combination of the manifold in it, and therefore, so far, contains no *determinate* intuition, which is possible only through the consciousness of the determination of the manifold by the transcendental act of imagination. . . .

This contrast reflects the general distinction, discussed earlier (Ch. 4), between sense and understanding. The senses present us with indeterminate appearances, which it is the function of understanding to determine or describe. The term 'appearance', which in its transcendental use is given to whatever is an object of the senses, is therefore quite neutral as to the description of what we empirically perceive. Kant's claim that the senses are inarticulate, or passive, amounts in this way to the stipulations that appearances are nondescript or indeterminate, while phenomena are described or differentiated appearances. If it is legitimate to make such stipulations about sense and understanding in general, then the same distinctions will arise between inner sense and understanding. Just as the senses generally may be said to present us with nondescript appearances, which are discriminated by the understanding, so inner sense is supposed to present us with an indeterminate manifold, which requires to be determined or described by apperception.

This general reliance on the distinction between sense and understanding does nothing particularly to explain what inner sense is. But the effort to explain or illustrate this particular sense raises a difficulty. For to speak specifically of inner sense is to contrast it with outer sense, and this contrast is regarded by Kant as empirical and not transcendental (cf. A 379; also Ch. 9, pp. 135–136). Since both inner and outer sense are exemplified in our experience, the contrast between them cannot be of a transcendental kind, so that neither of the specific senses could properly be contrasted with transcendental apperception. Inner sense should, therefore, be contrasted not with transcendental, but with empirical, apperception. In this way it is possible to explain the contrast between inner sense and understanding quite specifically, but on a purely empirical level. To speak of the distinction between inner sense and empirical apperception as a feature of our ordinary experience has the advantage that the transcendental notion of apperception can be approached through familiar features of our experience. Kant often speaks of apperception empirically as a feature in our experience. At B 422, note, he says that 'I think', which is the basic formula of apperception, is an empirical proposition, and that it expresses an indeterminate empirical intuition. At B 419 he explains that apperception is something real, and at B 156, note, it is explained in terms of 'attending to' something. There are also several accounts of the contrast between empirical and transcendental apperception (e.g. B 132, B 140). In these explanations it is natural to connect empirical apperception with such familiar performances as judging, or attending to, something in our sensible experience. The possibility of attending to some item in our experience is linked with that of discriminating one thing in that experience from another, and such discriminations are standardly expressed in the form of judgments. It is, therefore, legitimate to associate empirical apperception with the judgments that might be made about some sensibly perceived item.

The contrast between empirical apperception and inner sense can now be explained as that between our discriminating or judging what appears sensibly to us, and a certain mode of such sensible presentation. This mode of sensible presentation is that through, or in, which we discriminate among a set of inner characteristics, such as pains, emotions, thoughts, or experiences generally. Kant complicates this conventional picture in one way by including such things as thoughts among the items presented to inner sense. For these are naturally associated with empirical apperception. Kant held that our knowledge of apperception is just as much derived from inner sense as our knowledge of pains or emotions, but that this does not prevent us from drawing the distinction between sense and apperception. Even on this empirical level, therefore, apperception cannot be said to be knowledge. We have knowledge of apperception, as we have knowledge of anything empirically, through a combination of sense and understanding. In a situation where we attend to, or judge on the basis of, some item in our sensible experience, we naturally distinguish between the attention or the judgment and the sensible presentation of the item. Kant insists that if we talk of knowing that we are attending to, or judging, something, then we should also distinguish between the judgment about our attention and its sensible presentation.

Kant's motives for adopting this view of apperception are complex. He adopts it in part because he wished to insist that our knowledge even of apperception was phenomenal and not of noumena or intelligible objects (cf. B 156: 'If then . . . not as it is in itself'). But whatever his motives, Kant's views about inner sense are unlike those which some modern philosophers are inclined to give of our self-knowledge (e.g. Wittgenstein: *Philosophical Investigations*, Sect. 246, or Strawson: *Mind*, January 1954, p. 84). It might be objected to Kant, for example, that there is or could be no such thing as inner sense. And this objection might rest upon the belief that to speak of inner sense is to speak, incoherently, of some inner procedure modelled on what we believe about some outer sense, such as seeing. Some contemporary philosophers might agree that there are outer senses, or that seeing is a mode of sensible presentation, but refuse to admit any counterpart inner sense.

One reason for such a view, which accepts outer but rejects inner sense, lies in the known defects of Descartes' account of such an inner sense. For he talked incoherently (*Regulae*, XII) of the understanding seeing what is impressed physically on the brain, as an explanation of what we ordinarily mean by 'seeing'. He advances, in this way, a crude theory of an inner observer which yields an objectionable account of an inner sense (cf. Ryle: *The Concept of Mind*). But although it is true that Descartes invites such criticism, through a momentary carelessness in his choice of words, it does not follow that all doctrines of inner sense are similarly or equally objectionable. Kant's doctrine in particular is ultimately quite as much a rejection of Descartes' theory as Ryle's is. Kant asserts only that we can identify certain inner characteristics, which we ascribe to ourselves, and can empirically contrast them with other characteristics, which we ascribe to objects in space. The idea of an outer or of an inner sense is only that of the way in which we are presented with such different features in experience.

It might still be objected that we have no genuine idea of a way in which we are presented with such inner characteristics. But it is a delusion to think that while we understand with perfect clarity the mode in which we are presented with outer objects, we do not understand the so-called inner mode of presentation at all. Indeed it would be a mistake to think that outer and inner objects can be easily separated from each other. When, for example, we are presented sensibly with, or see, an outer object, we can also discriminate in such a situation a visual experience, which belongs to inner sense. The experience of a pain belongs to inner sense, but the pain may be quite specifically located in a body, which belongs to outer. Many of the inner characteristics are associated with specific bodily locations, and all are associated with a body. This may help to suggest that what we understand by 'outer sense' can certainly be no clearer than what we understand by 'inner sense'. To speak of a way in which objects are sensibly presented is not to suppose that we know all there is to know about such a mode of presentation. It is to talk only of our relations to different kinds of object that we discriminate in our experience. Our relation to outer, or to inner, objects is, on Kant's view, an empirical matter, which belongs rather to science than to philosophy. An enquiry into the ways in which we are presented with inner objects belongs just as much to such a science as physiology, as an enquiry into our relation to outer objects. And if it is denied that such a science can ever give an adequate explanation of inner sense, the same denial will hold just as much of outer.[1]

What has been given so far is only an empirical account of inner sense and apperception. That these terms have an empirical use of this kind can be seen from the fact that they, and their natural contrasts, are all exemplified in our experience. Inner sense can be contrasted with outer, and empirical apperception with unconsciousness or inattention. These contrasts are given in our ordinary distinction between judging and perceiving, although the

[1] It was suggested above (Ch. 2, p. 31) that Kant, like Ryle, ascribes the responsibility for the philosophical mind–body problem to a category mistake. But whereas Ryle suggests that the (Cartesian) mistake is that of faulty assimilation of one category to another, Kant indicates that it is one of faulty differentiation between them. That is, Ryle suggests that Descartes wrongly over-emphasised similarities between minds and bodies; Kant believed that Descartes wrongly over-emphasised the differences between them. Kant also held that there was no genuine philosophical problem about the relation of minds and bodies. Genuine problems about their relation reflect scientific difficulties about our understanding of space and time, or of outer and inner sense.

situations in which these terms are exemplified contain references to both sense and understanding. When we judge that something is so, we may do so on the basis of our perception, and in any case can be said to know that we judge only on the basis of our inner sense. Similarly we cannot ordinarily consider perception without presupposing some linguistic resources, and cannot be said to know that we are perceiving without appealing to them. Consequently our empirical distinction between judging and perceiving is not totally sharp. It occurs within a framework in which we can know, or speak of, anything empirical only on the presupposition that it is possible both to perceive and to judge (cf. Ch. 9).

These empirical situations, and a recognition of the importance of these two items in them, indicate at once a transcendental distinction between sense, in general, and understanding, in general. For we may abstract (see note p. 174) from such situations general ideas of both sense and understanding. These abstract concepts of sense and understanding provide a quite sharp distinction, but one which is not exemplified in our experience. For to talk of sense and understanding in this way is to talk of sense, without reference to understanding, and of understanding, without reference to sense. Such a distinction is, for this reason, not empirical but transcendental; its terms express only general conditions of our ordinary experience, and do not name items in that experience. It has already been argued (Ch. 9, pp. 145 ff.) that there is no possibility of identifying sense in general, without some reference to concepts, and similarly no possibility of identifying understanding in general, without some reference to sensible experience. But we can employ the transcendental concepts of sense and understanding to express the two aspects of what is presupposed in our empirical account of perceiving and judging, and also to indicate that both features are required for our knowledge of experience. The function of this transcendental contrast is not that of naming discriminable objects in our experience, but rather that of expressing certain abstract or formal conditions in which we are able to discriminate such objects.

To speak, in this abstract or formal way, of understanding independently of sense, is to speak not of empirical but of transcendental apperception. Evidently such a transcendental concept has a peculiar philosophic function, which may easily be misunderstood. For such a concept may mistakenly be thought of as the name of some item either in or beyond our experience, when properly it has a function of a quite different sort. The limits so far placed on the proper use of this concept are just those which Kant himself indicates. At A 350, for example, he says of transcendental apperception: 'There is not in this representation the least trace of intuition distinguishing the "I" from other objects.' The notion of a transcendental apperception is that of an understanding from which every reference to sense experience has been removed or abstracted. It is an abstraction[1] (A 397–398, B 426–427, B 429, etc.) which may nevertheless be used to express a formal or logical presupposition of our experience (B 401, A 355–356, A 363, B 421–422). Most importantly, perhaps, such a concept is not the name of any object (A 350, A 356, B 401, A 354). At A 356, for example, Kant says of it: 'It concerns only the condition of our knowledge; it does not apply to any assignable object.' Associated with this transcendental concept of apperception is a transcendental concept of an ego, or personality. To speak, in this transcendental way, of an understanding may naturally seem to be to speak of a person, in that special sense of 'person' indicated in the Transcendental Deduction (B 132–133, Ch. 9, pp. 136–138). Our references to experiences ordinarily presuppose the notion of a person who has them; but it may seem impossible for *this* notion of a person to be exemplified *in* any particular experience. The idea of a person, presupposed in our ordinary reference to experiences, seems to be that of a whole set of experiences, and not that of the content of any one experience. In this way the concept of a person, of that to which experiences belong, is a problem. For there is no doubt that we are prepared to speak in this way of persons, and yet, since there seems to be no question of experiencing such an object, it may not be clear what we are speaking about.

It is very tempting to think that this special sense of 'person'

---

[1] It would be natural to think that if such a concept can be regarded as an abstraction from our ordinary experience, it must be of an empirical origin. But Kant gives an important explanation of his use of 'abstraction' and 'abstract' at Ak., Vol. 8, p. 199, note, in which it is made clear that this is not so. It is made clear that in speaking of abstracting concepts Kant is saying something quite irrelevant to the traditional theory of the 'origin' of ideas. It is too long to quote in full, and one brief motto must suffice: 'It is wrong to speak of abstracting a concept as a common mark, but right to speak of abstracting from the complexities of a concept in using it.'

could be elucidated, and its problem solved, by a simple reference to the notion of a transcendental apperception. But this is certainly a mistake, for the notion of transcendental apperception, like that of a transcendental personality, is empty. It would be quite wrong to think that these concepts name any item in our experience; and no less mistaken to think that they name items in an intelligible world beyond experience. To think in these ways would be to make just the mistake of hypostatisation which Kant indicates at B 409: 'The analysis of consciousness of myself in thought in general yields nothing whatsoever towards knowledge of myself as an object. The logical exposition of thought in general has been mistaken for a metaphysical determination of the object.' To use these concepts to solve the problem of personality would be to misuse them. From such a pseudo-solution it would be tempting to make the untestable claims of the Paralogisms that persons in this transcendental way are simple, substantial, and even immortal. These paralogistic claims, on Kant's view, mistake a metaphysical way of talking about empirical objects for a way of talking about supposed metaphysical objects.

This negative account of such transcendental concepts does not exhaust Kant's argument. He himself believes that the notion of transcendental apperception may help in the explanation of personality, but this belief does not involve the claim that such concepts have any conventional naming function. Part of the function of these concepts is, indeed, to express a problem about the conditions in which it is possible to speak of and discriminate persons in our experience. When Kant refers to the 'transcendental subject = X' (B 404), he is not speaking of any object which could solve the problem of personality, but only of a problem which requires solution. Just as he had used a similar device in the Transcendental Deduction (A 404) to express a general problem about the term 'object' (cf. Ch. 5, pp. 76 ff.), so in the Paralogisms it is used to express a general problem about the terms 'subject' or 'person'. It is in the attempt to answer this problem that Kant gives a more positive account of personality.

This set of critical qualifications placed upon the notion of transcendental apperception led Strawson to say of Kant that he had understood the problem of personality more clearly than Hume (*Individuals*, p. 103). Strawson says: 'It was this (transcendental apperception), too, to which Kant, more perspicacious here than Hume, accorded a purely formal ("analytic") unity; the unity of the "I think" that accompanies all my perceptions, and therefore might just as well accompany none.' Kant certainly does speak in this logical or formal way of the transcendental concept of apperception, though he would not have said that it was merely an analytic unity (B 130–133). Kant would not have admitted either that 'I think' does accompany all my perceptions. In the Transcendental Deduction he says that it must be able to do so (B 131), and this claim has been discussed above (Ch. 9, pp. 126 ff.). But it will not do to conclude from this that apperception might just as well accompany none of my perceptions. If Kant were speaking transcendentally of apperception, then there is properly no question of its occurrence at all; and perhaps it is this view that Strawson meant to reflect. But empirical apperception does sometimes occur, and does accompany my perceptions, though it would be false to say that it always does. I may, for example, say truly that I saw something, but did not notice it at the time. Apart from these inadequacies, however, Strawson indicates only the negative side of Kant's views about apperception.[1] When Kant says that apperception is real and important in its own way (B 419), he claims not only that the transcendental concept has an empirical counterpart in experience, but also that the former can in some way explain the latter. For the latter, like every claim about personal attributes, presupposes the special concept of 'person', which is expressed in the former. The transcendental concept has its own importance, in this way, as the expression of a problem, namely that of elucidating the conditions in which it is possible to discriminate persons in our experience.

## (ii) CATEGORIES AND PERSONS

Kant's conclusions about personality are easy to state, although the arguments that support them are often difficult to follow. There is, for example, no doubt that in intention Kant's views on this topic are radically opposed to those of Descartes. In this respect

[1] Strawson suggests that Kant was content to say that because the concept of apperception has these odd properties, there is no genuine problem of personality. What has been said so far argues that this is wrong; the transcendental concept of apperception is a way of expressing such a problem. Strawson indicates later (*Individuals*, p. 134) that Kant does have something else to say.

Kant is in sympathy with many modern philosophers who have also wished to reject a Cartesian account of persons (e.g. Ryle: *Concept of Mind*, Ch. VI. Strawson: *Individuals*, Ch. 3). But Kant's arguments against a Cartesian doctrine are not at all the same as those which modern philosophers have used. For this reason Kant's treatment of this problem has a particular interest. It is sufficiently modern to be intelligible, and sufficiently unfashionable to be stimulating.

Kant, like many modern philosophers, emphasises not only the differences between self knowledge and knowledge of others, but also the superiority, or priority, of the latter over the former. At A 362, for example, he says:

> In my own consciousness, therefore, identity of person is unfailingly met with. But if I view myself from the standpoint of another person (as an object of his outer intuition) it is this outer observer who first represents me in time, for in apperception, time is represented strictly only in me. Although he admits, therefore, the 'I' which accompanies, and indeed with complete identity, all representations at all times in my consciousness, he will draw no inference from this to the objective permanence of myself.

When Kant speaks of the 'I' (not 'I think') which accompanies all representations at all times in my consciousness, he indicates the odd tautological character of appeals to a unity of consciousness. The same feature of such appeals is noticed on several occasions by Kant (e.g. B 135, B 138, B 404, B 408–409). It is what makes him refer to the transcendental concept of apperception in terms of an 'analytic' unity, which nevertheless points to the further problem of explaining the synthesis which it presupposes. This is only to repeat what has been said already in the critical account of personality, that the notion of a transcendental unity of consciousness is only a metaphysical way of expressing claims about personal identity, and cannot except tautologically be used to explain these claims. Such transcendental concepts of personality might conceivably be of use if they named any discriminable objects in our experience, but they do not. We do not have an intuitive intelligence.

Kant insists, in this passage, not only that self knowledge is different from knowledge of others, but also that the latter is prior to the former. To say, as Kant does, that an outer observer of me will draw no inferences about my objective permanence implies that it is his knowledge of me, and not my knowledge of myself, which sets the standard for knowledge of persons. For the inferences which I might be tempted to draw about the permanence of myself, on the basis of my privileged position, are on Kant's view fallacious and paralogistic. The same priority is also expressed by saying that it is this outer observer who first represents me in objective time. Kant does not appeal to the existence of other people to promote me to such an objective time order. It would be quite possible for me to represent myself in such an order, so long as I view myself from the standpoint of an outer observer, that is, view myself as an object of outer intuition. To speak of the difference between my relation to myself and my relation to others, is also to speak of the difference between the way I appear to myself in inner sense, and the way I appear to myself as an outer object. In this way the priority of outer sense could be expressed by saying that I can have knowledge of myself only so long as it is possible to view myself as an outer object.

This claim, that our recognition of outer objects is in some way prior to our recognition of inner states, even in the case of oneself, is the conclusion of the Refutation of Idealism.[1] For the various arguments of the Refutation are designed to show that the application of categories is primarily to outer sense, that is, to spatial objects. If Kant were right in this, then he would have shown that our knowledge of ourselves is not, as Descartes believed, prior to and the basis of our knowledge of spatial objects. It would be the case rather that our knowledge of ourselves is in some way dependent upon our knowledge of outer phenomena. In asserting such a priority Kant is not denying that all our knowledge can be said to be based upon our personal experiences. But in the transcendental way in which this claim is true, our experiences may themselves be described in inner or outer terms. Kant's claim is that our outer descriptions and outer knowledge are prior to our inner descriptions and our inner knowledge.

Empirical idealism attempts to construct our knowledge of the external world on the basis of our knowledge, or descriptions, of inner phenomena. Kant's refutation of such an empirical idealism is a firm rejection of this priority, but his rejection of it does not consist simply in reversing it. For Kant the objects of both inner

[1] There are several arguments of the same kind apart from the official Refutation at B 272–277. Cf. Kemp Smith: *Commentary*, p. 298.

and outer sense are given immediately, and neither can be said to be constructed or inferred from the other.[1] When he says, therefore, that outer sense is prior to inner sense, he is not speaking of the priority which a premiss has over a conclusion based on it. The priority should instead be expressed by saying that since the categories apply primarily to outer objects, we could have no knowledge of inner experience without some knowledge of outer.

Kant's proof of this priority is expressed with great simplicity. At B 276 it is argued:

> All determination of time presupposes something permanent in perception. But this permanent cannot be an intuition in me. For all grounds of the determination of my existence which are to be met with in me are representations; and as representations require a permanent distinct from them, in relation to which their change, and so my existence in the time wherein they change, may be determined.

Again, at B 291–292 the same point is expressed in a slightly different way: 'For space alone is determined as permanent, while time and everything that is in inner sense is in constant flux. . . . all alteration, if it is to be perceived as alteration, presupposes something permanent in intuition, and in inner sense no permanent intuition is to be met with.' These arguments exemplify the importance which Kant finally attaches to space, or spatial discriminations, at the end of the Analytic of Principles (B 291–294). They correspond to the claims in the Transcendental Deduction (B 156) that we can understand time only in accordance with a spatial model. Consequently the categories, and the principles associated with them, make time discriminations possible only through their application to spatial phenomena. Kant is certainly right to say that we do understand temporal relations in spatial terms. We speak, for example, of events as 'taking place', and think of time as a continuous one-dimensional line. But the reasons which Kant gives for this may not seem wholly clear. For the present, however, it is better to consider how this conclusion influences his account of the way in which we discriminate persons in our experience.

Kant acknowledges (B 294) that the claimed priority of spatial discriminations in our experience is important for his account of

[1] A 371: In order to arrive at the reality of outer objects I have just as little need to resort to inference, as I have in regard to the reality of the object of my inner sense, that is, in regard to the reality of my thoughts.

personality. It is this priority that justifies the claim that it is an outer observer of me who first represents me in a time order. If it is accepted that temporal discriminations depend upon the categories and their associated principles, particularly the Analogies, then all our experience, so far as it is temporal, will depend upon them. And if this is true, then our experience or discrimination of persons will also depend upon them. But the categories and their temporal discriminations are connected more closely than this to our recognition of persons. For this latter recognition itself depends directly upon our discrimination of time. The notion of a person is, for Kant, that of a subject of inner characteristics, or empirical experiences. When he speaks (cf. B 131–133) of a basic synthesis of ideas that are mine, as the ground of my recognition of my own personality, he thinks of this as a synthesis of inner characteristics. But it would be impossible to conceive such a synthesis if it were impossible to discriminate between those experiences which are inner and those which are outer. This latter distinction between inner and outer experience, on which the notion of a person depends, itself depends directly upon discrimination of time in experience. For inner experiences are conceived as temporal, or in time but not necessarily in space, and are distinguished from outer experiences, which are essentially spatial. It follows from this that our distinction between inner and outer experience, and so our recognition of persons, depend upon the temporal discriminations of the categories. Even in the case of myself, therefore, recognition of my personality depends upon discriminations which the categories effect in spatial phenomena. I could not regard myself as a person, or speak of inner experience, if I could not discriminate outer phenomena. I could not regard myself as in time, if I could not regard myself as an outer object.

In this doctrine Kant has both an explanation of the sense of 'person' and an account of the conditions in which we can make such a discrimination in our experience. To speak of a person is to speak of that to which inner experiences belong. But it would be impossible to speak in this way, or to give this term 'person' such a meaning, if it were impossible to recognise outer phenomena. The Cartesian view that our knowledge of outer phenomena might be built up from our knowledge of inner experiences is, on Kant's view, quite wrong. It would be impossible to speak of inner experience at all if it were impossible to speak of outer experience. Kant insists, rightly, that this does not mean that we never make mistakes about the properties of outer objects, or even that our outer experience is more reliable than inner (B 278–279, note 3). His argument has nothing to do with illusions, or the general reliability of our senses, but claims only that we must be able to discriminate outer from inner experience, if we are to speak of persons. This argument may be supported by saying simply that we think of time in spatial terms, but Kant also provides some explanation of why we should think in this way.

## (iii) KANT AND STRAWSON

Kant's account of personality has some similarity to that given by Strawson (*Individuals*, Ch. 3), and it may be useful to compare them. Both accounts are intended to reject a Cartesian view of personal knowledge, and both emphasise the importance of outer or spatial discriminations in our use of the concept 'person'. But the arguments used to support these conclusions are not quite the same; nor are the conclusions themselves exactly similar. Perhaps the most obvious differences lie in the sense which is attached in the two accounts to the concept 'person'; and this difference is connected with another, namely that Strawson's arguments are intended to be 'purely logical' (op. cit., 99, note), while Kant's are not. For Strawson, in rejecting Descartes' account of a person as a subject of inner experiences, concludes that this concept *means* 'a type of entity such that *both* predicates ascribing states of consciousness *and* predicates ascribing corporeal characteristics . . . are equally applicable to a single individual of that type'.[1] Kant, however, also rejected Descartes' account of persons, but still held that a person is essentially that to which inner characteristics belong. But he claimed also that although this is what

[1] That this is what the concept *means* seems to be entailed by Strawson's account of the 'logically primitive' sense of 'person' (p. 102: '. . . persons, in the sense I have claimed for the word . . .'), and by his claim (99, note) that 'we are speaking of a class of predicates (which) defines a major logical type of individual'. Nevertheless this is not wholly clear. There is no doubt that the concept of a person *is* that of an entity accepting both physical and mental predicates, but Strawson does not make it clear what extra evidence is available to establish that this is what the concept *means*.

the concept means, it is a condition of our using it that we should be able to discriminate outer, spatial objects. Kant, therefore, provides an additional reason for this condition of the use of the concept 'person', namely that without it we should have no temporal concepts of the kind required to discriminate outer from inner sense.

Strawson's argument is essentially very simple, and is conveniently summarised at p. 100: 'One can ascribe states of consciousness to oneself only if one can ascribe them to others. One can ascribe them to others only if one can identify other subjects of experience. And one cannot identify others if one can identify them *only* as subjects of experience, possessors of states of consciousness.' Kant has a similar argument which he uses to show the general fallacy behind the Paralogisms. The fallacious arguments are, in his view, of the following type (B 410–411):

> That which cannot be thought otherwise than as subject does not exist otherwise than as subject, and is therefore substance.
> A thinking being, considered merely as such, cannot be thought otherwise than as subject.
> Therefore, it exists only as subject, that is, substance.

Kant regards this argument as fallacious because it contains an ambiguity. In the major premiss the requirements for being a substance are that some item should be able to be conceived generally, by everyone, as a subject in intuition. But the notion of a thinking subject, as such, is not of this kind, since even if it were able to be given in intuition, it would not be the same item that was intuited generally. Such a notion as that of a thinking subject, therefore, does not contain that possibility of agreement which is required for an objective use of the concept 'substance'. This is very like saying that one cannot identify other thinking subjects *only* as such, that is, only as subjects of experience.

It is important to notice, however, that Kant's argument should be understood in two different ways. For what Kant is strictly considering in the Paralogisms is the transcendental concept of consciousness or personality. This concept fails to satisfy the requirements for naming a substance, simply because it names nothing whatsoever (B 411, note: 'In this latter sense, no object whatsoever is being thought'). This is to repeat the claim that such a concept is empty, and does not have a conventional naming function at all. But the empirical notion of a person cannot be said to name nothing, nor can it be said to be unrelated to intuition. As a person, empirically, I may be said to intuit myself as a condition of my having any self-knowledge. The argument of B 410–411 can be applied to this empirical concept of a person, but it holds for this case not because there is no such object as a person, but rather because the objects conceived as such are different for different persons. The paralogistic fallacy in this case would be that of inferring from the claim that everyone thinks of something as a subject, i.e. himself, to the conclusion that this subject is a substance. The inference fails in this case because the things so regarded as subjects are necessarily different individuals, while the notion of a substance requires that it should be applied to something which everyone admits to be the same thing. This requirement is what is meant to be stated in the major premiss.

This paralogistic fallacy applied to the notion of an empirical person corresponds to the argument of the Refutation of Idealism. For what it shows is that our inner intuition, or the notion of a person as the object of inner intuition, does not by itself satisfy the requirements for the application of the category of substance. It reflects the belief, which is reflected also in Strawson's argument, that one person cannot have intuitive access to the empirical experiences of another. But Kant's use of this belief is different from Strawson's. For Kant's argument is complex in a way in which Strawson's is simple, and Kant's conclusions are different. Strawson concludes that the concept 'person' *means* that to which both mental and physical characteristics equally belong. Kant concludes only that the primary application of 'substance' cannot be to persons, either in the transcendental or empirical sense. Kant thus imposes a restriction on the use of the concept 'person', but he still holds that this concept means 'that to which inner characteristics belong'. It is worth while, therefore, to consider Strawson's argument, for if it were correct, then Kant's conclusion would yield to his.

Strawson's argument, summarised above, consists of three claims, all of which are ambiguous because they may be understood either in a factual or in a logical way. Strawson evidently intends that they should be understood in a logical way, but it is worth noticing some of the ambiguities. The first claim, for example, might be understood to mean that one can ascribe states of consciousness to oneself, only if there are other people to which to ascribe them. For there is a sense of 'impossible' in which it would be true to say that if there were no such subjects, it would be impossible to ascribe states of consciousness to them. Construed in this factual way the first claim would be false; for there is no reason why I should not think of myself as a person, even if I were the only person in the world. The logical construction of this claim amounts to saying that if I have any concept whatever, then it must be logically possible for me to ascribe this concept to different items. For the notion of a concept entails that of the possible application of a term to different items.[1] In this particular argument, I can regard myself as a person only if I recognise it as logically possible that there should be other individuals of this type. If, to put it oddly, it were logically impossible for there to be others of this kind, then the supposed concept of such a kind would not be a genuine concept at all.

In a similar way the second claim might also be understood as a factual claim. To say that one can ascribe states of consciousness to others only if one can identify other subjects of experience might mean that one could ascribe such states to others only if one knew that some other item was a subject of experience. But again, if there were no other people, then this would not be known, but it would not prevent me from ascribing such states to myself, nor from admitting the logical possibility that there might be, or have been, other people. What the claim properly means is that one can ascribe states of consciousness to other items only if it is possible for there to be other items to ascribe them to. Recognition of the logical possibility that there are others entails the logical possibility of recognising that there are others. It is not clear, however, what is meant in this claim by 'others'. Strawson calls them 'other subjects of experience', but he has already expressed the view that it is impossible to identify other 'Cartesian egos' (p. 100), and he goes on to express the view that it is impossible to identify others *only* as subjects of experience. This may seem to commit him to saying that since it is impossible for this condition to be satisfied, because we cannot strictly identify other subjects of experience, we cannot have the concept of a person. But since it is evidently

---

[1] Strawson does not always express his claims in a purely logical way, so that some of them appear, misleadingly, as statements of fact. E.g., p. 104: 'The condition of reckoning oneself as a subject of such predicates is that one should also reckon others as subjects of such predicates.'

not Strawson's intention to draw this conclusion, it is better to avoid the ambiguity by speaking only of other 'items'. The claim then amounts to saying only that in order to be able to ascribe states of consciousness to others, it must be possible to identify other items to which to ascribe them.

The final claim also contains an ambiguity. What it is meant to reflect is the accepted view that it is impossible for one person to have access to the experiences of others. For on this view it would not be possible for me to identify other items *only* as subjects of experience, since I have no access to the experiences of which they are the subjects. This means that in order to be able to identify other items it must be possible to describe them in terms other than those of consciousness. For if I could describe them only in terms of their consciousness, then I could not identify them at all. But the claim might also be taken to mean that it is impossible, if one speaks of oneself as a person, to speak of anything else *only* as a subject of experience, or as the possessor of states of consciousness. And this claim not only does not follow from the other construction, but would ordinarily be thought to be false. For if I ever were to say of some other item in my experience 'That is a person (and not, for example, a wax dummy)' I could very well be said to have identified that item only as a subject of experience. There are, then, at least two senses of the word 'identify', and consequently at least two interpretations of this third claim in the argument. In one of these the argument holds, and in the other it does not. The argument might be expressed as 'it would be impossible to speak of other items if the only descriptions that could be given of them were in terms of consciousness'; or it might be expressed as 'it would be impossible to speak of other items if it were (ever) possible to describe them only in terms of states of consciousness'. Whereas the first interpretation is a faithful reflection of the belief that one person cannot have access to the experiences of another, the second is a distorted reflection of the same claim. It is, therefore, only on the first construction that the argument holds.

Although Strawson's claims are ambiguous, there is, therefore, at least one interpretation in which the argument holds. The only question is whether, on this interpretation, it follows that the concept of a person *means* an entity such that both mental and physical characteristics can be equally ascribed to it. There is no doubt that what can legitimately be inferred from the argument is that the concept of a person presupposes outer, or spatial descriptions, so long as it is with such descriptions that states of consciousness are specifically contrasted. This is the conclusion that Kant wished to draw from his argument. But it seems doubtful whether it follows from this that the concept 'person' has the meaning that Strawson, but not Kant, ascribes to it.

There are several ways of reinforcing this doubt. One is to say that when we speak of persons, we think of them as the possessors of inner characteristics essentially. If I say that some item is a person, and not a wax dummy, then ordinarily I would be taken to be saying that the object is conscious or possesses inner characteristics. The fact that what I point out as the object is something which also has certain physical features is not, it might be argued, relevant to the question of what 'person' means. For these spatial or physical features are also shared with many other items, which we do not regard as persons. It is as much of a common belief that persons are essentially the possessors of consciousness (cf. A 357–358) as it is that one person cannot have access to the experiences of another. Such a belief is not incompatible with the argument, since it could be held that spatial descriptions are conditions of the use of the concept 'person', in this sense, and not that the concept means something quite different.

It may seem natural to think that an explanation of what we identify as a person must be an explanation of what the concept 'person' means. If to identify something as a person is to refer necessarily to spatial descriptions of the object, then it may seem that in identifying something as a person we are necessarily ascribing spatial characteristics to it. Or again, it may seem to follow from the fact that we cannot identify persons only as subjects of experience, that a person cannot be only a possessor of inner characteristics, or that the concept 'person' cannot mean only 'that to which inner characteristics belong'. But these inferences seem to hold only because of the ambiguity noticed already in the claim 'It is impossible to identify something only as a subject of experience'. For the sense in which this claim is needed, if these inferences are to hold, is just that sense which has already been rejected in the argument. All that the argument shows is that in order to speak of persons we must be able to discriminate spatial objects. But from this it does not follow that any spatial characteristics form part of the meaning of 'person'. This would follow if the impossibility of identifying something only as a subject of experience were the same as the impossibility of describing something in terms only of inner characteristics. For if it were impossible to describe anything in terms only of inner characteristics, then it would be impossible for 'person' to mean only 'possessor of inner characteristics'. But it is precisely this required meaning for the impossible condition which has been rejected in the original argument.

Strawson's difficulty arises from a rejection of the claim that a person is essentially that to which inner characteristics belong. For if it is now asked: What is that to which inner features are ascribed? it is natural to answer in terms of the physical bodies which we refer to in ascribing inner characteristics. From this it may seem right to conclude that persons are essentially subjects of both mental and physical characteristics, for neither of the apparent alternatives seems satisfactory. The question arose because it seemed impossible to speak of persons purely as subjects of experience. For Strawson claims that it would be impossible to speak of persons at all, if they are thought of as Cartesian egos, to which only private experiences can, 'in correct logical grammar', be ascribed. And to speak of persons as purely physical objects will seem equally wrong, since these two notions are ordinarily contrasted with each other. But from the claim that it would be impossible to speak of persons only as Cartesian egos, it does not follow that it is impossible to speak of them as Cartesian egos. For it would be quite possible to hold both that persons are essentially subjects of experience, and that it would be impossible to speak of them in this way, if this were the only way.

What is wrong, however, with the argument is not so much the alternative answers to the question, as the question itself. Once it has been stated that a person is essentially that to which experiences belong, it makes no sense to ask further: What is that to which experiences are ascribed? Such a question would be like asking: What is that which lasts for twenty-four hours? once it has been stated that a day is that which lasts for twenty-four hours. If such a question were admitted, it may seem inevitable to argue that since any object which lasts for twenty-four hours must be identifiable in spatial terms, a day is something spatial. But since it clearly will not do to say that a day is only a spatial object, it might seem natural to conclude that the concept 'day' means something which has both spatial and temporal characteristics. Such a conclusion might naturally seem to conflict with the ordinary belief that the concept 'day' stands for something which is only a period of time. But the conclusion is not inevitable, since it might be held both that a day is essentially something temporal, and also that it is a condition of using the concept in this way that it should be possible to identify spatial phenomena.

It would not be difficult to confuse the senseless question about the concept 'day' with the question: How do we measure a period of twenty-four hours? or: Under what conditions is it possible to discriminate periods of time? And in the same way there is a difference between asking: What is that to which experiences belong? and: What conditions are required in order to be able to discriminate persons in our experience? Kant answers this latter question by saying that one condition is that we should be able to discriminate between inner and outer characteristics. This is equivalent to Strawson's argument that it is possible to speak of persons only so long as it is possible to identify spatial or physical items in experience. But this might be held to be a condition of the possibility of using the concept 'person', rather than a part of what the concept means. It is indeed, on Kant's view, a condition of using the concept 'person' to mean 'that to which inner characteristics belong'.

## 12

# THE TRANSITION TO
# MORAL PHILOSOPHY

'Freedom as a property of a being to which I attribute effects in the sensible world is, therefore, not knowable in any such fashion (through empirical observation)' (B xxviii).

'Practical freedom can be proved through experience' (B 829).

THROUGHOUT the Dialectic Kant deals with a number of mistakes and conflicts in philosophy; and his treatment of them generally follows the pattern outlined previously (Ch. 5). The mistakes and conflicts arise generally from a failure to distinguish between phenomena, of which we have knowledge, and supposed intelligible objects, of which we know nothing. We have, on Kant's view, certain concepts or Ideas which cannot apply in our experience, but which are sometimes wrongly held to apply to an intelligible world beyond the reach of our senses. Kant argues, for the most part, that such Ideas, which have in a way outgrown our experience, serve properly as heuristic fictions regulating our enquiries. To think that such concepts stand for noumenal objects in a world beyond our senses is an illusion; to make claims about such objects in such a world is to speak emptily; and to argue or dispute about such claims is futile.

It is easy to think, however, that in the Third Antinomy (B 473– 474, B 556–586) Kant either contradicts or radically amends this account of dialectical Ideas and their purported objects. For it is in this argument that Kant seems finally to admit the existence of intelligible objects in a new and committal way. In this passage Kant tries to resolve a conflict between our theoretical or scientific language of causal explanation, and our practical or moral language of freedom and responsibility. Kant suggests, in his solution to the Third Antinomy and in a corresponding passage in the Preface (B xvi–xxx), that to talk of freedom is to talk of a property belonging to intelligible objects. This issue, and Kant's method of resolving it, should not be regarded as merely peripheral to the *Critique of Pure Reason*. The notion of freedom is for Kant the keystone of the whole Critical structure (Ak., Vol. 5, pp. 3–4), for it is on this notion that the transition from theoretical to moral philosophy depends. If Kant uses the concept of a noumenon to effect this transition in a new and committal way, it cannot be brushed aside as a secondary issue. Kant's difficulty in the Third Antinomy is a version of the traditional conflict between free will and determinism, but his account of this conflict has some peculiarities. In the next section Kant's approach to the problem will be outlined, and in the final section something will be said of the force of his solution.

### (i) CAUSALITY AND FREEDOM

Kant's problem about causality and freedom does not arise because he sometimes speaks of causal laws as necessary. It has been explained already (Ch. 9, pp. 143 ff., and Ch. 10, pp. 164–166) that whatever Kant meant by calling particular empirical laws of this kind necessary, he certainly believed them to be falsifiable. But to say that a causal explanation of some event might have been false would not have settled Kant's difficulty about freedom. For this difficulty arises precisely on the supposition that a causal law is true, but not necessarily true, of an event to which freedom is also to be ascribed. Again, his problem does not arise merely because he held that every event has a cause. This belief certainly influenced his idea both of the problem and its solution, but the ways in which it does so are complex and will be considered later. But the difficulty would still arise even if there were only some events that had causes, so long as freedom were also to be ascribed to the same events. The difficulty is one about the compatibility of concepts. It is concerned with the propriety or possibility of ascribing freedom to an event, on the supposition that causality can also be ascribed to it.

Kant indicates some of the peculiarities of his problem in the

Preface (B xvi–xxx), where he speaks of the projected 'Copernican Revolution' in our modes of thought. The revolution, in a theoretical context, consists in supposing that we impose laws on nature, and do not merely derive them from it. This doctrine, which is given a sense in the Transcendental Deduction and Analytic of Principles, has a close connection with the distinction between phenomena and noumena. For Kant held that this imposition of laws could be understood only if nature is regarded as phenomenal and not noumenal. Kant proposes that his Copernican hypothesis, and the associated contrast between phenomena and noumena, should be tested by an experiment. But since the claims to be tested are not merely empirical propositions about experienced objects, the experiment cannot be of the conventional scientific kind. It is instead a 'conceptual' experiment (B xviii, note) concerned with the compatibility of concepts and not with any matters of fact. The test is to discover whether the distinction between phenomena and noumena can be used to settle what Kant calls 'conflicts of reason'. These conflicts are to be found in the Antinomies, but it is the conflict in the Third Antinomy which is picked out for special mention (B xxvii).

It is clear from this argument that Kant's problem in the Third Antinomy is recognised to be of a special kind. Whatever the outcome of such a philosophic conflict Kant recognises that our ordinary views about conduct, for example, will remain unaffected (cf. B 772). The problem is on a theoretical or transcendental level, and is consequently insulated from our ordinary empirical beliefs. It is, as the conceptual experiment suggests, a problem about the logical relations of concepts, and not about their relations to any objects in our experience. This implies that no factual evidence will be enough to settle the issue about freedom on this level. The fact that we sometimes do not hold a man responsible for his acts, where there is an accepted causal explanation of them, is of no more relevance than the fact that we do sometimes hold a man responsible, even though we accept an explanation of his behaviour.

Kant's conceptual experiment presupposes the account given already of the distinction between appearances, or phenomena, and noumena. Sometimes, however, Kant explains this contrast in a way which may seem more committal than has so far been admitted. At B xxvi–xxvii, for example, Kant says: 'But our further contention must also be duly borne in mind, namely that though we cannot *know* these objects as things in themselves, we must yet be in a position at least to *think* them as things in themselves: Otherwise we should be landed in the absurd conclusion that there can be appearance without anything that appears.' It has sometimes been argued (cf. Adickes: *Kant und das Ding an sich*, Ch. 1, p. 6) that in this passage Kant commits himself to the existence of noumena in a quite new way. But this is not so. All that Kant says is that while we cannot know things as they are in themselves, we must be able to conceive them. It has, however, already been granted (Ch. 5, p. 76, and Ch. 2, p. 34) that intelligible objects are conceivable, that is to say not logically impossible. Kant wishes to insist that we may without contradiction speak of intelligible objects, and even of appearances as appearances of such objects. His argument in this passage asserts only that such a way of speaking about appearances would be inconsistent if the concept of a noumenon were itself inconsistent. But to say that noumena are not logically impossible is not to admit that there are any such objects, nor to suppose that we could have knowledge of them. In a footnote Kant repeats his general warning that logical possibility is not the same as material possibility, and not at all the same as actual existence.

This passage does not commit Kant to the existence of noumena in any new way, but it throws some light on his use or choice of the term 'Erscheinung' or 'appearance'. It has been argued (Ch. 3, p. 46 ff.) that Kant employs this term in his account of perception in a way quite different from that in which the term 'appearance' is normally used. To speak of what we perceive as an appearance is to say neither that all our perceptions are illusory, nor that we have to infer objects and their empirical properties from their appearances. In the transcendental context appearances are not related to their objects in the way in which ordinarily appearances are related to their empirical objects. It is clear, from this passage in the Preface, that Kant chose the term 'appearance' at least partly because it suggests the notion of a thing which appears. But in the transcendental context in which 'appearance' is contrasted with 'transcendental object' or 'noumenon', this suggestion indicates only the conceivability of such transcendental objects and not their actual existence. Kant's conceptual experiment, in which this transcendental contrast is an important part of the apparatus, does not require the actual existence of noumena but only their logical possibility.

The experiment is carried out properly in the solution to the Third Antinomy, although the results are reported in advance even in the Preface. Kant reaches the conclusion that freedom and causality are compatible, because we can conceive a situation in which the same event is phenomenally caused but noumenally free. Or again, that we can give a sense to the notion of intervention in a causal chain, by conceiving the chain to be phenomenal and the intervention based upon noumena. Or again, that the two apparently conflicting notions can be said to be compatible, because we can conceive the same person to be phenomenally determined but noumenally free. The experiment, on Kant's reading, yields a confirmation of the transcendental contrast between phenomena and noumena, because it is in terms of this contrast that the two apparently conflicting concepts can be reconciled. The world of theoretical knowledge is restricted to that of phenomena, and for this reason there is room in the noumenal world for faith (B xxx).

The natural responses to this solution are to say that it is unsatisfying and wrong. Kant seems to have assigned the world of practice or morals to the realm of noumena (cf. B 579, note), about which we are supposed to be totally ignorant. To speak of moral judgments or of moral concepts as applying to such a world may seem to make the notion of morality not more but less intelligible. Kant generally treats claims about supposed noumenal objects as illusory or empty, but in this transitional context he seems anxious to promote claims which are intended to be true of such objects. It would be entirely natural to say on the basis of this argument either that Kant's problem does not arise, or that his solution to it contradicts what he says elsewhere of intelligible objects and dialectical Ideas.

Kant's argument will seem objectionable in these ways so long as it is understood as a straightforward defence of freedom. It would be natural to argue, for example, that the problem only seems to arise because Kant held that causal laws were necessary, or that every event has a cause, although these claims have been already disputed. Yet Kant certainly appears to claim that we are sometimes free agents, but that this is true only of our noumenal

193

selves or intelligible characters. But Kant states a number of qualifications to this outline of argument, which show that it is very far from being a simple defence of this kind. He makes considerable efforts, for example, to avoid the charge of inconsistency, by stating exactly what he has, and what he has not, been able to prove. He makes it clear that he has not been able, and has not even intended, to prove that we are free agents in any intelligible world. He claims also, at the end of the Third Antinomy, that the conflict between causality and freedom is an illusion (B 586). This may suggest that his attitude towards this Antinomy is not wholly different from his attitude to the others, and that he does not regard the problem of freedom as a genuine problem. But this raises obvious difficulties, for if Kant recognised that to speak of freedom in an intelligible world is an illusion, then it is hard to see what the appeal to an intelligible world is designed to do.

Kant states that his argument has not shown that freedom in an intelligible world is 'real', or even 'possible' (B 585–586). These provisos are analogous to his persistent claim that the logical possibility of noumena does not amount to an admission of their material possibility or actual existence. All that the argument can show in the Third Antinomy is that the concepts of freedom and causality, however much they may seem to conflict, cannot be said to be incompatible. This is to insist again on the claim that the problem, and the associated experiment, are concerned with concepts and their relations. Such a problem can quite properly be discussed without considering whether the concepts in question are exemplified in our experience or are empty. To discuss whether two concepts are compatible is quite different from discussing whether any objects actually satisfy them. Since Kant's problem is of this logical kind it would be a mistake to think that the claims about intelligible freedom in his argument are stated to be true of any intelligible world. Since he is required to argue only that a situation in which causality and freedom are both ascribed to the same event is logically possible, he is committed to saying only that such a situation is conceivable and not that it actually obtains. It may be disputed whether such a situation really is conceivable, but at least this is not the same as disputing whether freedom actually obtains in some intelligible world inaccessible to our senses.

This qualification is supported in a number of passages in which

Kant restates our inability to know anything about intelligible freedom. He makes it clear (e.g. Ak., Vol. 5, p. 57) that in appealing to the world of noumena he has not licensed any extension of our knowledge beyond phenomena: 'Thus the application of the categories to the super-sensible, which occurs only from a practical point of view, gives to pure theoretical reason not the least encouragement to run riot into the transcendent.' This emphasises that the argument to resolve the Third Antinomy is still supposed to conform to standards previously adopted in speaking of the unknowable world of noumena. And this is shown in other claims made about intelligible freedom, for example (*Grundlegung*, Ak., Vol. 4, p. 463) that the notion of such freedom is incomprehensible, that it may be a mere ficton (B 573–574), and that in any case we have no means of knowing whether it is or not (B 829–830). There are also other passages (in the *Grundlegung*) where the notion of freedom is spoken of as a limit, in much the way in which the concepts of transcendental or intelligible objects are also spoken of as limits. These claims, in the new transitional context, are the same as the qualifications made about intelligible objects in the corresponding arguments of theoretical philosophy. They suggest that Kant had only one account, and not two incompatible accounts, of noumena and dialectical Ideas.

It is also important to recognise that Kant's problem about free will arises at a transcendental and not at an empirical level. In stating the Third Antinomy (B 473–474) and introducing its solution (B 561–563) Kant relies upon a distinction between transcendental and empirical, or practical, freedom. This contrast is analogous to that discussed already between transcendental and empirical objects. Kant makes it clear (B 828–830) that there is no philosophic problem about practical freedom, which is exemplified and proved in our experience. The Antinomy arises only over transcendental freedom, and this problem is speculative and of no concern in our ordinary practical judgments. But although the transcendental concept of freedom is, in this way, a philosophical or speculative problem it would be a mistake to think that it can be solved. This transcendental concept is, like that of a noumenon (cf. B 311 and B 343 and Ch. 2, pp. 25–27), a problem which we have no means of solving. Kant seems to claim, therefore, that we may speak of freedom in two ways, either empirically or transcendentally. Practical freedom needs no philosophic arguments to support its existence, for this is recognised empirically, and no argument can establish the existence of transcendental freedom, for this can occur only in a context where we have no knowledge.

The concept of transcendental freedom has the status of a dialectical Idea, and shares the characteristics of such Ideas. Their function is heuristic and regulative; they serve to stimulate enquiry by expressing a goal, or setting a task, in the way in which, for example, the Idea of the origin of the universe may stimulate astronomical discoveries. The notion of freedom in the transcendental sense has also a regulative function; it is associated with a 'regulative principle of reason' (B 582) which is part of Kant's account of freedom in an intelligible world. The same point is made in the *Grundlegung* (Ak., Vol. 4, p. 458), where Kant describes freedom as the embodiment of a point of view: 'The conception of a world of understanding is then only a point of view, which reason finds itself compelled to take outside appearances in order to conceive itself as practical.' This point of view, nevertheless, requires to be safeguarded in some way from the charges that it is itself inconsistent, or that it is incompatible with the notion of causality. But Kant's method of defending this point of view is not the naive way of saying that human beings are free either in experience or in any intelligible world.

The strategy adopted by Kant in his defensive exercise is expressed in a passage at B 767:

> By the polemical employment of pure reason I mean the defence of its propositions against the dogmatic counter-propositions through which they are denied. In this case it is not a question whether its assertions may not perhaps also be false,[1] but only that no one can assert the opposite with apodeictic certainty, or even, indeed, with a greater degree of likelihood. We do not here hold our possessions on sufferance; for although our title to them may not be satisfactory, it is yet quite certain that no one can ever be in a position to prove the illegality of the title.

An exactly similar argument, related specifically to the problem of freedom, is given at B 781. Kant explains that when he hears that someone has 'demonstrated away' the freedom of the will, he knows in advance that the argument will fail. But the reason for this is

---

[1] This seems a more accurate translation than Kemp Smith's.

... not because I believe that I am in possession of conclusive proofs of these important propositions, but because the transcendental Critique has convinced me that, as reason is incompetent to arrive at affirmative assertions in this field, it is equally unable, indeed even less able, to establish any negative conclusion in regard to these questions.

Finally, in the *Critique of Practical Reason* Kant indicates the same strategy (Ak., Vol. 5, pp. 93–94), which involves no simple assertion that we are transcendentally free, but only the claim that no proof of its impossibility can be given. Just as no argument can establish the existence of transcendental freedom, so no argument can disprove it.

On these grounds Kant seems to have evolved a solution to the problem of freedom, which is designed to show not that determinism is false, but that it cannot prove what it asserts to be true. Kant is evidently not arguing simply that we are as a matter of fact free in some intelligible world, but only that, in the sense of 'free' that he is concerned with, we cannot be shown not to be. This explains why Kant says that his argument has not proved that such transcendental freedom is real, or that we could be said to know that it exists, but only that it cannot be said to be incompatible with causality, or that no one can prove that it is. Kant intends, therefore, neither to assert nor to deny that we are free transcendentally and it is only in this transcendental way that freedom and causality may seem to conflict. For no argument is needed to defend the belief that we are free in an empirical sense, for such freedom is established in our ordinary experience. In this way the impossibility of a proof either for or against transcendental freedom does not mean that we are unjustified in speaking ordinarily of free acts, or of ourselves as free agents. In the sense in which we use 'free' in experience we are not talking about any supposed intelligible world, and there is no problem about our freedom. Kant certainly held that there was a relation between transcendental and practical freedom, such that the empirical concept presupposes the transcendental. Transcendental freedom is, on Kant's view, required to be admitted if practical philosophy and our practical judgments are to be possible. But the way in which such freedom is required is not that in which it is proved or asserted to exist, or even to be possible, but only that in which it remains a problem and so at least cannot be denied. To say this is not to contradict what Kant says elsewhere of noumena, but to reiterate it.

## (ii) KANT'S SOLUTION OF THE THIRD ANTINOMY

Despite the arguments already given in the preceding section, it may still be held that Kant's treatment of the Third Antinomy is radically different from his treatment of the others. In the two 'mathematical' Antinomies Kant has no particular interest in defending either the thesis or the antithesis. He consequently takes the view that both thesis and antithesis may be regarded as false (B 557–559). But in the Third Antinomy he seems to be committed to both the thesis and the antithesis; for he has shown in the Second Analogy that every event has a cause, and yet also plainly wishes to justify our belief in freedom. In this case, then, he is prepared to say not that both thesis and antithesis are false, but that they may both be true (B 560). It may therefore be doubted whether Kant wished to say only that the problem of free will was insoluble, or not genuine. And this doubt may serve to reinstate the naive view that Kant had to assign freedom to the intelligible world, simply because he had already proved that the principle of the Second Analogy was true of all phenomenal events.

It would be easy to counter this objection by saying that Kant does not admit both thesis and antithesis in the Third Antinomy to be true, but says only that they may both be true, if they are interpreted correctly. Again, to say that both arguments may be true is to say only that they are compatible, or that the conflict between causality and freedom is an illusion. But these claims, though true, conceal the difficulty that Kant seems to be involved in the Third Antinomy because he accepts a proof of the principle of the Second Analogy. It was suggested earlier that Kant's problem does not arise merely because he held that every event has a cause. Now it should be said that if this claim is intended as a statement of the principle of the Second Analogy, then it is not involved in the Third Antinomy at all. For the principle which is involved in this conflict is a cosmological principle of totality, which has been already distinguished from that of the Second Analogy (Ch. 5, pp. 70–71).

The principle of the Second Analogy is an expression of a necessary truth, which Kant usually formulates in terms of an event's presupposing a cause. The least misleading formulation, however, would be one which recognised its conceptual status, by expressing it as 'The concept "event" presupposes that of "cause"'. It is natural to express this principle loosely as 'Every event has a cause', but it is misleading to do so. For from the conceptual truth it does not follow that we know the causes of any event. The causal law, which the principle of the Second Analogy expresses, is not itself a causal law, and does not state or mention any particular causal factor's presence in any particular event. In order to be able to know the cause of any particular event it is required not only that the conceptual truth should hold, but also that certain regularities should have been observed and tested in our experience. The expression 'Every event has a cause' might, however, be understood as an assertion that we know the causes of every event. If it were understood in this way, then it would not be equivalent to the principle of the Second Analogy. For from the conceptual truth of the latter it follows neither that we know the causes of every event, nor even that it is possible to know the causes of every event.

It is a claim of this latter kind which is involved in the Third Antinomy, and which the cosmological principle of totality expresses. For at least one major difficulty about free will is thought to arise on the supposition that we might, or will one day, have a complete explanation of every event. It may sometimes seem natural to argue that if we ever achieved such complete knowledge, or even if it were possible to achieve it, then there would be no room for the ascriptions of freedom that we normally make. The possibility of such an achievement may incline us to think that our current belief in freedom is only a result of our ignorance about behaviour. If we were better informed, or if it were possible to be totally informed, about the explanation of such behaviour, then we could no longer continue to speak in terms of freedom or responsibility. The conflict in the Third Antinomy between determinism and freedom is, in this way, not a conflict between the conceptual truth that the concept 'event' presupposes that of 'cause' and our ascriptions of freedom. It is a conflict between our ascription of freedom and the belief that it is possible to give a complete explanation of every event. The conceptual truth does not entail a belief in this possibility, but the belief would not arise if the conceptual truth did not hold. We succumb to the tempting belief in a total explanation, irrationally, because we can give partial and incomplete explanations.

That Kant is speaking in the Third Antinomy of this cosmological principle is made clear in the introduction to the Antinomy of Pure Reason (B 442–443). For there the cosmological Ideas that generate these rational conflicts are all Ideas of the completeness of a certain series. Such a series might be that of spatial or temporal sequence, and so give rise to conflicts about the extent of the universe, or its origin in time. But the completeness involved in the Third Antinomy is that of a causal series, or explanatory sequence. It is possible to set oneself as a task or goal the discovery of the causes of every event. Such a goal might be expressed in the claim that every event has a discoverable cause, but such a conviction is only a heuristic device and not a constitutive truth. It is a regulative Idea which perhaps enjoins us to extend the search for causes as far as possible, but it is not equivalent to the principle of the Second Analogy. It is easy to see why such total or complete aims should be regarded as heuristic fictions. They do not express a limited goal which might be attained at some foreseeable future time. They express an absolutely unlimited goal the attainment of which seems to make only dubious sense, however effective a stimulus to enquiry it may be.

The conflict in the Third Antinomy arises in this way from an incoherence or unclarity in the determinist Idea of a total or complete explanation of phenomena. On the one hand this determinist Idea implies that no phenomenal event is unexplained, since if any such event had no explanation, the explanatory series would not be complete. But the notion of an explanation for any particular phenomenal event is that of a prior condition which determines it; and if this prior condition is itself a phenomenal event, then it too must be explained. In this way the Idea of a complete explanation of phenomena seems to imply an interminable series of explanatory conditions, which cannot be completed so long as the conditions are themselves phenomena. Yet the idea of a point at which no further explanation can be given is also apparently required in the notion of a complete explanation. Only if there were such a terminus to the explanatory series would it be possible for the explanation to be complete. Such a terminus, however, could not itself be a member of a phenomenal series of events, since it is required that every phenomenal event should have an explanation. And so the Idea of a complete explanation of phenomena seems to imply on the other hand that there should be a condition which cannot be further explained, and is, therefore, not a phenomenon.

This apparent incoherence in the Idea of a complete explanation may seem to have little to do with our ordinary belief in freedom. But Kant has already explained that the conflict is a speculative and not a practical matter; and also that it concerns not practical but transcendental freedom. It presents a difficulty in our understanding of such concepts as 'cause', 'explanation' and 'complete', as much as in our understanding of 'free' or 'responsible'. The Idea of transcendental freedom may nevertheless be introduced as that of a terminus in explanation, of a dimension in which it is not possible to ask for any further explanation. It should not be thought that Kant's argument is designed to establish the existence of such a terminus. It shows on the contrary that the existence of such a terminus never can be established in our experience. The argument concludes that the apparent conflict between causality and freedom rests on an incoherence in the determinist Idea of a complete explanation. If it is held that such an Idea shows freedom to be impossible, then Kant's argument shows by contrast that the same Idea might just as well be held to imply transcendental freedom.

The incoherence in this determinist Idea can be seen at a more concrete level in the kinds of conflict that it generates. So long as the question: Is it possible to give a complete explanation of phenomenal events? is treated as a straightforward question, it cannot be settled. For to answer either that such an explanation is, or is not, possible leads at once to the kind of dispute argued above (Ch. 5, pp. 69–70) to be futile. A determinist, who believes in the possibility of a complete explanation, might, for example, challenge his opponent to produce an example of an event which it is impossible to explain. And the opponent might naturally in turn challenge the determinist to produce an explanation for every event. Any such conflict must end in deadlock, for neither challenge can be met. To give either of these simple answers to the original question is to be unjustifiably dogmatic, for what is wrong in such disputes is not so much either of the answers as the question itself, or the determinist Idea that prompts it. This is the reason for Kant's refusal to defend freedom by arguing that some events, for example, those in which decisions figure, are not explicable. To give such an answer, on his view, would be a 'wretched subterfuge' (Ak., Vol. 5, p. 96), for there is as little ground for saying that there are such inexplicable events as for saying that every event is explicable.

Kant's appeal to a noumenal world is in this way not a straightforward assertion that we are, or could be known to be, free in such a world. He does not adopt a dogmatic defence of this kind, but argues only that the determinist Idea which seems to require such a defence is itself incoherent. But it would be as much of a mistake to think that an appeal to a noumenal world could by itself establish that the concepts of causality and freedom are simply compatible. For such an appeal could be used, or misused, to establish the compatibility of any two concepts whatever. All that would be needed to show, for example, that the concepts 'heavy' and 'weightless' are really compatible, would be to say that objects are phenomenally heavy but noumenally weightless. Such a simple device to reconcile two apparently conflicting concepts is worthless, but it is clear that the argument in the Third Antinomy is not of this absurd kind. For the appeal to noumena in the Third Antinomy is forced by the incoherent Idea from which the conflict springs. The only ground for calling the conflict illusory in this case is that the Idea which generates it is incoherent; it can be said to imply the very concept which it is intended to reject.

Kant's appeal to a noumenal world is, therefore, not radically different in this case from the same appeal in other sections of the Dialectic. Since the principle of the Second Analogy is not itself directly concerned in the Antinomy, Kant has no need to safeguard freedom and causality by assigning the latter to phenomena and the former to noumena. Just as in the case of the other conflicts about dialectical Ideas, the reference to noumena is a sign that the conflict is not genuine. For to say that such a dispute could be settled only by discovering the properties of intelligible objects beyond the reach of our experience is equivalent to saying that the problem is insoluble. Freedom in the transcendental sense can be safeguarded from such determinist attacks not dogmatically by asserting its existence, but by showing that the attacks cannot succeed. The only guarantee of such a concept, and the only way in which it is required, is to say that it remains a problem which we have no means of solving. In this way alone can we be assured that no proof of the impossibility of freedom can be given.

Kant's treatment of free will has a bearing upon some recent disputes about this concept (cf. *Analysis*, Vol. 18, pp. 25, 34, and 41). On one side it has sometimes been argued that the problem of freedom can be resolved simply by appealing to our ordinary language. That we speak of free acts would, on such a view, establish that we are free. But this has also been disputed, on the grounds either that our ordinary language might be mistaken, or that since it is this language which is in dispute it cannot simply be assumed without begging the question. Kant's attitude to the problem conveniently straddles both of these positions. For he claims both that we are quite justified ordinarily in speaking of free acts, and also that this practical freedom is not concerned in the philosophical problem about free will. For such a philosophic problem involves transcendental and not practical freedom. Kant would agree with those who say that the appeal to our ordinary use of 'free' cannot settle such a philosophical problem; but he admits this only at the expense of saying that such a philosophic problem cannot be settled, or is not a genuine problem at all.

The ascription of practical freedom cannot settle the philosophic problem because it does not rule out the possibility of causal explanations. It could not then establish that free acts, in this practical context, were examples of an inexplicable event, or of a terminus in explanation. Indeed to speak of a man acting, for example, out of prudence in refusing something which he would have liked to accept, is already to give some explanation of his behaviour. Yet it is in such cases that we would ordinarily speak of a free action. If, therefore, there is a further question about the compatibility of the concepts of causality and freedom, it cannot be settled by an appeal to such ordinary cases. The Idea of a complete explanation of phenomena might be used to raise such a further question, which could be answered in favour of freedom only by establishing the existence of a terminus in explanation transcendentally, that is, the existence of a point at which no further explanation is possible. Kant argues that it is only in this way that a philosophic problem about freedom can arise; but once such a problem has arisen all that can be done is to recognise that it is insoluble.

It is true that Kant does not simply abandon the notion of freedom in his metaphysical accounts of morality in the *Grundlegung* and *Critique of Practical Reason*. For he recognises that we speak of ourselves as free agents, and think of at least some of our actions as spontaneous. We believe it possible ordinarily to intervene in causal sequences, and think of such intervention sometimes as a terminus in explanation. Once it has been shown that a certain person did something, we do not always require any further explanation of the occurrence. But although we do not always require such a further explanation it does not follow that there is no further explanation to be given. To speak of a point at which no further explanations could be given would be to speak of freedom in a transcendental way, but such an Idea cannot be shown to be true of any event in our experience. Properly understood the Ideas both of a complete explanation and of transcendental freedom serve only to direct our enquiries, or to regulate our conduct. We enquire into phenomena as though there were nothing which is exempt from causal explanation; we conduct ourselves as if there were points at which there are no further explanations to be given. Kant's argument tries to show that just as the acts which we ordinarily regard as free cannot be shown to be outside the scope of explanation, so we cannot know that there is nothing outside it. The kind of knowledge that would show our ascription of freedom to be a result only of ignorance about behaviour is a myth. But this resolution of the apparent conflict allows, and even invites, further analysis of the ways in which the Idea of freedom is involved in our conduct. It is this further analysis which is provided in the *Grundlegung* and *Critique of Practical Reason*.

# LIST OF BOOKS

THE following is a list of books cited in the text, and not a bibliography
on Kant. References to Kantian texts, other than the *Critique of Pure
Reason*, have been given generally to the Akademie edition (Berlin,
1900– ). I have used, and sometimes deviated from, the translations of
the *Critique of Pure Reason* by Norman Kemp Smith (London, 1929);
of the *Prolegomena* by P. G. Lucas (Manchester, 1953); of the *Critique of
Practical Reason* by L. W. Beck (New York, 1956); and of the *Fundamental Principles of the Metaphysic of Ethics* (Grundlegung) by T. K.
Abbott (London, 1934).

ADICKES, E., *Kant und das Ding an sich*, Berlin, 1924
AYER, A. J., *Language, Truth and Logic* (2nd. ed.), London, 1948
AYER, A. J., *The Foundations of Empirical Knowledge*, London, 1940
BERKELEY, G., *Works*, ed. A. C. Fraser, Oxford, 1901
DESCARTES, R., *Descartes' Philosophical Writings*, translated by Norman
    Kemp Smith, London 1952
GEACH, P. T., *Mental Acts*, London, 1957
GEACH, P. T., and BLACK, M., *Translations from the Philosophical Writings of
    Gottlob Frege*, Oxford, 1952
HAMPSHIRE, S., *Thought and Action*, London, 1959
HUME, D., *Enquiries*, ed. L. A. Selby-Bigge (2nd. ed.), Oxford, 1902
JACOBI, F. H., *Werke*, Leipzig, 1812–1825
KÖRNER, S., *Kant*, London, 1955
LOCKE, J., *Essay*, ed. A. C. Fraser, Oxford, 1894
MARTIN, G., *Kant's Metaphysics and Theory of Science*, translated by P. G.
    Lucas, Manchester, 1955
PATON, H. J., *Kant's Metaphysic of Experience*, London, 1936
PRICHARD, H. A., *Kant's Theory of Knowledge*, Oxford, 1909
REICH, K., *Die Vollständigkeit der Kantischen Urteilstafel*, Berlin, 1932
REID, T., *Essays on the Intellectual Powers of Man*, ed. A. D. Woozley,
    London, 1941
RUSSELL, B., *Logic and Knowledge*, ed. R. C. Marsh, London, 1956
RYLE, G., *The Concept of Mind*, London, 1949
RYLE, G., *Dilemmas*, Cambridge, 1954

SCHOPENHAUER, A., *Werke*, Leipzig, 1873–1874

SMITH, NORMAN KEMP, *A Commentary to Kant's 'Critique of Pure Reason'*, London, 1918

STENIUS, E., *Wittgenstein's Tractatus*, Oxford, 1960

STRAWSON, P. F., *Individuals*, London, 1959

VAIHINGER, H., *Kommentar zu Kant's Kritik der reinen Vernunft*, Stuttgart, 1922

VLEESCHAUWER, H. J. DE, *La Déduction Transcendentale dans l'oeuvre de Kant*, Antwerpen, 1934–1937

WELDON, T. D., *Kant's 'Critique of Pure Reason'* (2nd. ed.), Oxford, 1958

WITTGENSTEIN, L., *Tractatus Logico-Philosophicus*, London, 1922

WITTGENSTEIN, L., *Philosophical Investigations*, Oxford, 1953

# INDEX